NATIONS AS ZONES OF CONFLICT

John Hutchinson

SAGE Publications
London • Thousand Oaks • New Delhi

First published 2005

SAGE Publications Ltd
1 Olivers Yard
55 City Road
London EC1Y 1SP

SAGE Publications Inc
2455 Teller Road
Thousand Oaks, California 91320

SAGE Publications India Pvt Ltd
B-42, Panchsheel Enclave
Post Box 4109
New Delhi 110 017

British Library Cataloguing in Publication data

A catalogue record for this book is available
from the British Library

ISBN 0-7619-5726 X
　　 0-7619-5727 8 (pbk)

Library of Congress Control Number available

Typeset by C&M Digitals (P) Ltd., Chennai, India
Printed in Great Britain by The Cromwell Press Ltd, Trowbridge, Wiltshire

Contents

Acknowledgements

This book has been some years in the making. I would like to thank my editor, Chris Rojek, for his patience during this time.

Many people have contributed to the writing of this book. One spur came from Wayne Hudson with whom I taught a course in world history at Griffith University, which gave me a new appreciation of the long range and recurring processes in history. In developing my arguments, I have been much indebted to the pioneering scholarship of John Armstrong and Anthony Smith on the ethnic origins of nations, and to Michael Mann's insights into the multiple sources of social power. I am grateful to Steven Grosby for comments on an article I published in *Ethnic and Racial Studies* in which I introduced some of my ideas, and to Kosaku Yoshino, whose 'consumption approach' to nationalism has influenced Chapter 4 of this book. I have benefited from responses to early versions of these ideas presented in the form of conference or seminar papers in Australia, Britain, Italy and Turkey. This study was composed since my arrival at the London School of Economics, and I must pay tribute to the stimulus provided by ASEN, the Association for the Study of Ethnicity and Nationalism, run by talented and enterprising postgraduate students who have made the LSE such a powerhouse for the study of nationalism.

Finally, I would like to thank my parents for the support they have always offered so unstintingly, and to my brother Geoffrey for managing to persuade me of his interest in the progress of this book.

Earlier versions of some chapters have appeared elsewhere.

Chapter 2 is an extended version of 'Myth against myth: the nation as ethnic overlay', *Nations and Nationalism*, 2004, 10 (1–2), 109–24, and I would like to thank *Nations and Nationalism* for permitting me to reproduce material from this article.

Some of the arguments in Chapter 5 were presented first in my 'Nationalism, Globalism and the Conflict of Civilisations', in U. Ozkirimli (ed.) *Nationalism and its Futures*, London: Palgrave Macmillan, 2003, pp. 71–92.

Chapter 5 also contains material published as 'Enduring nations and the illusions of European integration', in W. Spohn and A. Triandafyllidou (eds) *Europeanisation, National Identities and Migration: Changes in Boundary Constructions between Western and Eastern Europe*, London: Routledge, 2002, pp. 36–51. I am grateful for permission to reproduce this material.

John Hutchinson
London
January 2004

To Geoffrey

Introduction

E. H. Carr recounts with malicious wit the example of the eminent historian Herbert Butterfield who, in 1931, published *The Whig Interpretation of History*, a devastating polemic against that quintessential English national myth: the conception of English history as a story of the realisation of a spirit of liberty under the leadership of a patriotic landed class. Butterfield denounced this interpretation, which he claimed was prevalent in English historiography, as unhistorical and a sinful effect of the study of the past from the standpoint of the present. In doing so he was charting a path followed by many modernist scholars of nationalism who seek to deconstruct the idea of the nation as an 'invented tradition' somehow foisted on a gullible people. Yet in 1944, when his country 'was engaged in a war often said to be fought in defence of the constitutional liberties embodied in the Whig tradition under a great leader who constantly invoked the past "with one eye, so to speak, upon the present"', he published *The Englishman and His History*. He decided not only that the Whig interpretation was *the* English interpretation of history, but he also wrote enthusiastically about the Englishman's marriage between the present and the past (Carr, 1964: 42–3). Here we see the contradictory impulses in our attitude to the national past – the first scientific, driven by the desire to emancipate ourselves and our societies from the authority of myth; the second quasi-religious, arising out of the desire to find in the past a meaning and direction that enables people to overcome the problems of the present.

The example of Butterfield amuses but it does not surprise us, because we are aware of this oscillation in our own lives: how as thinking individuals we are sceptical of the received myths of our tribe, yet at times of stress can be swayed by mass patriotic emotions. In spite of the deconstructive work of scholars, national identities remain embedded as a living force in many (though not all) societies, organising individual and collective activities. In this book I wish to explore why this is so.

In doing so, I wish to take issue with the dominant modernist school of scholars, who view nations as peculiar outgrowths of modernity and attachments to 'ancient' ethnic myths and symbols as a form of false consciousness.

We must be grateful for the searching insights of scholars such as Ernest Gellner, Eric Hobsbawm, Benedict Anderson and John Breuilly, but they tend to view national identities either in functional or instrumental terms, as mechanisms through which a 'modernisation' process comes into being or is sustained. Instead, I put forward a view of nations as products of powerful and usually protracted experiences, occurring well before the modern period, that are centrally involved in directing the pathways of modern societies.

Modernists acknowledge the dual aspect of nations: on the one hand, the orientation to an allegedly ancient ethnic past, and, on the other, their commitment to collective autonomy and progress. They discount, however, nationalist claims to continuities. Nations are, they maintain, radically distinct from ethnic groups, which are quasi-kinship groups, perpetuated by myths of common descent, a sense of shared history and distinctive culture. They are, above all, 'rational' political organisations, and though they may employ selectively ethnic symbols, this is for instrumental or decorative rather than substantive purposes.

From this perspective, nations are relatively recent products of modernisation or rationalisation as exemplified in the rise of the bureaucratic state, industrial economy and secular concepts of human autonomy. Nations are culturally homogeneous, and products of a linear process through which regions and social strata are steadily incorporated, in the course of the nineteenth century, into unified and sovereign societies by state and market.

Such interpretations frequently are allied to globalisation perspectives that perceive the nation as a transitional unit between traditional localism and planetary interdependence. Ethnicity is dismissed as a characteristic of 'simpler', 'pre-political' societies, or of marginal groups destined to assimilate into existing states. Hobsbawm (1990: ch. 6) acknowledges the reality of current ethnic revivals, but he characterises them as temporary irrational reactions to disruptive social change with no capacity to negotiate the future. With the further rise in scale of political, military, economic and cultural integration and mass international migrations, national sovereignty has become a thing of the past, and the future lies with regional and global institutions, such as the European Union and the United Nations (Hobsbawm, 1990; McNeill, 1986).

These scholars offer powerful insights, but their stress on the novelty of nations and their emergence as an outgrowth of 'modern' organisational forms leads to several weaknesses that together suggest a systemic failure of explanation.

First, their emphasis on the modern character of the nation fails to account for the power of ethno-historical memories (real or imagined) of premodern periods to mobilise mass political campaigns to restructure the modern state. Such revivals often reinforce powerful premodern institutions and values, particularly religious, which define the modern state and conceptions of citizenship.

Secondly, modernists, in focusing on the political and economic revolutions of the modern world, neglect the profound cultural struggles engendered by nationalism, which result in the formation of the new moral community of the nation. The nation is not an 'invented tradition' or even an 'imagined community', but rather is built, sometimes with great difficulty, on an earlier ethnic substratum.

Thirdly, although modernists are aware of regional and other diversities, because of their focus on cultural homogeneity, they fail to emphasise that most nations are riven by embedded cultural differences that generate rival symbolic and political projects.

Finally, modernists' view of nation-formation as culminating in a sovereign and unified society is problematic. It fails to address variations between 'mature' nation-states in the range of social spheres explicitly governed by national norms. It overlooks the oscillations between national and imperial, class, regional and religious identities throughout the modern period (Connor, 1990).

Because of these weaknesses, these interpretations cannot satisfactorily explain the current national revival sweeping much of the globe. Moreover, since this national differentiation is occurring in a period of an allegedly global homogenisation of peoples, we need a more nuanced account of the possible forms of accommodation between national and transnational organisations than one that assumes the supersession of the former.

An Alternative Model

One of the faults of these interpretations is of an over-coherent model of what is called the modernisation process. According to this, populations are increasingly mobilised in support of a national state (either existing or prospective), and, once formed, a national state operates as a unitary society, directing development from a centre. As Michael Mann (1986: ch. 1) argues, we have to reject such unified models of society; throughout history populations inhabit four overlapping and competing networks of power – political, military, economic and ideological – each with different boundaries and institutions, and developing in uneven and unpredictable means. Neither in the nineteenth century nor in the present have nations or national states been autonomous social wholes, but have instead been subject to unforeseen shocks (wars, economic revolutions, ideological ferment and migration flows), which have instigated a periodic redrawing of the boundaries between 'insiders' and 'outsiders' and a questioning of the status order within political communities. The recurring shocks of the modern period have periodically both undermined the authority of national identities with respect to others, and triggered nationalist movements to restore autonomy and a stable and distinctive collective identity.

For these reasons we should consider an alternative model of national-formation: one that conceives of the nation as a species of ethnic project, only contingently related to the state, and which recognises that the power of states to regulate populations is limited and fluctuating. This model should explicitly address:

- the enduring character of nations based on a sense of being embedded in much older (ethnic) communities that have survived centuries of vicissitudes;
- the internal cultural revolutions required before nationalists are able to overcome established identities, including ethnic traditions;
- the persistence and functions of cultural difference in nations; and
- the episodic character of nationalist resurgences throughout the modern period.

From this comparative historical perspective we can throw new light on contemporary debates about the future of nationalism, nations and national states in a world marked by globalisation, regionalism and religious resurgence.

This book argues that nations are zones of conflict. National identities are so deeply implicated in our modern consciousness because the collective identities on which they are based are embedded by centuries of conflicts, memories of which are carried into the modern world by several institutions. Because they are so deeply institutionalised, the rise of nationalism is accompanied by struggles of legitimacy with traditional power holders, and there remain tensions between traditionalists and national modernisers in many societies. Moreover, the modernist assumption that national cultures tend to homogenisation underplays the role of cultural wars within nationalism as protagonists look to alternative pasts as inspiration for their programmes. Although it is true that populations are increasingly regulated by states through the granting of citizenship rights, this in itself does not create unitary and sovereign national societies. Nationalism is an episodic movement, provoked by periodic incapacities of states to protect the nation throughout the modern period. This suggests that so far from being 'passive' outgrowths of modern forces, nations are dynamic entities that structure our response to the multiple and unpredictable processes we encounter. These insights are brought to bear on current debates about the future of nations, which are allegedly threatened by globalisation, regionalism, continentalism and religious resurgence.

This episodic interpretation seeks to combine two apparently antithetical approaches. The first is the *longue durée* 'ethnosymbolic' framework developed by such scholars as John Armstrong and Anthony D. Smith, which views nations as dynamic, long term historical processes that structure the forms of modernity. The second is a 'postmodernist' framework (see Özkirimli, 2000; Yuval-Davis, 1997), which emphasises that collectivities and individuals have multiple and conflictual identities over which there can be no final consensus. I agree with the postmodernists in rejecting the notion of a modernisation process that results in a world of unitary sovereign nation-states and in the importance of looking at contest and conflict in shaping collectivities. But I reject their idealist and asociological voluntarism that ignores the binding power of identities when they are institutionalised. I also see no evidence that an acknowledgement of multiple identities should lead us to suppose we are witnessing a shift to a multicultural postmodernity.

In integrating the insights of postmodernists within an ethnosymbolic framework, I seek to combine an appreciation of the enduring character of modern nations with the important role of conflict in their formation, and to argue that the preservation of persisting differences and rival cultural repertoire is one of the important reasons for the adaptability of the nation throughout two centuries of tumultuous change.

A definitional note: throughout the text, I refer to national states rather than nation-states. This is in acknowledgement that almost all states have national or ethnic minorities. A national state is a state organised by the norms of its dominant nation.

Organisation

Chapter 1, although accepting the modernists' argument that as politicised ethnicities nations are relatively recent, rejects the contrast modernists frequently make between a highly stratified and static premodern world, and a highly mobile post-eighteenth century one. It argues that nations are based on older ethnic formations, which have crystallised in the process of conflicts arising from missionary religions, imperial expansion, warfare, long distance trade and mass migrations and colonisations. Exposed to multiple challenges, most ethnicities that survive have layered or multiple pasts that may be embedded by several institutions. Although modernist scholars tend to view nations as products of modernising and anti-traditionalist states that erode older identifications, modernisation also intensifies the challenges to state autonomy. To secure the survival of the nation political elites must ally with older ethnocommunal identities, which then have a directive effect on modern societies.

Chapter 2 rejects the modernist conception of nations as 'invented traditions' capable of easily overriding pre-existing loyalties. It suggests that a revivalist nationalism crystallises from the conflicts between traditionalism and modernisation, mentioned above. Rejecting the assumptions of European and Christian superiority, revivalism proposed a revolutionary ethnic model of a humanity built on self-actualising nations whose origins were in the 'East', each of which contributed or would contribute to human progress. This was a dynamic ideology legitimising the regeneration of declining nations by cultural exchange. Cultural minorities, including religious minorities, ensured the global diffusion of this ideology. Revivalism gained wider resonance when traditional societies, faced with external challenges, had to innovate by cultural borrowing. It used two strategies to overcome ethnic traditionalism. One was internal moral transformation by employing an alternative (dynamic) past to redefine what is authentic tradition. The other was 'mythic overlaying': the creation of a counter tradition of heroic activism based on a cult of national sacrifice that legitimised political revolution when traditional elites seemed powerless. However, this overlaid and did not eradicate older, often religiously-based ethnic identities, and divisions between secularists and religious bedevil many nations.

Chapter 3 shows how many nations, because of their multiple heritages, are riven by long running cultural conflicts that espouse radically different views of the structure of politics, the status of social groups, relations between regions, the countryside and the city, economic and social policies and foreign policy. By relating these rival visions to traumatic historical cleavages, it explores the functions and consequences of such conflicts in the shaping of modern societies. On the one hand, these conflicts institutionalise cultural pluralism, but, on the other, they can lead to a polarisation that at times erupts into civil war. It argues that their persistence undermines the modernist assumption that nations demonstrate a trend towards homogenisation. The persistence of these conflicts can be explained in part by the geopolitical position of nations, and in part by the fact that nations are shaped by several historical legacies.

Chapter 4 rejects the dominant linear conception of nation-formation that assumes a shift from an ideological nationalism of elites to the routinised identities of sovereign national states as rival class, regional and religious groups are incorporated from above into solidary mass nations. Such an approach confuses statism with nationalism: in fact these two phenomena regularly come into conflict. It maintains that throughout the modern period nations and national states have been beset by class, regional and religious conflicts and that national states have never been sovereign actors. It suggests the co-existence in time of two forms of nationalism – the 'sacred' transformational movement produced during crisis, and the 'profane' or banal nationalism that people unselfconsciously consume as part of giving meaning to the experiences of everyday life. In seeking to explain fluctuations in the salience of national identities, it identifies unpredictable factors such as warfare, famines and large-scale migrations of populations that trigger movements from below for and against the nation and national state.

Chapter 5 applies these findings to contemporary debates about subordination of nation and national state loyalties to more extensive global, regional (e.g., the EU) and religious identities. It argues that in the *longue durée* ethnies and nations have been agents of global, European and religious networks and that the historical processes of globalisation (warfare, imperial expansion, trade and missionary religions) are precisely those that have resulted periodically in the crystallisation of new ethnic layers. Because many national heritages are multilayered, and globalisation itself is not unitary but multiple, disaggregated and contradictory in its forms, nations can select from a range of options by which to preserve their identity and achieve social progress. I argue too that a sense of nationality and a mission to Europe historically have been intertwined, and in the past religious and secular conceptions have gone hand in hand. What we call globalisation in the contemporary period is likely to lead to the intensification of nationalism and national identities rather than to their erosion.

1

Zones of Conflict

Introduction

In *Imagined Communities*, Benedict Anderson (1991: 6) likens the style of imagining of the nation to that of kinship. Indeed, nationalists invariably depicted the nation as 'a family', which calls on the 'natural' solidarity of its members. The names of nations are drawn largely from ancient peoples – England from Angles, Finland from Finns, France from Franks, Russians from Rus, Vietnam from Viet – with the implied claim that the nation is a primordial unit of humanity. Nations inhabit not just a territory but a Fatherland or Motherland that contains the blood and bones of their ancestors. They are bound by 'memories' of common triumph and disaster, recalled in yearly rituals and commemorations: for Jews Yom Kippur, for Ulster Protestants the Battle of the Boyne, for Serbs their calamitous defeat of 1389 in Kosovo. They claim a unique cultural mission, sometimes expressed in the form of being a chosen people; Ireland was an *insula sacra*, Russia a Holy Mother, Georgia the location of the Garden of Eden, and Sri Lanka, sacralised by a legendary visit of the Buddha, means 'Island of the Good Law'. Their character as self-governing peoples is justified by ancestral polities or founding charters: the Scots extol the Declaration of Arbroath (1320); the Basques their *fueros*; and Icelanders their tenth-century *Althing* (assembly).

All this suggests that nations are a species of ethnic group. Yet most scholars argue that nations are products of novel political, economic and cognitive processes. These modernist scholars, as we shall call them, agree that nations are Janus-faced: on the one hand, oriented to an ancient ethnic past, on the other, futuristic in mobilising populations for collective autonomy and progress (Nairn, 1975: ch. 9). They, however, reject as mythical, nationalist claims to continuity with ancient (ethnic) communities (Anderson, 1991; Breuilly, 1982, 1996; Calhoun, 1994; Gellner, 1964, 1983; Hobsbawm, 1990; Kedourie, 1960). Nations are radically distinct from ethnic groups, which are quasi-kinship groups. They are, above all, 'rational' political organisations, and though they may employ selectively ethnic symbols, this is for decorative rather than substantive purposes (cf. Hutchinson, 1994: ch. 1). A modernist politics is concerned with the construction of new identities, conceived in the enlightenment norms of universal equality, self-emancipation of the individual through the 'rational' institutions, and abstract freedoms of a 'scientific state'.

In this chapter I will argue (against the modernists) that there is a clear relationship between ethnic and national formation, after examining first the modernist critique of ethnic-based approaches, and then an alternative ethnosymbolic framework. I seek to demonstrate three points. First, ethnic-formation is a recurring phenomenon in history, engendered frequently by conflict. Secondly, ethnic communities have been enduring cultural and political actors in the premodern period, assuming forms often comparable to the modern nation. Thirdly, though nations have novel features, they are products of factors cutting across the premodern–modern divide, and earlier ethnic identities may have a directive effect on nation-formation.

The Modernist Critique

Modernists reject what they see as the 'primordialist' assumptions that have pervaded the scholarship on nationalism: that nations are historical givens, have been a continuous presence in human history and exert some inherent power over both past and present generations. They also reject a more moderate 'perennialist' position, that nations can be found in many eras before the modern period. From the modernist perspective, nations are outgrowths of modernisation or rationalisation as exemplified in the rise of the bureaucratic state, industrial economy and secular concepts of human autonomy. The premodern world is one of heterogeneous political formations (of empire, city-state, theocratic territories) legitimated by dynastic and religious principles, marked by linguistic and cultural diversity, fluid or disaggregated territorial boundaries and enduring social and regional stratifications. This putatively disappears in favour of a world of nation-states. Such interpretations emphasise five major aspects of these formations (Hutchinson, 1994: 4–6). Nations are

- secular political units, infused with ideas of popular sovereignty, which seek realisation in the achievement of an independent *state*, united through universalistic citizenship rights;

- consolidated territories, that exemplify the new scales of organisation brought about by the bureaucratic state and market economy that have eroded regional and local loyalties and engendered more intensive networks of communication;
- ethnically homogeneous compared with earlier polyethnic societies, by virtue of state policies, including the promotion of official languages, the inculcation of a patriotic ethos in education and the expulsion of minorities;
- high cultural units based on a standard vernacular language, literacy and print capitalism, whose new genres of newspaper and novel provide the necessary basis of an extensive industrial society of strangers;
- industrial urban societies with a high degree of territorial integration, whose large-scale career pathways create a new mobile middle class that dominates national life.

Modernist scholars are dismissive of continuities with ethnic groups. These are small scale and are essentially *prepolitical*, at best providing raw materials on which nation-builders can draw. The significant premodern political units were dynastic monarchies and empires whose ethos was aristocratic. These might employ ethnic groups for specialised tasks in state administration, but ethnic considerations *per se* had little influence on their governance. Before the eighteenth century the major forms of identification were religious, and in Europe, the Middle East and much of Asia, the universalism of Christianity, Islam and Buddhism ensured a marginal position for ethnicity in the regulation of public institutions and the legitimacy of rulers. For modernists the primary institutions of national culture are products of relatively recent processes. Anderson (1991: 25–36) contrasts the mythic and recurring temporality of religious premodernity with the linear homogeneous empty time experienced by national communities. The crucial aspect of national culture is not language as such but printed vernaculars that allow for the creation and transmission of high cultures based on the language or dialects of the people. Anderson explains this as the effect of print capitalists, and although such languages emerge in the early modern period at the time of Luther, it is only with the larger extension of literacy and the formation of urban middle-class genres such as the newspaper and the novel that the mass anonymous nation becomes imaginable. In these accounts national cultures are passive and malleable, forged by modern institutions and social strata. Although nationalists may employ ethnic idioms and symbols, this is for instrumental reasons, as part of the construction, even invention, of novel political communities.

11

Underlying modernist models are assumptions that before the eighteenth century the mass of the people lived in highly localised worlds, detached from elites who had broader horizons. There was an intercontinental network of urban trade connecting Northern European Christianity, the Islamic Levant and (via the silk and spice routes) the Indian subcontinent and China, but the vast proportion of the population lived in agrarian village-based subsistence economies, insulated from such influences (Abu-Lughod, 1993: 77). The dominant belief systems after the coming of Karl Jaspers's 'axial age' were universalist religions, which bound peoples into civilisations regulated by clerisies whose languages (Arabic, Latin, Sanskrit) came to bear little relation to vernacular cultures. Given the limited penetration of state structures, which were often imperial, such populations had little political awareness outside their own villages. For this reason they not only lacked national identities but, when they possessed ethnic identities, these had little extensive or intensive social and political salience. It is the radical mobility of industrialism and the large-scale organisational capacities of states that explain the rise of nations. The world of nations therefore is an invention of modern processes.

These interpretations cannot be dismissed lightly. Compared with their predecessors post-eighteenth-century nations, undoubtedly do have distinctive social, economic and political features. Centralising states play a decisive role in their formation and persistence, and the interstate system as it has developed globally is constitutive, at once constraining minority populations and driving them to find a protective state roof of their own. But the stress on the novelty of nations and their emergence as an outgrowth of 'modern' organisational forms, leads to several weaknesses that together suggest a systemic failure of explanation for several reasons.

1. In many periods in history ethnicity provides an important framework of collective identity and of collective political action.
2. Modernists fail to acknowledge the many different sources of dynamism and unpredictability in the premodern era that can act as catalysts of ethnic formation.
3. Although many ethnic identities do face erosion, others become embedded in vernacular literatures, religious institutions and legal codes and take on a larger social and political salience, similar, in many respects, to the modern nation.
4. Because the sources of ethnic formation are multiple, most long-lived ethnic cultures are multilayered, which provides ethnic communities with alternatives at times of crises.

5. An overemphasis on the statist character of the nation fails to acknowledge the vulnerability of the state in the modern world that leads to ethno-communal revivals seeking to restructure the modern political community, redefining its territorial extent, cultural character and conceptions of citizenship. Since these movements may arise within dominant (e.g. Russian) as well as minority nationalities (e.g. Basque and Catalan), this means ethnicity cannot be dismissed as a residual or reactive principle. It is an important regulatory principle of contemporary politics, concerned with questions of the moral content and the boundaries of a collectivity over which power is exercised, rather than of power, *per se*.
6. Older ethnic principles define to a considerable degree the nature of such revivals, and hence have a directive effect in the formation of the modern nation.

There are two important issues here. One is a question of definition. By making the idea of popular sovereignty and the political integration of the masses central to the concept of nation, modernists 'win' their case by default, since it is clear that the pervasiveness of such ideas emerges with the European Enlightenment. But this evades the issue of whether *sentiments*, as opposed to the ideology, may have a much older basis and affect the formation of later national ideologies. For ethnosymbolists such national sentiments are formed over long periods of time from the coming together of myths, memories, symbols and cultures.

The second issue is empirical and linked to the first: because of the stipulative and narrowly *Political* (as opposed to political) nature of the definition, modernists have felt little need to examine the historical record before 1800. A cursory glance will show that the static localised conception will not hold for many periods in many areas of the world, and that political and social institutions have attached themselves and 'carried' ethnic sentiments.

Ethnosymbolists and Recurring Factors

I adopt, instead, an ethnosymbolic framework, building on the work of John Armstrong (1982) and Anthony Smith (1986: ch. 1, 1999: Introduction). This approach seeks a middle ground between opposed primordialist and modernist stances. It views the post-eighteenth-century nation as a *novel* species of ethnic group whose formation has to be understood in *la longue durée*. From primordialists such as Clifford Geertz (1963), ethnosymbolists have an appreciation of the long term affective power of ethnic sentiments and symbols, and from the perennialists such as Adrian Hastings (1997), the salience of complex ethnic polities in history and their role in providing the building blocks of modern nations. But they agree with modernist arguments about the distinctiveness of the post-eighteenth-century world of nations and the crucial role played by the ideology of nationalism and novel social processes such as secularisation, bureaucratisation and industrialisation.

Smith's definition of nation differentiates between the ethnie (ethnic community) and nation. An ethnie is 'a named unit of population, with common ancestry myths and shared historical memories, elements of shared culture, a link with a historic territory, and some measure of solidarity, at least among the elites'. A nation is 'a named human population sharing a historic territory, common myths and historical memories, sharing a mass public culture, a common economy and common legal rights and duties for all members' (Smith, 2001: 19). There is thus a strong definitional overlap between the two entities. This overlap is still closer in later definitions: Smith (2002: 15) drops the necessity of a common economy. We shall see that they are affiliated in two other ways. First, ethnic and national formation results from recurring factors cutting across the premodern–modern divide and, secondly, pre-existing ethnic identities shape the formation of modern nations.

The central focus of ethnosymbolism then is the relationship between ethnie and nation. Smith and Armstrong differ somewhat in their approach. Armstrong, influenced by Fredrik Barth, views ethnic communities as boundary marking groups, and in *Nations before Nationalism* he examines the ways such identities crystallise and persist because of encounters on frontiers: between nomadic and sedentary societies, between religious civilisations, between warring empires and between language areas. Smith instead focuses on the inner springs through which populations develop an 'awareness' of being unique: for example, a sense of being religiously chosen or the process of settling in a new land causes populations to form and maintain boundaries with others. An ethnic group thus is not defined solely by physical descent or even the myth of physical descent, nor is it accurate to dub it 'pre-political'. For both an ethnic group is a *moral* community characterised by a sense of common origins, identification with a territory, and a commitment to a specific culture. It is also political since there is always a structure of authority to be legitimised, though the political order can vary enormously from that ruled by a military chieftain (a Mongol Khan) to that maintained by a kingdom or Commonwealth.

Whatever their nuances, these scholars stress the importance of viewing formation and persistence of ethnie and nations over the long duration that can result in the embedding of many sets of collective repertoire out of which a national consciousness may develop. They also accentuate the subjective dimension of ethnic and national consciousness as presented in myths, memories and symbols which, when given force in institutions and activities of communities, 'objectify' populations.

Ethnicity is thus meaning-directed, revealed in assemblages of myths, which define for populations unique origins (where they have come from), location (why they are where they are), a golden age (their unique historical achievements), degeneration (why they have fallen) and regeneration (how they can return to their former glory). They explain the group to itself and fulfil many functions, including the intergenerational reproduction of a sense of group honour that enables survival. Memories are important, especially as portrayed in commemorative rituals of epochal events and heroes that provide role models and lessons for the present. Symbols, when encoded in the urban architecture of capital cities, sacred religious texts or sites, legal codes, languages and political charters and constitutions, persist over long expanses of time and space and thereby communicate a sense of group meaning. Finally, a key role is played by social institutions such as states, churches, legal systems, vernacular languages and literatures whose organisations and communication networks form populations into distinctive cultural communities, which differentiate themselves from others. In Steven Grosby's terms, a stable ethnicity is dependent on the constitution of a collective imaginative core that, even though it may contain conflicting elements, orients populations through time (Grosby, 2002: 244–5).

This framework is useful for bringing out hitherto underexplored aspects of nation-formation. Although I tend to favour an emphasis on the dynamic moral qualities of ethnicity, on which Smith concentrates, Fredrik Barth's boundary approach to ethnicity (employed by Armstrong) can be exploited to explore hitherto neglected aspects of nation-formation, including the functions of internal cultural conflicts, the shifting salience of national identities in the modern world, and compatibility of national with global, regional and religious identities.

The main purpose of this chapter is to highlight many of the neglected factors and processes that cut across the premodern–modern divide and help explain the ethnic resurgence in the modern period. An emphasis on a sense of difference and historical self-consciousness implies a sense of interaction and competition between populations, and of the existence of extensive networks of communications. One of the weaknesses of the modernists is the depiction of the premodern world as essentially localised, immobile and historically frozen in its social stratifications. Many historical periods, however, are marked by profound social changes. Robert Bartlett (1993: 3) portrays the high middle ages (950–1350) as one of the establishment of states by conquest, and of migrations into the 'periphery' of Europe, including the English colonisation of Ireland, the German movements into Eastern Europe, the Spanish reconquest and the struggle of Crusaders against Muslims in the Eastern Mediterranean. Although by the fourteenth century populations in the centre of Europe – England, France, Germany Scandinavia, North Italy and Spain – were becoming more homogeneous, on the margins ethnic conflict continued on issues of language, law and religion (Bartlett, 1993: 313).

Ethnogenetic Factors

In fact there are many periods of world history characterised by large scale disruption and trauma, in which the processes responsible – religious evangelism, imperial conquests, warfare and state expansion, migrations and long distance trade, many of which are the subject of Bartlett's analyses – were the catalysts of ethnic formation.

Religion

Although the rise of universalist scriptural religions has been regarded as eroding ethnic affiliations to territory and culture, they have often been catalysts of ethnic and, some would argue, national formation.

Adrian Hastings recognises the universalist thrust in Christianity that permitted it to ally with imperial polities (e.g. the Roman Empire) and enforce a transethnic high civilisation that smothered local ethnic cultures. Nonetheless, he claims a special nationalising role for Christianity (Hastings, 1997: chs. 1, 8). Evangelism, inspired by the biblical recognition of linguistic diversity, effected the translation of the scriptures into local languages and the proliferation of written vernaculars in order to reach the people. In presenting Israel as the exemplary political community of unified kingdom, sacred territory and holy people bound by distinctive culture, the Old Testament diffused the model of the nation, first in Western Europe, then, as Christianity expanded with European imperialism, world wide.

The central aspect of ancient Judaism was the idea of being a chosen people by virtue of its covenant with God through which the Israelites undertook to obey His commandments. The model had various translations. Medieval dynasties claiming descent from biblical figures transferred the aura of election to their kingdoms as embodied in the ruler, and sacred kingship formed in the personages of Charlemagne, the Holy Roman Emperor, St Louis of France, St Stephen of Hungary and St Sava of Serbia. Arguably, it is in later Protestant populations, with their emphasis on the community of believers rather than episcopacies and rulers, that the covenantal model is strongest, for example during the seventeenth century in Cromwell's English Commonwealth and the Dutch Republic, which proclaimed themselves to be new Israels (Gorski, 2000). The consequences of being a people of the Covenant are a historical consciousness, legalism, mass literacy and scripturalism (Akenson, 1992: ch. 1). The priesthood must be formed to enforce the holy laws and practices that separate the community from profane others; the history of the people, especially its relationship with God, becomes sacred, to be recorded in writing (scriptures) and consulted at times of crisis; since the covenant is with the people, not with rulers, a mass literacy is promoted so that all believers can read the scriptures in written form. By these means a sacred ethnic community is formed embedded at a demotic level, which can survive political disaster. The idea of being a providential group preserving God's sacred values in a world of evil appealed especially to colonising groups such as the Pilgrim Fathers, Afrikaners and Ulster Scots, for whom the biblical story of exodus provided justification of their claims to territory in their new lands and a calling as a 'redeemer' people.

Christianity, however, was not unique. All evangelising religions have had to accommodate the ethos and practices of the previous cultures in order to reach the people. They have been used by rulers to build culturally cohesive populations, differentiated from neighbouring groups. Their tendency to schism and internal differentiation can contribute to the transformation of ethnic categories into rival ethnic communities, and wars between political communities of different faiths have often generated ethnic myths.

In the early medieval period, many Eastern European rulers – Prince Ratislav of Moravia, Tsar Boris of Bulgaria, King Stephen of Hungary, Mieszko of Poland – used Christianity in order to form diverse pagan groups into a solidarist 'nation' and, in turn, were sanctified as saints. Tsar Boris selected Byzantine Orthodoxy, hoping to create an ethnic Church that would unite his Slavic peoples and break the power of his nobility. Mieszko converted to Catholicism in 996 to forestall a German crusade against his pagan tribes, and chose his priests from his fellow Slavic neighbours, the Czechs. Prince Ratsko, youngest son of King Nemanja of Serbia, founded a Serbian Orthodox Church, independent of the Byzantines, and was its first primate. In turn, Christian figures sanctified these kingdoms by turning the rulers into saints (Petrovich, 2000: 1359–61). In the seventh and eighth centuries AD Tibetan rulers used Mahayana Buddhism to create a unified state and wrest control of territories from T'ang China, as did the Vietnamese from the tenth century, after breaking from Chinese rule, in order to distance their populations from neo-Confucianism. The resulting wars inspired the rise of a historical literature and of a vernacular script (Farmer et al., 1986: 326–31). The institution of kingship in Sri Lanka developed in association with the spread of Theravada Buddhism in the third century BC and Buddhist monastic orders participated in wars against Tamil invaders (Carrithers, 1984).

Just as Christianity had, Islam, Buddhism and Hinduism fissured into different traditions, creating or re-inforcing ethnic identities whenever rival traditions took root in adjacent and competing populations or states. Islam, by prescribing Arabic as the sacred language of the Koran, did in general undermine the status of local vernaculars. In Iran, however, the new Safavid dynasty in 1501 tapped a Persian resentment at the Arab conquest, already expressed in a nineth-century Persian literary revival, by making the 'heretical' Shi'ism the official religion of the state. This was followed by a large-scale Persian ethnocultural revival, including traditional representational art forbidden by Islamic teachings, which was given intensity by the wars against the Sunni Ottoman Empire (Savory, 1992). A Sikh ethnicity arose as a break away from Hinduism in the sixteenth century, gradually forming into a distinctive ethnocultural group with sacred centres (Amritsar), identification with a homeland (the Punjab) and a distinctive way of life (Van der Veer, 1994: 53–6).

As John Armstrong (1982: ch. 3) demonstrates, the global ambitions of rival proselytising religions brought them into military conflict, and states on the fault lines defined themselves as elect polities, destined to be the border guards of their civilisation. The wars of the Crusades are well known. Conflict between Islam and Christianity continued for over one thousand years from the eighth century onwards in two major zones: the Iberian-Mediterranean and Eastern Slav frontiers. The intermittent but recurring conflicts saw several Christian polities (Byzantium, Castilian Spain, Poland, Hungary and Tsarist Russia), define themselves as *antemurale Christianitas*, and Muslim states such as the Ottoman Empire, Safavid Iran and Mameluke Egypt claim *ghazi* ('warrior of the faith') status. A series of different mythomoteurs (constitutive myths of a polity) developed in these zones of conflict. After the Arab conquest of much of Iberia in the eighth century a Castilian Conquistador mythomoteur formed, followed in the eleventh century by one presenting Christian Castile as the defender of a pluralist society including Muslim and Jewish *millets* (religions communities), and finally, in the fifteenth century, by a myth of the united kingdoms of Castile and Aragon as defenders of an Iberian Catholic purity. The shattering defeat of the Rus polities by the Mongols in the thirteenth century created the myth of the Tatar yoke and a permanent Russian fear of the Eastern steppe and drive to conquer this threat by expansion. The successful Russian rebellion against the Muslim Tatars from the late fourteenth century led to the Russian rulers assuming control of two traditions, one of Orthodox crusade against Islam and the other of establishing an Empire of the steppe.

Armstrong observes that one of the features of such border polities, engaged in long-range religious warfare across shifting frontiers, is a concern with quasi-racial purification and fear of cultural contamination. In the Spanish case this was reflected in a concern with blood purity and their expulsion of the Moors and Jews, and their militant attack on heresy during the Counter-reformation; in the Russian case it was expressed by a fear that they were losing their 'European' characteristics as they absorbed more Asian populations.

Antemurale myths also re-emerged from wars between Catholic and Orthodox and between Catholic and Protestant states. England and Holland saw themselves as the bulwarks of Protestant liberty against Catholic despotism. Poland formed its myth of being the *antemurale Christianitas*, in defending Christianity against the Tatars and Turks, and Catholicism against Asiatic Russian Orthodoxy and German Lutheranism. All of these identifications have strongly shaped the trajectories of the modern nations.

Empires

Empires, likewise, have been considered as the enemy of a politicised ethnicity. The expansion of the Romanov state into an Orthodox multi-ethnic empire, absorbing imperfectly other Christian ethnicities including Ukrainians, Georgians and Armenians, tended to swamp the development of a Russian national identity as well as that of the populations they ruled. The state claimed a mission to the Slavic peoples, symbolised in the architecture of St Basil in Moscow and its massive Kremlin complex, which sought to appropriate the legacy of Rome.

Nonetheless, empires, when viewed in dynamic geopolitical terms, as they undergo patterns of territorial expansion and contraction in rivalry with each other, periodically reinforce an ethnic consciousness (Collins, 2000: ch. 3). An ethnic consciousness could arise as an unintended consequence of

19

imperial expansions. Peter the Great's attempts to create a secular basis for his empire and his onslaught on its Orthodox identity allowed the transfer of ethnoreligious symbols from the state to opposition groups among the Russian people (Hosking, 1997: 207–8). Since empires generally expand from a dominant ethnic core, smaller ethnies on the periphery are most affected by such rivalry, often developing a consciousness as 'natural victims' (Pearson, 1983: 190–1). A powerful ethnicity was forged in Armenian and Jewish populations, caught on exposed trade and communication routes between rival Roman and Persian empires, who suffered collective subjugation and 'exile' (Armstrong, 1982: ch. 7). Indeed, the recurring struggles of empires, especially those on the religious fault lines, could create shatter zones in which populations were intermingled and ethnicities played off against each other. One example is the Balkans region fought over by the Habsburg and Ottoman Empires, where Croats saw themselves as the defenders of Catholic Christianity against the Muslim Turk and differentiated themselves from their Orthodox Serb neighbours with whom they shared a common language.

Empires, Michael Hechter (2000, chs. 2, 3) claims, may consolidate ethnic communities through systems of indirect rule that reinforce indigenous leaderships. Expanding polities in Europe and elsewhere tended to respect local legal systems and rules. Where imperial conquest destroyed political institutions of peoples, churches played important roles as embodiments of ethnic identity and independence. Examples include the Uniate Catholic Church as the fortress of Ukrainian ethnicity against Poland after the Union of Brest in 1596. The Jews in Poland were given substantial religious and civil self-government in sixteenth-century Poland (Petrovich, 2000: 1367).

The classic example is the millet system of the Islamic Ottoman Empire, which was a military theocracy that devolved power to religious organisations since it (erroneously) equated people and religion. This could work to reinforce or erode ethnicity. The Armenians and Jews were given their separate millets. Since the Orthodox millet was administered by the Greek patriarch of Constantinople, the system reinforced Greek power and identity, but suppressed the ethnicity of other Orthodox peoples including the Bulgars. When the Serbian Orthodox Church was given independent status within the Empire in 1557, it took on the functions of a 'surrogate ethnic state' (Petrovich, 2000: 1363).

The transcendental myths of ancient and later empires (e.g. Mesopotamia, Rome, Byzantium), conveyed in the urban architecture of their capital cities, rubrics and insignia (Armstrong, 1982: ch. 5), had an extraordinary persistence in time and diffusion in space, providing models for their successors that included not just empires but also territorial states. Roman symbols provided a repertoire for the medieval European polities that sought legitimation by claiming descent not just from biblical figures but also from the Trojan founders of Rome. Armstrong finds a precocious nationalism developing in the later Byzantium Empire which, as its territories shrank, was reduced to the Greek-speaking population that dominated its administration in Constantinople and expressed a distinctive ethno-religious mission differentiating it both from Latin Christianity that had sacked Constantinople during the Fourth Crusade and also the encroaching Islamic enemy.

Interstate competition

That said, such empires tended to suppress the political expression of ethnic identities, which were more visible in those areas and periods where power were decentralised in the form of competing states, often arising either out of the collapse of such empires. As the Chinese T'ang Empire went into decline from the eighth century, several strong independent polities formed with an ethnic character – Tibetan, Viet, Turkic and Korean (Farmer et al., 1986: 328–34). Before that Anthony Smith locates an interstate system developing in the ancient Middle East that gave rise to such ethnic polities as Sumer, Babylon, Egypt and Israel. Historians, however, focus above all on the rise of an interstate system developing in medieval Europe where, following the collapse of the Roman Empire in the west, the conflict between the Papacy and Holy Roman Empire prevented any possibility of politically unifying European Christendom under a successor Empire.

As Michael Howard (1976) has argued, military competition between kingdoms in Western Europe, combined with the rise of new technologies of warfare, created the matrix out of which the modern European national states emerged. Smith (1981) recognises the impetus given by state centralisation, but concentrates on the importance of interstate warfare as a crystalliser of ethnic and national images and identities. Warfare has ethnicising effects by mobilising localised groups into a state army and thereby creating an identification with a larger territorial 'homeland', by generating propaganda through which mutually opposing ethnic stereotypes are constructed between opposing populations, and by throwing up heroes and epochal battles. Such epic events, when celebrated subsequently by poets, historians and artists such as Froissart and Shakespeare, develop a legendary status and through commemorative rituals become institutionalised in the group consciousness. The social effects of warfare on populations were more limited when it was conducted by mercenaries or a small aristocratic stratum, or, indeed, a corps of professionals. But recurring and protracted interstate wars between feudal states such as the Hundred Years War between the French and English kingdoms could result in a social penetration of ethnic sentiments. Even when wars resulted in the overthrow of a state, an ethnic consciousness could persist, especially where groups defined themselves in religious terms, interpreting their defeat like the Serbs at the Battle of Kosovo as a test of their commitment to the true religion. A religious sense of election thus explains away defeat, and indeed instils a reinforced drive to defend collective traditions as a means of eventually regaining divine favour.

Others (Howard, 1976; McNeill, 1984; Mann, 1986; Tilly, 1975) have explored the relationship between warfare, the formation of efficient centralised states and the gradual emergence of a national territorial consciousness. Competition between kingdoms in Western Europe and the development of new military technologies began to privilege efficient centralised political administrations with consolidated territories, culturally united populations and prosperous economies. Susan Reynolds argues that recurring warfare in the thirteenth and fourteenth centuries transformed the kingdoms of England, Scotland and France into enduring regnal communities with widely shared myths of descent (see also Ichijo, 2002: 59–62). As rulers sought to extend royal powers to raise taxation over the territory, they inspired movements of resistance led by the nobility who, in the name of the community of the realm, won charters of rights such as Magna Carta (Reynolds, 1997: ch. 8). In the early modern period technological improvements, such as rifles, resulted in infantry replacing cavalry as the crucial component of armies, and infantry required drilling and permanent establishments. This, together with innovations in artillery and fortifications, further put a premium on powerful territorial states with efficient administrations and taxation systems.

State centralisation then crystallised and diffused a sense of ethnic consciousness in populations with existing cultural affinities. A key factor in the transformation of dynastic polity into a centralised and sovereign state was the establishment of a fixed capital and/or cathedral cities with a unified administration, architectural buildings (palaces and cathedrals) which acquired 'sacred aura', royal courts, judicial or parliamentary institutions and universities. Paris's establishment as a capital in the late thirteenth century rapidly became the focus of, in Armstrong's words, a 'protonational identity' – its theological and legal schools making it the studium of Christendom, the

Song of Roland mythologising it as Charlemagne's capital, and its closeness to the burial ground of St Denis, fabled counsellor of Charlemagne, providing a sacred status. Such centres provided important avenues of social mobility, drawing the ambitious from more distant areas and forming them into a cohesive elite by socialising them into cultural and linguistic practices: by the fifteenth century the Parisian bourgeoisie provided the main support of royal centralism (Armstrong, 1982: 170).

In England London played as significant a unifying role, not just as the political but as the mercantile and cultural centre of the kingdom (Hastings, 1997: 40, 47). It was the seat of monarchy and of parliament, the legal profession and merchants who were to combat royal authority by invoking the traditions of liberties granted to the community of the realm. By the late sixteenth century antiquaries, drawn heavily from common lawyers, had constructed an Anglo-Saxon myth of English liberties, which rejected the increasing claims of royal authority as an importation of a Norman usurpation (Hill, 1968: 67).

Long distance trade and migrations

Premodern economic patterns are regarded as limiting the possibility of large-scale ethnic attachments since the long-range urban trade in luxury goods stretching from Northern Europe to China had little relation to the subsistence agriculture of the countryside. Ethnic groups, such as the Armenians, Jews, Greeks, Chinese and Indians, were crucial for maintaining this trading network as 'middlemen' minorities providing scarce specialist skills as financiers, brokers and merchants, but they stood outside their surrounding and frequently suspicious agrarian societies (Curtin, 1984: 5–8). W. H. McNeill (1986: 1–31) argues that until the modern period metropolitan civilisations were polyethnic and contrasted with barbarian exceptions in the Eurasian periphery (e.g. England or Japan). It required a demographic explosion in eighteenth-century Western Europe to change this state, resulting in a mass migration of a rural co-cultural population into the cities and hence the emergence of a homogeneous national society.

Nevertheless, the development of long distance trade brought an awareness of the riches of advanced centres, excited the ambitions of groups to control it and brought far-distant cultures into conflict (Bayly, 2002). Waves of steppe migrations or invasions into the wealthy agrarian civilisations of Asia and Europe followed the land-based silk and spice routes which were the land channels of the premodern Eurasian trading network. The Mongol drive for world empire in the thirteenth century and the later conquests of Tamerlane have been explained by historians as motivated in part by a desire to seize control of the silk route. The memory of the 'Mongol/Tatar yoke' had a deep impact on Muscovite Russia, Magyar Hungary and the kingdom of Poland. The Mongol unification of the silk route, it has been claimed, created an information circuit linking Asia and Europe, inspiring European states to discover a more secure seaward route to the fabulous riches of the East recounted in Marco Polo's tales (Adshead, 1993: ch. 3). Columbus's venture led to the accidental European 'discovery' of America, large-scale colonisations that led to new ethnic crystallisations in the New World, and wars between the European great powers in their struggle for overseas wealth and empire. This, together with the religio-dynastic wars of the Reformation on the European subcontinent, was the context from which early modern national identities developed.

Large-scale migrations and invasions could be triggered by many factors, including demographic increase and ecological fragility. McNeill (1963: ch. 10) highlights that one of the patterns of world history from earliest recorded times up to the eighteenth century has been a struggle between warlike steppe nomads and settled agrarian civilisations. Magyar and Russian polities would define themselves as defenders of European Christendom against the Asiatic East. The history of Europe itself has been shaped by a long series of migrations and colonisations, including the Indo-European bands who replaced the indigenous peoples of Greece, the Balkans and Italy; the Celts, who settled in lands from Bohemia to Ireland in the fifth century BC; Germanic peoples, who from the first century BC began to supplant the Celts; Roman invaders, who colonised much of Europe and Asia Minor; Slavs who, from the third century AD settled in the Alps, Carpathian basin, Balkans and Greece; Magyars and Scandinavians, who appeared by the end of the first millennium; and the Turkic peoples who invaded Greece and the Balkans in the fifteenth century (Geary, 2002: ch. 1).

Many of the formative myths of ethnies derived from such experiences, both on the part of the 'invaders' and of the 'indigenes', though after a sometimes lengthy interval. The conversion to Christianity of the Frankish leader Clovis and his coronation by the Bishop of Reims in 496 was later used as the foundation myth of the French kingdom. The Norman conquest of Anglo-Saxon England provoked a British Arthurian mythology that suggested ancient Britain as a seminal European culture that had taught the Romans, and later a countervailing myth of Anglo-Saxon liberties (MacDougall, 1982). Other settlers such as Ulster Scots, English in America and Afrikaners would bind themselves to the new land by claiming it as the fruit of their Covenant with God to uphold a holy mission.

Ethnie as Social and Political Actors

What can this very schematic and selective discussion of world history tell us about ethnic identities? It suggests that they are historically pervasive and can be found in all periods of the premodern world, from oldest recorded civilisations through to the seventeenth century. This pervasiveness arises because they can arise or be reinforced by many different processes, and they take many different forms. The previous discussion has identified many different kinds of ethnie. We have nomadic warrior ethnie from the deserts and Asian steppes such as the Mongols, Seljuk Turks and Magyars; religious ethnies, distinguished by a sense of chosenness valorised by religious institutions such the Jews, Armenians and Sikhs; aristocratic ethnie of sedentary agrarian communities, tied to the fortunes of dynastic states such as medieval France, England and Spain; colonising ethnie – Hispanic in Latin America, Afrikaner, English Puritans in the American colonies – whose identities are formed through the process of conquest and its justification (e.g. by the biblical story of exodus); and diaspora ethnies such as the Jews and Armenians crystallising from experiences of conquest and exile, who survive by filling social and economic niches as financiers and traders, using kinship and religious networks.

But though historical processes such as warfare, religious evangelism, migration and imperial expansion proliferate ethnie, they also extinguished them. The Romans enforced a genocide on the Carthaginians, and the Celtic peoples of central Europe were absorbed by incoming Germanic tribal confederations. Although all but a few of 25 or so states in Europe can trace their names back to peoples of the middle ages and sometimes of antiquity, in the Middle East Arabic Islamic expansion eroded in popular memory all but a few of the ancient cultures of this region, destroying their religious heritage and replacing their written languages with the holy language of the Koran: even the Pharaonic heritage of Egypt and its language was submerged (Lewis, 1998: ch. 4). The impact of universalistic religions can be such that even if the ethnie survives, much of its earlier heritage may be lost. Just as triumphant Muslims effaced the depictions of Medes and Persians in the friezes of Persepolis, the ancient capital of Persia (Lewis, 1998: 72), the spread of Orthodox Christianity in the Balkans was accompanied by a destruction of many pagan artefacts of the Hellenic past.

25

Because of the many different threats that populations face over time, most identities are transformed. If the heritage is one of layers rather than of obliteration, ethnie will likely have rival pasts. Magyars were nomadic steppe warriors maintaining a descent from an Arpad dynasty who, on settling in (present day) Hungary, became sedentarised, converted to Christianity in 1000 and developed a myth of descent from a legendary St Stephen, a Christian warrior king who was law giver to the clans. In this legend Magyars became a Christian *antemurale* of Europe against steppe infidels. Nonetheless, sections of the Magyar aristocracy were unwilling to abandon their nomadic raiding, and tensions remained between different traditions.

Why do some ethnie survive, incorporating older pasts within their culture, when others do not? Even if the names and some symbols remain, can we speak of ethnic continuities if there are radical demographic, linguistic, religious or territorial changes? At one level, continuities exist when they are constructed by subsequent eras 'returning' to the past (via movements of ethnic restoration) as part of collective social or political projects. A Persian cultural revival two centuries after the Arab conquest looked back to a mythical post-Creation past that was combined with a 'heretical' Shi'ite form of Islam. A new Persian identity was expressed in Firdausi's eleventh-century canonical work of Persian literature the *Book of Kings*, an anti-Arab diatribe that recounts a mythic history of Iran from the creation to the Arabic conquest. Similarly, the crisis of the Byzantine Empire, threatened both by the Latin West, whose Crusaders sacked Constantinople, and the Islamic Turk, reduced increasingly to a Greek-seeking base, resulted in a neo-Hellenic revival by the twelfth century (Campbell and Sherrard, 1968: ch. 1). But there may be an artificiality to such 'revivals', and the question remains: what allows ethnies to survive the transformations that threatened to destroy them?

Hastings (1997: 25–6) argues the transmutation of oral languages into written vernaculars that become the language of public culture (including literature, laws, religious writings and administration) provides the threshold of survival. Such vernacularisation creates a self-conscious culture that is maintained by a diversified educated elite. Having a vernacular language, however, is neither necessary nor a sufficient condition of survival, since there are cases of disappearing ethnic high cultures (e.g. Phoenician). Religion can be a still more potent guarantor of persistence: as we have seen, universalist religions have become particularised, canonising the ethnie's territory and culture as holy (as in the case of Sri Lanka, Armenia and Georgia), and in such cases give a transcendental dimension to the preservation of an ethnic heritage.

Smith argues that aristocratic-vertical ethnies, identified with the honour of state displayed above all in war, are more vulnerable to political vicissitudes than demotic ethnies defined by religion. The former are narrowly based on an official class and are often exclusive, whereas the latter are embedded in the community and, identifying with a religious mission, are more capable of surviving defeat, able to re-interpret it as a divine message to return to authentic ethnoreligious/religious traditions. He contrasts the disappearance of the northern Israeli kingdom of Samaria, associated with the charismatic kingship of David and Solomon, with the survival of Judah, organised round the Temple priesthood and prophets, whose demotic reach allowed the Jews to overcome repeated defeats and even enslavement during the Babylonian captivity (Smith, 1981). This seems plausible, but as the Irish case suggests, no single factor is essential: ethnicities are more likely to survive if strongly embedded in collective life, whether by means of language, literary, religious or legal traditions.

Ireland is an interesting example of how the introduction of Christianity by St Patrick to a Celtic pagan warrior society in the fifth century did not destroy existing culture, but rather created a Celtic-Christian synthesis. When Christian monks transformed the oral Irish language into a written vernacular in the sixth and seventh centuries, they recorded the ancient Irish epics, known as the Ulster and Fenian cycles, that celebrated an earlier heroic, aristocratic, pagan world, as well as genealogies, poetry and the great legal codes that had effect throughout the island in spite of a multitude of kingships. The key to the creation of a complex ethnic community was the existence of an earlier intellectual tradition of poets and legal scholars from pre-historic times whose high status was recognised by (Irish) Christian missionaries. This tradition continued unbroken after the introduction of Latin Christian culture (Richter, 1988: ch. 12). It culminated in the eighth century when Ireland became an evangelical centre for European Christianity and produced the great illustrated manuscripts known as the *Book of Kells*.

In Ireland we see how, in certain circumstances, radical changes may result not in the obliteration but in the further diversification of ethnic traditions. In many cases the past should be seen as a set of overlays of different and sometimes rival traditions that live as alternative repertoires available to be used at times of crisis. In the Magyar case rivalry between pagan and Christian heritages surfaced at the time of invasions first of the Mongols and then the Ottoman Turks. One option was for the Magyar aristocracy to identify with a nomadic golden age (claiming descent from Attila), rejecting a 'decadent' Christianity, and to ally with their fellow

27

steppe warriors; the other (preferred) option was to maintain themselves as an *antemurale* people against infidels. Armstrong argues the availability of these alternative traditions may have enabled Magyars to resist assimilative pressures both from the steppe and from Christian German forces (Armstrong, 1982: 47–51).

In Ireland the fusion of vernacular-pagan and religious traditions sustained in the absence of political unity a continuous and self-conscious Gaelic culture from pre-Christian times to the seventeenth century, in the face of severe disruptions – ecological, religious, military and demographic. The early medieval Christian-pagan cultural synthesis, Richter suggests, was triggered by a catastrophic epidemic in the seventh century, in response to which there was an attempt to compile records and return for inspiration to the ethnic heritage. He observes that there were two periods of similar disruption: the Anglo-Norman military penetration in the late twelth century and the long term Anglicisation of Ireland in the seventeenth century. The first, introducing new monastic orders into Ireland, brought an end to Irish artistic traditions but stimulated the production of a more comprehensive account of Irish history, including a history of Brian Boru, the Irish High King who had defeated the earlier Viking 'invaders', manuscripts such as the *Book of the Dun Cow*, the rise of a new bardic order and forms of bardic poetry. This Irish (or, as it normally is called, Gaelic) revival affected the descendants of the Anglo-Normans, with many adopting the ways of the native Gaelic aristocracy. The second and decisive rupture followed the seventeenth-century English Protestant conquest of Ireland that resulted in the replacement of the Gaelic by an English aristocracy. This catastrophe inspired scholars to a last recording of their heritage in the *Book of Invasions* and the *Annals of the Four Masters*. The destruction of Irish secular institutions all but destroyed a native high Irish language culture, but an Irish ethnicity was not destroyed. Instead, the Catholic Church, claiming descent from St Patrick, became the custodian of native memory, including that of the early medieval golden age, carrying it into the modern period.

This example reveals the existence of a continuous self-reflexive Irish ethnic collectivity that even without a state was able to regulate legal and social life. But how representative was Ireland? This perhaps attests to the long survival of an ethnic *culture*, whereas it might be argued we should be primarily interested in political ethnie and their comparability to modern nations. Can we say that there are such ethnie that are comparable to modern nations in the premodern period, for example in Western Europe? Modernists are rightly suspicious of any easy comparisons with premodern ethnie, for modern nations are political and socially penetrative and culturally homogeneous.

Patrick Geary (2002: ch. 3) argues that the ethnie of the Roman and post-Roman period from which modern nationalists claim descent were often fictive, fluctuating and dynamic. They were in origins multi-ethnic federations of wandering groups whose political elites appropriated the names, origin myths and glorious heroes of earlier peoples. Certainly descent myths are pervasive in the medieval period, but are often related to territory, dynasties and kingdoms than to peoples. Many kingdoms, even though they espoused an *antemurale* myth (as in the case of Hispanic kingdoms before the reconquest), were polyethnic. Ethnic myths, where they are associated with a premodern dynastic state and its affiliated aristocracy, may have little penetration, in part because of the limited capacity of the polity with poor communications outside its capital. More seriously, during the sixteenth and seventeenth centuries one finds the gentry in many parts of Europe seeking to differentiate themselves from the rest of the population by adopting exclusive myths of origins that identified the gentry as a foreign conquering group – the Scandinavian myth of the Russian gentry, the Sarmatian myth of the Polish *szlachta*, the Frankish myth of the French aristocracy – to justify class monopolies (Davies, 1997: 144).

In a subtle discussion Josep Llobera (1994: ch. 2) reasons that although one cannot speak of nationalism (in the modern sense) in the middle ages, from the ninth century national identities attached to territorial states gradually developed in Western Europe out of five cultural clusters, Germania, Gallia, Brittanica, Italia and Hispania. These units overlapped and were internally heterogeneous; the national identities that eventually emerged were products of contingent factors; only a small part of the population was aware of them; and the Germania and Italia clusters were 'late successes'. Nonetheless, he makes the following points in favour of the existence of early medieval national identities. From early on terms like '*natio*' and '*patria*' (albeit with different meanings from modern usage) were being employed, and by the end of the middle ages their use was commonplace. During this period monarchs made vernacular languages the media of court chronicles, from which they gradually became the languages of territory. Myths of descent became widespread, legitimising peoples' identities and their right to reject foreign rule, and towards the end of the period there developed at the popular level sets of national stereotypes and concepts of national character. A sense of continuity was created by the persistence of 'names' and a set of cultural attributes alongside them. By the late middle ages one can identify a popular sentiment against foreign domination, a formative influence being the Hundred Years War between England and France, and evoked in popular heroes such as Joan of Arc (though it is likely that the myths of the wars were more potent as ethnicising factors than the experience itself). By the fourteenth century religion and politics were being intertwined, usually through a close association between a saint (such as St Denis) and nation. This evolved into a theory of Gallican liberties in France and took more radical forms after the Reformation.

In a detailed analysis of the emergence of France from 'Francia' Liobera cites Colette Beaune's 1985 study of medieval France, which argues that a French collective identity formed by the fifteenth century around three major axes: France and its history, France and its God and France and its symbols. Chroniclers from the twelfth century promoted the view of France as a divinely inspired kingdom, founded by St Clovis and descended from an original people (the Trojans) that sustained its independent status *vis-à-vis* the Holy Roman Empire. During the middle ages there was an increasing sacralisation of the French monarchy, arising from the monarch's anointing (during the coronation ceremony) with the holy ampulla of oil, the cult of St Denis, as the patron saint of kings and (later) the kingdom, and the canonisation of King Louis IX. Finally, there developed a set of symbols to denote France, including the heraldic lilies of the French royal arms. By the fifteenth century, as a result of the Hundred Years War, this had broadened to an idealisation of the territory as a paradisial garden, which demanded sacrifice from its people (Llobera, 1994: 51–6). The French case is important as it subsequently became the most powerful European state, and it exerted an immense influence as the definer of political, social and cultural norms.

As Llobera acknowledges, this collective consciousness was not pervasive; it co-existed with a confusing web of regional, religious and local jurisdictions and identities. Critics are sceptical of how it can be designated a national as opposed to a regnal identity. But this picture suggests that by the late middle ages political units were forming that evoked from time to time a more extensive ethnic awareness. By the time of the Wars of Religion that galvanised populations during the sixteenth and seventeenth centuries, we find a broader national consciousness in England, Scotland, France, the Netherlands and Sweden focused on an increasing sense of territoriality, the development of state institutions (as opposed to merely dynastic rule) and capital cities, a distinctive religious mission and the rise of vernacular literatures (cf. Hastings, 1997: ch. 5). In several instances there is a gradual confluence of a lateral aristocratic ethnie attached to state with the more demotic ideals attached to religion and community. This is an important point because it shows how the variegated processes of ethnic formation (religious, political, military, economic) can be *mutually reinforcing* in many cases, so that in England and the Netherlands a intense and socially pervasive national Protestantism strengthened allegiances to the political constitution.

The Rise of States and Modern Processes

To document the existence of solidary ethnic communities and even ethnic polities before the eighteenth century does not of itself establish the case for the ethnic origins of nations. Modernists have argued on three grounds that modern nationalism and nations are essentially different from earlier formations and must be explained by novel factors. First, earlier ethnic identities were never dominant and, lacking autonomous institutions, were subordinate to the religious, class and dynastic institutions that carried them, whereas modern nationalism has been the hegemonic ideology of the modern state and state system. Secondly, the core of nationalism is a novel political ideology of self-determination. This subverts older ethnic traditions, tied to religion and dynasty, in the name of popular sovereignty, and seeks to create a congruence between a unified and distinctive cultural community and the state. Thirdly, whereas earlier ethnic identities were predominantly connected to religion, for nationalists it is language that becomes the key index of collective identity. This is linked to the rise of state centralisation since the eighteenth century that now made the language of administrations of crucial significance for the life chances of their populations.

In short, nationalism is directly related to the emergence of the modernising territorial state. An alliance with industrial capitalism expands the capacities of the state enabling it to penetrate a localised rural and hierarchical society of difference and create a culturally standardised nation of citizens living on a unified territory. Advances in communications, census and cartographic surveys, taxation and policing, the development of territory-wide standardised educational systems promoting novel vernacular high cultures, mass conscription in the military institutions, and the creation of border controls and fortification resulted in distinctive bordered power containers (see Giddens, 1985: 120). The rationalist legacy of the Enlightenment shaped the policies of French republican nationalists, for whom traditional forms of allegiance, including those of 'backward' ethnic and regional cultures (for example, Breton and Basque), were now viewed as part of the savage state from which human communities should progress to urban civility. As the French model proved itself in war so a world interstate system developed in which all populations were gradually caged within new political units. The centralising state is a revolutionary new instrument that destroys systems of indirect rule, and nationalism is essentially civic with its goal the construction of a sovereign and meritocratic society. It represents a repudiation of the ethnic principle of membership by descent (*ius sanguinis*): citizenship is acquired largely by the principle of territorial membership (*ius soluis*).

From the modernist perspective, then, nationalism is really a movement associated with 'modernity', and with the bringing into being of political societies characterised by an adherence to universalistic scientific norms and technological efficiency. The fascination of nationalists with golden ages and with the preservation of continuities with earlier generations seems backward-looking and merely sentimental. As Ernest Gellner (1996) has put it, nations need have no 'navels' in the ancient world. He also suggests that although some premodern nations may have existed as contingent entities, in the modern world nations are necessary. This perspective is allied to an invented or constructivist conception of nationalism. For Hobsbawm the first liberal European nationalisms are 'rational', and focused on incorporating populations into the large territorial polities that enable industrial progress. Only subsequently does ethnicity become the salient and 'irrational' mode of identification among populations fearful of the world of progress in which they cannot compete, and giving rise to separatist nationalisms that make no sense in a world extending in scale. The ethnicity of these smaller nationalities, moreover, is essentially invented (Hobsbawm, 1990: ch. 4).

This is not to say that modernists fail to acknowledge the importance of national identity and culture. To Ernest Gellner the possession of a national identity has become intrinsic to a definition of the human person, and a national culture is the communicative basis of a mobile, extensive and socially differentiated industrial society of strangers (1983: 6). Gellner, Benedict Anderson and Eric Hobsbawm have broken new ground in investigating the central institutions and orientations of the modern nation. Gellner has explored the rise of high vernacular cultures and the educational systems that underpin and disseminate them; Hobsbawm (1983) the new symbols (anthems, flags, monuments and stamps), traditions and commemorative ceremonies that create the national community; and Anderson the genres of the print culture (of newspaper and novel), the bureaucratic pilgrimages and the map making of state administrations that construct the national imaginary community in space and time. But though they acknowledge nationalist evocation of the past, they give ethnicity no causal force in orienting populations through the transition. The real culture of modernity is science and the ethos of capitalism and administrative systems. The rational, disenchanting aspects of modernity are in tension with the mythic self-images of nationalism.

The major difference, however, between modernists and ethnosymbolists arises over the question of the invention or the construction of the nation and the centrality of modern political elites and state institutions in its formation. Ethnosymbolists are critical of what they see as a top-down explanation of culture formation, particularly visible in the interpretations of Gellner, Hobsbawm and Kedourie, that conflates nationalism with a political nationalism focused on the achievement of legal citizenship and the subversion of traditionalism. The terms 'invention' and 'construction' have strong connotations not only of novelty but also with intentionality and manipulation. Some modernists have implied that the nation in nation-state is epiphenomenal, a set of rhetorics that accompany what are designated as 'modern' social structures. But this raises the problem of why it seems necessary to invoke ethnic pasts, symbols and cultures in the modern world. Moreover, unless one assumes that symbols and cultural practices are always epiphenomenal (an extreme materialist position few would defend), it is hard to explain how nationalist ideologies are able to appropriate symbols at will from established cultural systems. As Quentin Skinner (1974) has argued, an account of politics as rational action has to acknowledge that leaders, in order to successfully mobilise populations, must appeal to moral sentiments widely acceptable to the community, and that elites once they appeal to such sentiments are then constrained in their actions, lest they appear to be opportunistic. It is implausible, therefore, to conceive of modernising nationalists as outside their society mobilising it from above. Once invoked, ethnic memories have an independent force with which they have to negotiate. What needs to be explored (see Chapter 2) is the relationship of nationalism to other belief systems and the complex symbolic mediations and appropriations by which nationalists are able to channel the past for their purposes.

This is to suggest that the nationalists do not operate within a *tabula rasa*. The case for exploring pre-existing ethnic sentiments as a causal force in the rise of nationalism is strengthened by the many examples where the latter forms as a communitarian revolt against modernising states, which are perceived to be assimilating populations to an alien dominant culture. In Ireland, the Czech, German and Slovak territories, a *cultural nationalism* has focused on the moral regeneration of the historical 'community', attempting an inner renovation of the ethnic base, promoting high vernacular cultures, educational centres and grass roots economic, cultural and political self-help organisations. This is distinct from *political nationalism*, which looks to the state and citizenship. Although the former is often small-scale, when able to ally with powerful traditional non-state institutions, such as churches, which articulate a special destiny for the community, cultural nationalist movements can create a *counter–cultural* centre against the state (Hutchinson, 1987: ch. 1).

Of course, modernising states have been central to the transformation of ethnic communities into nations by promoting and embodying the project of secular improvement that undermined the hold of religion, and creating a secular middle-class society. Modernists might reply that communitarian nationalisms also generally shift to a statist politics in order to institutionalise the nation, for national populations operating in a world of competing national *states* require a state to guarantee a national educational system and defence. Moreover, nationalist movements are able to succeed usually because of a crisis of the state, often through defeat in war. For many scholars this demonstrates that the communitarian project is secondary, and that we should focus on the 'dominant' state-led route or model of nation-building. In the long run the politics of citizenship is more compelling to populations than the concerns of a few romantic intellectuals.

To assume this, however, is to exaggerate the givenness of states and their capacity to provide meaning for and to exercise dominance over their populations. One of the faults of these interpretations is of an over-coherent model of what is called the modernisation process. According to this, populations are increasingly mobilised in support of a national state, and, once formed, a national state operates as a unitary society, in which development is directed from a political centre. As Michael Mann (1986, ch. 1) argues, we have to reject such unified models of society: throughout history populations inhabit overlapping and competing networks of power – political, military, economic and ideological – each with different boundaries and institutions, and developing in uneven and unpredictable ways. Indeed, throughout the modern period, states, whether they were long established empires or, indeed, avowedly national states, have been periodically shaken or even destroyed by unforeseen events such as warfare, economic crises, ideological challenges, migrations and demographic shifts or ecological changes.

Outbreaks of wars, hot and cold, have resulted in the overthrow and rise of states, the shifting of states into new geopolitical spaces, the turning of dominant groups into national minorities, and vice versa, and large-scale movements of population. This geographical, demographic and status mobility has required a continuous redefinition of political communities with respect to each other.

Waves of transnational economic revolutions have also transformed the status of regions and classes within 'national states' and the power of national populations *vis-à-vis* each other. The economic depressions of the 1870s, the threat to the traditional European landed order from an emerging world agrarian market, together with the growth in rapidly expanding cities of a large and politicised unskilled working class attracted to militant socialist parties, and large migrations of Jews, radicalised European politics.

Great ideological movements arising from the heritage of the Enlightenment and religious counter-challenges have swept across state boundaries. Transmitted through transnational institutions such as churches, revolutionary internationals, diaspora groups and print (and later satellite) media channels, these new visions have engendered cultural conflicts within populations and between neighbouring states.

Unexpected natural changes – diseases, famines, ecological disturbances, shifts in fertility patterns – have had a disruptive impact on the relations between populations. The inability of the British government to avoid the Great Famine in mid-nineteenth-century Ireland permanently alienated the Catholic Irish from the union with Britain. Changes in birth rates relative to 'significant others' have created anxieties about the future of the nation and heightened tensions between rival states and between ethnic populations within states.

Under these circumstances states and populations, in order to survive, have fallen back on ethnocommunal moral and political resources. In short, as the recurring crises of the modern state have led to ethnic ideals and sentiments becoming *regulatory*, so ethnicity has come recurrently to animate the *modernising* policies of national states. After the national calamity befalling the Danish state in 1864, when Prussia seized the southern provinces of Holstein and Schleswig, the Danes, adopting as a slogan 'What is lost outwardly shall be won inwardly', inaugurated a popular cultural revival via the Grundtvigian Lutheran folk high school movement and set about reclaiming their wastelands and marshes (Yahil, 1992: 100–1). This movement helped form the liberal populist character of the Danish state, based on a society of independent farmers.

I shall explore in detail the impact of these different crises in Chapter 4. Suffice it to say now that in the two centuries since the period of the French Revolution there have been very few European states that have not been traumatised, sometimes several times, by warfare. German national identity, for one, has exhibited a long-range instability. A modern German identity was born in the struggle against Napoleon, but its politico-territorial definition was contested throughout its history. The Prussian monarchy's victories over Habsburg Austria in 1866 and then over France in 1870–1 allowed it to impose a *Kleindeutschland* definition (excluding the German-speaking Austrians). But this was regarded by the advocates of *Grossdeutschland* as an unfinished nation-state, lacking full legitimacy and reflected in an ethnic rather than a territorial conception of citizenship, which excluded substantial ethnic minorities (Danes, Poles, Walloons) within the 1871 borders. A succession of maps for 1914, 1918, 1923, 1939, 1941, 1945, 1949, 1961 and 1990 illustrates the radically expanding and contracting nature of its borders in the twentieth century (Jarausch and Geyer, 2003: 350). The defeat of Germany in the First World War led to the loss of several territories, including Alsace and Lorraine and the Sudetenland under the Treaty of Versailles, and it stimulated a rejection of the new Weimar democratic republic by conservatives and National Socialists in favour of an 'authentic' national state including all ethnic Germans within its borders. Hitler's annexations of Austria in 1936 and the Sudetenland in 1938 began to realise the greater German vision, but defeat in 1945 produced new losses and the partition into West and East Germany (Alter, 1985: 103–9). The result is a history of territorial *overlays* where competing memories and projects of where Germany is and should be remain unresolved (Jarausch and Geyer, 2003: 350).

Nor is Germany singular. The series of world wars (including the Cold War) have ensured a wave of nationally conscious movements seeking to revive and redefine the nation and national state from below. Some 28 states fought the First World War (Bond, 1984: 133), and with the collapse of the Romanov and Habsburg Empires several new national states appeared, including Austria, Hungary, Czechoslovakia, Poland, Finland, Lithuania, Latvia and Estonia. After the Second World War there were substantial territorial and ethnic shifts, with the forced movements of many millions, and Poland, when 'restored' as a territorial state after its partition by Stalin and Hitler had moved westwards by over 150 miles on its eastern frontiers and by about 70 in the west, losing one-fifth of its territories, including former cultural centres of Wilno and Lwow to Lithuania and Ukraine (Sharp, 1996: 25–6).

This indicates that many of the factors and processes of historical change cut across the premodern and modern divide and help explain the persistence of ethnicity as a mobiliser of collective action that states must employ to 'restore' autonomy and a stable and distinctive identity. The recurring historical revivals are driven by the need to overcome radical uncertainty, by the search for concrete models to redefine collective goals, and are inspired by myths of destiny that can unify and energise populations in the task of regeneration.

For ethnosymbolists central to nations is a concern with identity and history as means of overcoming contingencies that have regularly threatened the physical or cultural survival of populations in the modern as well as in the pre-modern world. By identifying with a historic nation embodied in myths, symbols and culture, which has survived disaster in the past, individuals combine in a society to overcome contingency and find a unique meaning and purpose. Culture, then, for ethnosymbolists means not just symbols, traditions or rituals, but also the meanings and orientations to collective action that these evoke. Modernists, they believe, have understated the degree to which pre-modern states have adopted ethnic legitimations, and even where premodern ethnic identities have operated below the state level, when carried by religious institutions, written vernacular cultures and legal systems and professions, they have persisted into the modern era, providing nationalists with inspiration and resources in campaigns to capture the modern state.

To nationalists the national community assumes a sacred 'primordial' quality, which since it is prior to the state (a mere human artefact) cannot be extinguished by political conquest (Grosby, 1995). This romanticisation of the collective will has a real resonance. For while it is possible to overthrow a state and control a territory, it is difficult to expunge or penetrate a way of life when it is embedded by a dense web of religious institutions, linguistic practices, literatures, legal customs and rituals, which then can become sites of collective resistance. The long historical perspective of nationalists, which includes eras of defeat, enslavement and recovery, inspires the capacity of communities to overcome disaster by mobilising an inner world of spiritual energies. Such convictions, particularly when yoked to a distinctive national religion, preserve a sense of national community in spite of all the odds. Poles under the Soviet yoke rallied under the umbrella of the Catholic Church, remembering the survival and resurrection of their nation despite two centuries of division and occupation by empires.

Ethnic Continuities and Modern Nations

But is this wave of nationalist revivals in the modern world evidence of ethnic recurrence rather than one of ethnic continuities? It would be possible for modernists to admit that factors cutting across the premodern–modern divide engender ethnogenesis, but to claim that the ethnic identities of nationalism are novel in kind, even though they may appeal to the myths and symbols of the past. After all, as Patrick Geary has asked, how plausible is it for the modern French to claim any genuine continuities with 'our ancestors, the Gauls' (Geary, 2002: ch. 1)? To what extent are such ethnic identities constructed to meet present needs after the fact?

France is widely presented as the first modern society and the exemplar of the civic state, based on a rational voluntarist conception of the nation, and its Gallic myth and symbols, although having humanist origins, are construed as a democratic legitimisation directed against a Frankish king and aristocracy. In fact, the very universalism of the French Revolution fed off older ethnic conceptions of France as having a special mission to Europe, as heir of Roman and Carolingian civilisations and as the chosen defender of European Catholic Christendom (Armstrong, 1982: ch. 5). Moreover, although the French republic constructed a powerful centralised and secular state, it was never able to uproot a living Catholic culture that sustained a powerful counter-republican crusade up to the present. The post-revolutionary state, whether republican, monarchist or Imperial, was destabilised throughout the modern period by invasions, changes of regime, boundary changes, social revolutions and mass migrations, and in the face of such uncertainties, rival political projects invoked ethnic legitimations.

Republican fervour was initially expressed in universalist rather than national terms and on an attack of the *Ancien Régime* of monarchy, aristocracy and Church. But invasions by the European powers almost immediately nationalised the Revolution, which mobilised the French peasantry with the introduction of the *levée en masse*. Napoleon exploited disillusion with Jacobinism, and although avowing the French mission of universal enlightenment, replaced the republic with an Empire, laying claim to the legacy of Charlemagne and making a concordat with the Church.

After the restoration of the monarchy in 1815, republicans, recognising the damage done by Jacobin radicalism and violence, qualified their rationalism by rooting the Revolution in a historic French nation and appropriating traditional ethnoreligious symbols and heroes. By 1841 Michelet presented the Revolution as the culmination of democratic nation epitomised by the medieval 'heroine', Joan of Arc (Gildea, 1994: 154–5). Counter-revolutionaries sought to reground the legitimist cause in a period of increasing democratisation by reclaiming Joan as a symbol of popular Catholicism and monarchism. Before this Chateaubriand and Victor Hugo gave momentum to the romantic cult of Gothic France, as embodied in its great cathedrals, previously linked to the glories of Catholicism and cult of monarchy, but now perceived as quasi-natural outgrowths ('mystical forests') of an ancient Gallic civilisation. For republicans they expressed the democratic and national genius of its medieval craftsmen who had created a distinctive Gothic civilisation. Catholics, by the 1840s, extolled these cathedrals as the ultimate expression of their faith and as the product of the golden age of Philip Augustus and St Louis, when France discovered its destiny as defender of European Christendom (Vauchez, 1992: 63–4).

The catastrophic defeat of the Second Empire in the 1870s and the loss of Alsace and Lorraine to Germany, and German invasions in two World Wars, all resulted in mass revivals of St Joan as national liberator and the cult of cathedrals as the embodiment of the French spirit that united republicans and their opponents (Gildea, 1994: 154–65). To republicans and their opponents, the great cathedrals have been enduring symbols of an indomitable French nation – the cathedrals of Metz and Strasbourg, poignant reminders of provinces in captivity after 1871, and the shelled cathedral of Reims in 1914 a representation of a suffering people (Vauchez, 1992: 64–6).

In short, the evolution of France demonstrates how revolutionary nationalists felt compelled to root themselves in older ethnic traditions, which while not *capturing* the democratic project, have powerfully shaped it. What is noticeable is how older patterns of power continue into the modern period, notably the dominance of Paris and its northern symbolic centres (including the great cathedral city of Reims) over the regions. By the seventeenth century Paris had acquired a sacred aura, derived from the presence of the King and his court, which differentiated it from the mere 'provinces'. Although the Girondins early in the Revolution planned to subvert the prestige of Paris by decentralising power, this was defeated, and the Revolution enhanced the capital's authority over the rest of France by making its language and culture the bearers of the national civilising project. The sacral energies associated with kingship were transferred to the republic, for which Paris now became the creative centre of modernity and change. Paris was the training centre of state elites and Parisian functionaries, like earlier royal intendants, were sent to the departments to enforce the revolution in the localities. The introduction of universal suffrage in 1848 offered the regions a chance to curb what was seen as an imperial centre, and from time to time Parisian pretensions to be the voice of France (as during the Paris Commune) were curbed. During the Third Republic the south and east of France and 'la province' increased in political influence. But well before, Paris was the centre of administration, universities and the professions, and during the nineteenth and twentieth centuries its social power was extended by the growth of communications such as the railway and telegraph (Corbin, 1996).

It might be argued that the construction of Paris as a sacred centre of the nation demonstrates only the enormous authority of the modern state over its society. But just as in the ancient world, the power of such capitals derives in large part from their ability to mobilise sacral resources. Mustafa Kemal, wishing to build a secular nation-state on the French model, established Ankara as his capital, based in the new heartland area of Turkey – Anatolia – from which he pursued a crusade to undermine the public authority of Islam. He replaced Istanbul, the former capital not only of the failed Ottoman Empire but also of the Caliphate. But a Turkish nationality was thinly based compared to the memories of an Ottoman golden age, and was evoked through concocted ethnic mythologies of the Turks as bearers of the original sun language of humanity. Although today Ankara is the administrative centre, the cultural power still remains with Istanbul.

Embedded ethnic identities can display their affectivity also in impeding the development of a mass democratic national state whose ethnic and territorial borders coincided. A sense of Polish consciousness after the loss of the Polish Lithuanian Commonwealth in the late eighteenth century through two centuries of disastrous revolts was carried by two institutions: the Catholic Church and its gentry class (*szlachta*). The *szlachta*, by the seventeenth century, had claimed sole custody of the Polish nation, in declaring a myth of descent from Sarmatian warriors that destined them to rule over the multi-ethnic peasantries. Idealising the older Commonwealth as a great power ruled by a noble class that acted the Catholic *antemurale Christianitas* against the Tatars, Turks and Russians, they bound themselves to the Polonised sections of the Lithuanian and Ukrainian gentry in seeking to recover as the national core the Lithuanian and Ukrainian eastern borderlands, where historically they had their estates. They thereby divorced themselves from the Polish-speaking peasantry who were settled westwards in Prussian-ruled Poland. Such was the power of this idea that the *szlachta* rejected a proposal of the Congress of Vienna of 1815 to establish a limited kingdom because it excluded their heartlands. Polish nationalism in the nineteenth century was hobbled by the unwillingness of this class to identify with the Polish peasantry, who remained aloof in the revolutions of 1830 and 1863 and supported the Habsburg Empire against the gentry (Prizel, 1998: 38–58).

As the gentry became steadily impoverished, their downward social mobility meant that images of the eastern borderlands, portrayed in romantic poetry and painting, dominated all social groups (Kristof, 1994: 226–7).

Although driven to political consciousness in the late nineteenth century by nationalisation policies in Prussian- and Russian-held territories, much of the peasantry greeted the resurrection of a Polish state in 1918 with apprehension, fearing a return to serfdom. Despite being based on a Polish peasantry, the state was authoritarian – dominated by the notion of an aristocratic stewardship over the masses. Under Pilsudski's regime the inner core, drawn from the borderlands, expressed the *szlachta* vision of a multi-national Catholic Poland (though one that refused to acknowledge the national aspirations of minorities such as Lithuanians, Ukrainians and Jews): Poland was to be a great European power and, acting as a Christian *antemurale* nation, liberate small nations from Russian (communist) oppression. What eventually made possible a more democratic and ethnically homogeneous national state was the elimination of the ruling elite and mass ethnic cleansing during the Second World War, and after the war the shifting of Poland's border westwards, to the Polish-speakers' core (Prizel, 1998: 58–74).

There are many other examples of the directive effect of ethnic memories on the policies of modern national states. Ideas of being a chosen people, bound to a Covenant with God based on a distant past, have allowed Afrikaners and Ulster Scots to survive adversity, but at the same time, by limiting their willingness to compromise, threatened their long-term survival. In Ireland an ethnicity invested in an alliance of (peasant) people and Catholic Church provided a strong populist basis to the national state after independence. Catholicism was made the official religion, a patriarchal moral economy based on the peasant farm was privileged, and the Irish, looking outward to the world, 'renewed' themselves as a missionary people, exporting clerics to Latin America and Africa and taking a prominent role in international organisations.

How can we explain the continuing power of such memories? Two factors are important: first, the existence of embedded institutions that perceive themselves as custodians of an older ethnic culture; and secondly, the continued relevance of such ethnic identities when populations are periodically faced with similar challenges to their physical and symbolic survival. In spite of significant differences between premodern and modern societies, long-established cultural repertoires (myths, symbols and memories) are 'carried' into the modern era by powerful institutions (states, churches, armies, legal systems). Historic ethnic identities are revived and redeveloped when crises emerge in the modern world that can plausibly be interpreted as new manifestations of much older challenges.

Island settings, positions on trade or invasion routes, locations in shatter zones between powerful adversaries, exposure as a frontier state of a civilisation, all these have shaped the sense of a people and affected relations in

41

the long term with other communities. Recurring periods of warfare with neighbouring powers, particularly, create languages of sacrifice to inspire successive generations of combatants. Irish, Russian and Greek nationalists have appropriated the religious symbols, sacred centres and sense of collective mission generated by long-term religious competition with adjacent populations as part of their drive to prove the cultural uniqueness of their people. Even Stalin acknowledged the power of older, religious, Russian collective identities when he appealed to 'memories' of the 'great patriotic war' of the Russian peasants against Napoleon and the much older Orthodox traditions of Holy Mother Russia in order to mobilise the defence of Moscow against Hitler's armies. The island setting of England, 'protecting' it from invasion, allowed the development over centuries of a system of common law and parliamentary traditions distinct from its continental neighbours. Such continuities has given a deeply conservative cast to English national identity and a suspicion of its continental neighbours. Contemporary English nationalists, in resisting incorporation within the European Union, employ the language of Anglo-Saxon liberties embodied in common law traditions, just as did lawyers in Stuart England, when defending indigenous parliamentary traditions against European absolutist models.

As the Polish example indicates, ethnicity can work against the development of a democratic national state established within stable territorial boundaries. If in Western Europe over time, concentrated ethnic populations and consolidated territorial juridical and political structures came together, this was often not the case in Eastern and Central Europe. Here populations were dominated by Empires; there was strong ethnic differentiation between city and countryside; and in the Balkans they inhabited the Shatter zones between Islam and Christendom. In these latter cases, the formation of nations has come much later, if at all, and has been made possible by warfare and the large-scale movements of populations, voluntary or forced. In the Balkans it is unclear whether the legacy of shatter zones will be replaced by a normalised system of nation-state relations. In other regions of the world, such as Africa, where European colonialism has created an incongruence between state and ethnic boundaries, it is not clear whether nations can be created at all. John Armstrong claims that the genealogical myths of nomadic warrior identities of the Middle Eastern Desert and Asian steppes, when combined with Islam, has made difficult the development of stable territorial (and later national) states (Armstrong, 1982: ch. 2).

Conclusions

What then can we conclude about the relationship between earlier ethnic identities and modern nations? This analysis has ambivalent lessons. It emphasises the drive and sense of solidarity that can come from building a nation on the basis of earlier ethnic identities, and the directive power of such identities when strongly institutionalised in a historical community. It suggests that in the absence of such identities nations cannot easily be constructed, given the unpredictable challenges of the modern world that can so easily destroy states without such communal resources by which to mobilise their populations. It also suggests the possible limits of nation-formation in the modern world. But above all, it raises the question: given the potency of ethnic identities, how it is possible that nations are created at all?

2

The Revivalist Revolution

Introduction

So far I have argued for the embedded and limpet-like character of ethnic identities and their capacity not only to resist but also to direct the secular modernising projects of states. But nationalism is a modern ideological creed that has inspired waves of revolts from the early nineteenth century to the present, first in Western Europe and the Americas, then world wide. How is this emphasis on the persistence of ethnic identities compatible with the innovative character of nationalism and the rise of the territorially extensive, socially mobile and mass political units that we call nations? How can nationalism be revolutionary and yet be shaped by earlier ethnic identities?

I shall argue that the key to this conundrum lies in the romantic revolution which gives rise to a quite new vision of polycentric ethnicity. According to this, humanity is inherently organised into historical communities, each of which is imbued with its own unique life force, expressed through its distinctive culture, is based on natural homelands and is self-governing. This *organic* conception of the nation gave rise to a 'cultural nationalism'. Originating among humanist intellectuals of historical scholars, philologists and artists, this was generally a small-scale phenomenon, that employed bottom-up strategies to 'revive' the national community. Cultural nationalism emerged side by side with what might be called 'political nationalism', which conveyed a different Enlightenment *voluntarist* vision of the nation as a political community of will, built on the rational decision-making of equal citizens and expressed through the mechanism of the territorial state. The two varieties of nationalism were anti-traditionalist and, in practice, often combined: political nationalists asserted a cultural distinctiveness to mobilise their constituencies and justify their claims to political independence, and cultural nationalists, to defend the national ethos and institutions, required the support of a state. Both encouraged the rise of a civil society, of an educated citizenry engaged in a diversified 'public' sphere in which all could participate no matter what their social, economic or religious status.

We have come to associate nationalism with the achievement of a national state that institutionalises a universalist, liberal democratic vision and creates equal opportunities for its citizens. By comparison, cultural nationalism seems of minor and perhaps transient importance. But, as I have discussed elsewhere (Hutchinson, 1987, 1999) the rationalist attack of political nationalists on inherited custom, first observed in the French Revolution, regularly produced a powerful conservative resistance, often expressed through a return to ethnic and religious traditions; and a cultural nationalism crystallised in turn, seeking to unite modernisers and tradition-alists in a new activist conception of the ethnic community.

Cultural nationalists or national revivalists played an essential role in the formation of modern nations by harmonising the sense of rootedness given by tradition with the ideas of progress, in a new activist conception of the (ethnic) historical community as inherently dynamic and interactive. They provided an essential moral basis for the projects of political nationalists. They appealed to new educated groups who realised that in order for their ethnic communities to survive in a world of ceaseless change, they had to be modernised (turned into nations).

In this chapter I explore first the ideas of this national revivalism. We shall see that although in its origins European, it represented a revolt against the hegemony of Christendom in the name of a multicivilisational humanity whose originating centres were outside Europe. This, in part, explains the appeal of nationalism world wide. Second, I examine how this ideology became exported globally, in part by European critics of imperialism and in part by cultural minorities. Finally, I analyse two important revivalist strategies of cultural and political revolution. The first was 'inner': what, following Quentin Skinner (1974), I have called a strategy of 'moral innovation', where revivalists sought to transform the accepted meanings of 'traditions' so that they took on new activist meanings. They were dependent on discovering 'forgotten' layers of the ethnic past that potentially represented counter traditions. The second strategy was 'external': the creation of a cult of sacrifice for the nation by a revolutionary elite, whose moral authority would then enable it to override existing myth structures and systems of authority. This represented what I call a 'mythic overlaying' of ethnic tradition.

Both revivalist outflanking manoeuvres (relativising 'tradition' by returning to an older and more 'authentic' past or creating novel cults that demonstrated its exhaustion) resulted in a competition with, rather than an obliteration of ethnic traditions. In many contexts there remains a tension between national and older ethnic traditions.

Romanticism as an Ethnocultural Movement

The romantic search for authentic foundations in an ancient past was prefigured by humanist and Enlightenment scholarship. From the sixteenth century humanist scholars in a time of religious civil conflicts, invasions and social revolution rejected the biblical or 'Trojan' origins of kingdoms and peoples to claim 'national' descent from the vigorous barbarian peoples who had fought the Romans (Jordan, 2002: 76; Kidd, 1999: ch. 9). Enlightenment *philosophes* such as Voltaire, in seeking to expose the backwardness of European Christianity, stressed the rationality of non-European cultures, such as Confucian China. Central, however, to romanticism was a polycentric *Weltanschauung*, which rejected Christian exclusivity and the rationalist universalism of the Enlightenment. It was based on a conception of a living, not mechanical, universe, in which all natural entities were animated by a force that individualised them and endowed them with a drive for self-realisation.

A national revivalism emerged in the late eighteenth century from a confluence of neo-classical and pre-romantic European currents and spread world wide from its original centres in the metropolitan cities of Europe such as London, Paris, Berlin, Amsterdam and Copenhagen. One of its earliest voices was the German philosopher, Herder. For Herder, one of the natural entities was the nation – a primordial and unique cultural and territorial community through which individuals developed their full potential as moral and rational beings. Herder portrayed humanity as essentially diverse, and world progress as a result of the mutual interactions of nations, each of which had its own unique contribution to make (Herder, 1968: 50–60). Romantics prescribed a duty to recover and sustain all such cultures, for the loss of one was a loss to humanity.

This vision had revolutionary consequences. The depiction of a common human story to which all cultures have contributed justified mutual borrowing. The 'discovery' of golden ages of creative collective achievement made history a weapon of social innovation. Revivalists intensified and extended identification with territorial homelands as a reservoir of sacred energies that created a 'religious' attachment of the urbanised middle classes to the national territory. They vernacularised cultures with the goal of creating a common set of values to unite a socially differentiating collectivity. They demoticised politics and inspired counterculture movements of educated youth dedicated to moral and social transformation. The effects were to create the idea of the nation as a moral community knit by sacrifice, which in recurring periods of revolutionary disruption or military threat could inspire its followers to seize power.

Regenerating a national humanity

A primary motivation of romantic intellectuals was the regeneration of European cultures. From the late eighteenth century, European intellectuals, convinced that their civilisation was deracinated, sought for sources of inspiration outside an ossified Christianity and the mechanistic philosophies of the Enlightenment. Philhellenes found this source in Greek antiquity, but others looked to the 'founding' civilisations of Egypt, Persia and the Arabs. One outcome was momentous: the 'discovery' in the 1780s by British Orientalist scholars in Calcutta, led by Sir William Jones and Henry Colebrooke, of an Hindu Aryan Sanskrit civilisation in North India, developing from the second millennium BC, which they proclaimed as the 'original' civilisation of humanity (Schwab, 1984: 51). Their publication and translations of major texts, the *Shakuntala* drama, the *Bhagavad Gita*, the mystical poetry of the *Gita Govinda*, and its legal codes presented a Hindu genius of epic grandeur, metaphysical depth and moral purity (Schwab, 1984: 51). This inspired a proliferation of Asiatic Societies in London, Paris, Jena, Weimar and Heidelberg and formed the ideas of a generation of German thinkers, including Herder, Goethe and Schelling, many immersed in mystical and theosophical ideas (Schwab, 1984: 161). Jones' conjecture that Sanskrit was the mother language of Europe was given 'scientific' status in Franz Bopp's Indo-European language classification in 1816.

A vision of a human family tree based on ethnocultural principles spurred a internationale of thinkers and scholars to rediscover and record the most distant origins of the peoples of the world and their interrelationships, as a way of making sense of the present, thereby stimulating the rise of archaeology, philology, folklore and comparative religion. This had several effects.

First, it subverted the existing status order within Europe and between Europe and the rest of the world. Within Europe prestige had previously been based on the relationships of rulers and peoples to biblical figures or Greco-Roman antiquity. Jones' discovery was interpreted by the Schlegel brothers as declaring the Asian origins of the European peoples who had migrated in successive waves (Greeks, Romans, Celts, Germans and Slavs)

(Poliakov, 1974: 198). Even in the seventeenth century, German thinkers such as Leibniz sought to combat the prestige of France by declaring the German language as the purest and original language of the peoples who had overthrown the Roman yoke and established the early nations of Europe. German romantics now claimed direct descent from 'pagan' Aryans and cultural leadership of contemporary Europe against the imperial pretensions of Napoleonic France, which legitimised itself as the new Roman imperium. More grandly, Schelling stated the German mission to become the 'mother' Aryan civilisation of the modern age, fusing the mythological traditions of humanity (Indian, Greek, Scandinavian and Persian) into one mythology that would redeem a world distracted by rationalism (Schwab, 1984: 226).

The valorisation of non-European civilisations undermined the legitimation strategies of Imperial states that portrayed their subject peoples as backward barbarians, in the perception of 'colonised' intellectuals who claimed rights to freedom and dignity as heirs of the founding civilisations of humanity. French and British archaeologists, fascinated by the significance of ancient Egypt in forming the ancient world, resurrected the glories of Pharaonic civilisation: the discovery of Tutankhamun's tomb in 1922 shortly after the granting of limited Egyptian independence inspired in the upper and upper middle class a secular Egyptian territorial nationalism in the 1920s (Reid, 1997: 130).

Secondly, revivalism resulted in the transfer of modern academic resources from the advanced cultures of Europe, enabling intellectuals in the 'hinterland' to reconstruct their own histories and cultures. Developing an ethnic model of the nation against the 'civic' or political model of France, Germany became the heartland of romantic nationalism, its thinkers and universities inspirations for the intellectuals of the stateless peoples of Europe from Finland to Slovak territories, and beyond; most early Russian nationalists were educated in German territories (Prizel, 1998: 168–9). German and French thinkers wishing to understand the Celtic contribution to their early 'nations' turned to Ireland, whose Celtic culture survived until the seventeenth century, and pioneered the academic study of Ireland's Celtic civilisation, documenting its early medieval golden age when it played a major role in the rise of Christian Europe. Outside Europe, British Orientalist scholars in Bengal felt a duty to educate Indians about their forgotten golden age because of Britain's debt to ancient India. Indian scholars were excluded from membership of the Asiatic Society of Calcutta (founded in 1784) until 1827. However, some contributed to its journals, and the training college for East India Company officials, Fort William, employed Indian pundits to assist in the compiling of textbooks and the codification of laws and languages. Indians thus participated in the systematisation of Hindu high and vernacular culture. In 1816 Hindu College was established to educate the Calcutta elite, promoting a regeneration of the Indian heritage together with the study of a secular Western curriculum (Kopf, 1969: ch. 5).

Thirdly, a sense of ethnic or cultural affiliation led romantic intellectuals to participate in the cultural and political struggles of 'reviving' nationalities. Mazzini, after establishing Young Italy in 1831, developed international organisations that proposed the regeneration and freedom of all the major nationalities of Europe (Mansergh, 1968: 76). The early civil servants of the East India Company, many critical of Empire, explicitly sought to govern India on 'Indian' lines, and to revive Indian glories under a British protectorate, with the long-term effect that Bengal established itself as the centre of Indian nationalism. A sense of their Greek heritage inspired co-operation among European intellectuals who rallied public opinion in support of the Greek struggle for independence against the Ottoman Empire, depicted as the struggle of European liberty against Oriental despotism. Widespread philhellenic sympathy in Western Europe contributed to the intervention of Britain and France who, with the traditional supporter of the Orthodox cause, Russia, in 1829 compelled the Ottomans to cede independence.

Finally, the depiction of world civilisation as the product of national cultures, each of which played a special role, justified a mutual borrowing of cultures. Of course, societies throughout history coming into contact engaged in syncretism and exchange, but revivalism promoted rather than merely accepted it. Nationalists might claim that although currently backward, their nation had once been a teacher of the nations, so that borrowing from the advanced was no more than reclaiming their patrimony. This undermined an ethnocentric resistance to change and enormously expanded the repertoire of options available to modernising elites. At the same time, it rejected an uncritical adoption of external models: such borrowing must work to enhance nations, not to efface them within a single conception of development. Against what they saw as the uncritical adoption by Russian westerners of French liberal revolutionary principles, conservative Slavophiles extolled the model of early nineteenth-century England, where the landed gentry sponsored moderate reform. Such a perspective encouraged nationalist groups within independent non-European states such as Japan, the Ottoman Empire and China to look world wide for models by which to reconstruct their societies and stave off European imperial challenges.

'Borrowings' could be employed by nationalists to enhance their cultural prestige or, indeed, to substitute for the lack of an ancient ethnic heritage on which to ground the nation. An extreme case is Kemal Atatürk's attempt, in breaking with the long Ottoman heritage, to create a prestigious and more ancient pagan Turkish culture by claiming the legacy of the Hittites, Egyptians and Sumerians (Seton-Watson, 1977: 259). Such 'borrowings' could have explosive effects on populations that were ethnically mixed or adjacent, resulting in cultural wars over the appropriations of common histories, cultural figures and artefacts. Norwegians, Icelanders and Danes clashed over the 'ownership' of the Nordic Sagas; Irish and Scottish intellectuals over national claims to the *Ossianic Lays*; Ukrainians and Russians over cultural possession of the Kievan region; and more recently, the Macedonians and Greeks over the symbols of Philip II and Alexander the Great. Conflicts themselves help generate a national consciousness, since intellectuals are forced to look back into the past in order to justify their appropriations.

History as a charter of innovation

National revivalists produced a dynamic view of the ethnic community in history, in which a veneration of the past was the means to future development, and the source of power lay not in God and dynasties but in the originating peoples and their mythos. History replaced religion as the guide to collective identity and destiny. Historical scholars – Palacky for Czechs, Hrushevsky for Ukrainians, Iorga for Romanians – became fathers of the nation. Romantic nationalists undermined existing ethnic traditions by recreating the past as one of continuous creativity. This was achieved by placing the origins of the group back in time, discovering multiple pasts with alternative repertoire and role models, and, above all, by identifying a golden age that authenticated innovation.

Romantics sought to reveal the entire collective personality of the nation as it develops in space and time, and in Lord Acton's words they 'brought into action the whole inheritance of man' (Schenk, 1966: 42). Since the history of peoples was rarely recorded in the documents of elites, romanticism encouraged an explosion of genetic sciences, including philology, archaeology, folklore and topography. Historians, through publications, academies and museums, sought to recover all aspects of the nation's heritage, interpret it to the community, attesting to the status of the nation as a primordial and significant civilisation, and defend its heritage against foreign detractors. History was expanded, deepened and *systematised* as historians sought to identify a national telos, in spite of apparent discontinuities, in order to educate each generation and establish a distinctive repertoire of options and sets of role models for the present.

In search of collective authenticity, romantics focused on the earliest emergence of peoples when their original character was most clearly displayed. The poet Henrik Wergeland, in 1834, declared in a famous speech 'In Praise of the Ancestors' that Snorri's sagas, translated in the late eighteenth century, were 'the Norwegian patent of nobility among the nations', portraying a Viking warrior people, a great state, heroic kings and explorers, an extensive code of law, expressive pagan religion and impressive poetry, epic and lyrical (Sorensen, 1994: 26–9). The publication by Lonnrot in 1835 of the epic poem the *Kalevala*, which appeared to date back to prehistoric times and to evoke a distinctive mythology, was greeted as a charter of nationality. Finns could now say 'I too have a history' declared one activist (Wilson, 1976: 42). The German poet Klopstock claimed to find a separate Germanic religion in the Icelandic *Edda* (Poliakov, 1974: 94–5). This unearthing of new pasts could shake the legitimacy of established groups. The recording of older pagan origins before the arrival of Christianity (or other religions), validated the rise of a heroic conception of the community of which the later coming of a world religion was just another expression.

The core of the nation, however, was revealed in its golden age when the creative genius of the nation flowered. In certain contexts this might entail a return to the middle ages, but this did not mean a reversion to religious dominance. This was a period of a high cultural achievement, harmonising all dimensions of human experience (religious, scientific, artistic, military and economic), when the nation was in active contact with the other great centres, and making a permanent contribution to human civilisation. Nineteenth-century Irish nationalists evoked the eighth century when Ireland's Celtic and Christian cultures fused, producing great works of art in the *Book of Kells*, and when, famed for its classical learning, Ireland became the school of Europe. Arab nationalists might view the coming of Mohammed as inaugurating a golden age, but in order to view Islam as the creator of the Arab nation, as the content of its culture and the object of its collective pride (Gershoni, 1997: 8–9), one that defeated Western crusaders and became a centre of achievement in mathematics, medicine, philosophy and the sciences.

Periods of decline, even disaster, had their lessons. Serbs commemorated their defeat on the plains of Kosovo and subsequent servitude at the hands of the Ottoman Turks, just as Greeks commemorated the fall of Constantinople, as catastrophes characterised by a combination of betrayal and inner weakness. However, history showed that the nation would never die as long as people held true to its memory, and, above all, that of the golden age. Historical 'memory' was used to stimulate revival through invidious comparisons with the decadent present. A national consciousness developed amongst diaspora Greeks of the early nineteenth century aware of the humiliating contrasts European philhellenic visitors made between the Hellenic progenitors of Western civilisation and the backward peasant subjects of the Ottoman Empire (Campbell and Sherrard, 1968: ch. 1). Above all, the golden age provided an inspiration for a rising generation who, returning to its energies, would throw off the paralysis of tradition and recreate the nation as a politically autonomous and self-reliant society, that would be a model to the world.

Historical memory, then, evoked a call to action. By rooting themselves in an ancient and self-renewing collectivity that had survived countless disasters, a new educated middle class found the confidence that they could overcome a world of revolutionary uncertainty and were inspired to heroic sacrifice. They acquired stature in the modern world through membership of a nation whose heroic age had contributed to the civilisation of humanity. They found their own special mission as a generation who would restore the links in the chain to this great past, thus renewing the historical destiny of their people.

Creating homelands

Although ethnic groups typically view themselves as linked 'ancestrally' to the land, romanticism intensified, extended, diffused and embedded this sense of belonging, imbuing the defence and the regaining of the national territory as a sacred duty. It attracted a sense of devotion in the deracinated young of the cities and towns who viewed the countryside as a spiritual resource, rather than as a livelihood.

For romantics nations were outgrowths of nature, and thus explained by the characteristics of the land they worked. Equally the land national communities named and worked was an expression of the nation and its history. In pantheist fashion they viewed the homeland as a repository of a moral vision and primordial energies. Of course, this had precursors in the classical idea of nature as arcadia (envisioned during the eighteenth century as Tuscany), but romanticism broke with the universal claims of this model landscape, since each nation's homelands had unique characteristics that gave the community its individuality. Scandinavians and Canadians celebrated the darkness and austerity of their Arctic wastes as infusing their peoples with an inner mysticism; the Swiss the ruggedness of the Alps, as protectors of their republican freedoms (Kaufmann and Zimmer, 1998).

Since nature was so endowed, nationalists must undertake cultural voyages to record the distinctive qualities of their habitat and its cultures as part of the discovery of their collective self. This *extended* spatially the sense of homeland, filled out a sense of the life and activities of the communities who worked the land, and historically *deepened* the sense of attachment by exploring the layers of the past that 'scaped' the land. Serbian nationalists spoke of the graves of the Orthodox dead in Kosovo as their 'burial cities'. In nineteenth-century Denmark archaeological discoveries of the lur and golden horn (musical instruments), the sunwagon and the 'barrow' burial mounds became important symbols of a primordial folk culture (Sorenson, 1996).

One result was the unexpected 'revelation' of remote areas of natural beauty and of great cultural significance, which, because of their 'wildness' and 'hidden' quality, became mysterious and sacred reservoirs of the national spirit. Inspired by a sense of rebirth, travelling nationalist artists, musicians and poets saw it as their duty to *diffuse* and represent the moral vision of the land. Irish poets like Mangan and Yeats, using folk images, personified Ireland as a beautiful young woman, Cathleen ni Houlihan to whom devotion was due.

Such regions became ramparts of the nation to which groups, especially alienated, urban, educated middle classes, could turn to escape assimilation to foreign values and experience moral regeneration, thereby *embedding* themselves in the land. They provided pilgrimage sites during which young nationalists from different regions found a common national identity, celebrating seasonal festivals, founding educational colleges and sometimes even forming settlements, such as the Zionist kibbutz in Palestine. The defence of these regions from foreign cultural or political threat galvanised powerful nationalist movements. During the late nineteenth century tens of thousands of the Finnish middle class youth visited Karelia to tap its poetry, and after Finnish independence the Finnish nation-state fought two wars with the USSR in order to claim this sacred region for the nation (Wilson, 1976: 47, 141–3).

The cult of the land had thus a unifying effect, binding a new mobile middle class of the cities to the larger territorial unit by rooting them in a defence of a highly individualised homeland. New imperatives bound this group – the unification of all members of the nation, freeing the land from foreign rule, and ridding the land of aliens who by their presence adulterated its cultural purity.

Vernacularising the social world

Although some vernacular cultures predated the era of nationalism, the romantics pioneered a general vernacularisation of high culture, creating a unified field of exchange by which new educated elites sought to integrate a society differentiating through the division of labour.

Herder's plea to the European peoples to preserve their national vernaculars, as the lifeline of their heritage and the expression of their unique collective consciousness, had a great impact, particularly on the Slavs. In Eastern Europe nationalism generated an explosion of philological research and the publication of dictionaries and grammars, as the nationalists sought to identify the authentic language of the people, purified of foreign borrowings, and to make it the public medium of modern science and culture (Anderson, 1991: ch. 5). The transformation of 'dialects' into a common literary standard served to unify dispersed populations into communities and differentiate them from neighbouring 'others'. Linguistic nationalism mobilised resistance of ethnic minorities against (often imperial) centralising states that sought to impose an alien official language on their territories for purposes of administrative efficiency.

However, the vernacular revolution went much deeper than this. Language was only one of several means to a larger goal: the resurrection of the *Volksgeist* that expressed the unique creative genius of the nation in all its plenitude. Because of national decay, this *Volksgeist* was submerged and lost to sophisticated society, but the remnants could be found in the untamed imaginative life of rural folk living close to nature. In shaping these fragments into a unified whole, a romantic might turn to many sources – fairy tales, songs, melodies and proverbs. But James Macpherson's 'discovery' of the *Ossianic Lays* (1762) triggered a competitive craze throughout Europe to rediscover early epic literature, whose myths and legends were portrayed as the earliest and purest expression of the anonymous genius of the people. The Irish responded by rediscovering their ancient Celtic Red Branch and Finn Cycles; Norwegians the *Edda* (translated 1766–8); and in 1813 Germans rekindled their interest in the thirteenth century *Nibelungenlied* (Schwab, 1984: 214).

If the historian provided a map of the national identity, it was the artist who exemplified the nation's creative energies. Artists, romantics believed, were the original conscience and voice of the people, whose role had been usurped by established religions and, subsequently, scientists and journalists. They had a special mission to restore the ancient unity of being, lost to the modern world by the division of labour, to return individuals to their national archetype and thereby to recreate a unified way of life. Kollar for Slovaks, Mickiewicz for Poles, Yeats for the Irish, Bialik for Zionists, Wagner for Germans had iconic status within their national movements. They were often encylopaedic intellectuals, recorders of folk culture, dabblers in mystical cults, founders of cultural institutions (theatres, opera houses, schools of art) and active supporters in the reformation of everyday life (through national sports, dances, dress, applied arts and design).

As creative artists they could not simply reproduce the past: they had to find new cultural genres and institutions appropriate to their changing society, a society that was increasingly literate and diverse. Sir Walter Scott, hailed as the Scottish Shakespeare, became a cult figure in nineteenth-century Europe as the inventor of the historical novel, and thus the progenitor of Tolstoy's *War and Peace*, which, set against the backdrop Napoleon's invasion of Russia, became the canonical work of Russian prose. Both authors set heroic individuals against the backdrop of key historical moments in exploring the struggle of national progress against tradition (Bate, 1997, 145). The lyric poem and ballad, often modelled on traditional oral literature, were also pervasive poetic forms.

An influential genre was the drama – inspired by Shakespeare who, in the eighteenth century, had been criticised for his uncouth breaches of the classical rules. To the English he exemplified the national genius of an Elizabethan golden age that was empirical, sceptical and unsystematic, and they revered the patriotism of his history plays, particularly *Henry V*. Intellectuals European-wide, rejecting the hegemony of French classicism, now likened him to Homer and Ossian in his artlessness, protean energy, sense of mystery and social range (Bate, 1997: ch. 6). Impressed by the Elizabethan drama's nation-building effects, Schiller, regarded as the poet of German freedom, argued that a national theatre would provide a means of promoting a national mythos to the people, and his play, *Wilhelm Tell*, (1804) based on Swiss legends, became a coded plea for German freedom (Jarausch et al., 1997: 32). The poet Yeats argued that a theatre, by bringing individuals into a collectivity and immersing them in the national legends, could perform for a literate age the equivalent of the ancient epics, whose communal recitations had bound older oral societies. Yeats founded the Abbey Theatre to present the heroes and gods of the Irish epic cycles, above all the warrior-seer Cúchulainn (Hutchinson, 1987: 134). In this he was influenced not just by the Czech and Norwegian theatres, but also by the composer Wagner who established his Bayreuth Theatre as a religious centre for the German nation, in the belief that his legendary operatic cycle based on *Nibelungenlied* would dissolve everyday reality and reveal to Germans their heroic collective essence.

Wagner, like Yeats, hoped that from such legends he could create a single, collective, national personality. In Finland the *Kalevala* epic, after its publication in Karelia in 1835, became the lodestar round which a unified but also diversified national identity was constructed. In the next 50 years this inspired a mushrooming of patriotic societies to study the *Kalevala*, the promotion in schools of a knowledge of the Finnish language, history, geography and folklore, the rise of a Finnish language press, and the identification of the Karelian region as a sacred centre for Finns. During the campaigns against cultural and political Russification in the late nineteenth and early twentieth centuries, the poet Leino, the painters Gallen-Kallela and Halonen, and the composer Sibelius, turned to the *Kalevala* and the Karelian landscape to create a distinctively national high culture (Wilson, 1976: 58–60).

The vernacular revolution was more than about language or the arts. This was a revolt against the prestige of existing languages of culture, religious and secular, and those who deployed them – the Latin-educated clergy and the French-speaking aristocracies of Europe. A new humanist elite formed to express a distinctive vision based on popular traditions that would guide a society undergoing rapid differentiation under the impact of technological change. They established societies to promote native dress, national sporting associations, gymnastic, arts and crafts societies. All aspects of the human personality were to be explored and brought into balance with each other. The physical was to be developed in association with the spiritual, as a preparation for service to the nation, paving the way for cohorts of a virile and revolutionary shock force.

Forming a political community of sacrifice

Romantics revolutionalised politics by transferring authority from the state to a national community animated from below, thereby encouraging an upsurge of populist energies. It gave rise to grass-roots organisations in localities outside existing political structures that could influence existing power holders in national states, or act as centres of disaffection from which to mount a revolutionary attempt on the state.

By the late eighteenth century 'enlightened' dynasts like the Habsburg Emperor Joseph II justified their rule by improving the welfare of the people, but for romantics politics was not just a means to serve the nation but an authentic expression of its collective will. The nation was not viewed in rational terms as the sum of unmediated individuals, but as an organic unity differentiated by regional, gender, religious and occupational identities.

National revivalists rejected the centralising bureaucratic state as a threat to life forces of the community. Equally, the forces of tradition had to be over-thrown in each social sector, which must be vitalised by the national will. Social decay came from within, from a loss of national identity that resulted in anomie and social conflict as the nation dissolved into its constituent interest groups. A healthy national identity, the Irish revivalist Thomas Davis maintained, was not something that crystallised in the rational exercise of political power (through voting or participating in political institutions). Heroes rather than mere citizens were the key to national survival and progress. Only the formation of a heroic leadership in each national sector would ensure the formation of a solidary community protected against the anomie and class conflict of modern life (Hutchinson, 1987: 104–5).

Theirs was a grass-roots strategy of educational permeation. Revivalists spoke of a return to the people, and valorised those whom they regarded as the custodians of the nation's continuity, usually the peasantry. In practice, the future of the nation lay in nationalising the educated leaders of society. In many poorly-educated agrarian societies this stratum was tiny, and to obtain social leverage they had to appeal to the gentry and clergy. Where these strata responded, as in Poland and Croatia, the nationalism took on a conservative hue. In much of Eastern Europe, however, the gentry might be ethnically different or foreign-speaking, and nationalists were forced to turn to a peasantry that had a low political consciousness. Here revivalism took on the form of a self-help movement. In this spirit the leading organisations of nineteenth-century Ukrainian and Latvian revivalism, the Shevchenko Scientific Society and the Riga Latvian Association, in constructing a modern vernacular literary and scientific culture out of a largely illiterate oral culture, promoted a vigorous lay movement among the peasantry, including an explosive expansion of libraries, agricultural and credit co-operatives, newspapers and support for (in the Ukrainian case) a native university at Lemberg (Plakans, 1974: 464–9; Rudnytski, 1977: 141–54.) In Denmark, by contrast, the cultural nationalist Grundtvigian movement of Lutheran pas-tors and folk high school teachers found fertile ground in the prosperous farmers. It became a major training centre for Danish political elites and thereby helped to form the distinctive populist and libertarian character of that nation-state (Ostergard, 1994: 46–7).

In practice, their politics were pragmatic and directed at the educated from whatever social group. They found sympathisers in groups of religious and social reformers, particularly lower clergy seeking a revitalising of their religion by directing it to the welfare of the people. Their core constituency was young middle-class men (educated professionals such as civil servants, teachers, lawyers and journalists) who became the political cadres of nationalist organisations. As the names of these organisations suggest (Young Italy, Young Poland, Young Ireland, Young Egypt), nationalism was an ideology of the educated young (Kedourie, 1960: 99–102). Alienated from traditional values by their secular education, imbued with new expectations of social and political mobility, they sought to reconnect with their society by leading it from backwardness. Yet only too often they were blocked from power by established holders of office and status. Nationalism offered them an alternative moral vision of integration achieved by a novel form of training, conveyed by the term *bildung*, a drawing out of the essence of the individual through an immersion in the life energies of the nation, as captured in its history, arts, customs and whole way of life. It offered them an alternative vocation as nation-builders. The effect was to create a new moral community, based on disaffected male youth, organised around a cult of national sacrifice.

Revivalism created a new symbolism and set of ceremonies and an overlapping range of cultural and social agencies (literary societies, musical choirs, sporting associations) as part of this holistic vocation to train body and mind for a life of sacrifice for the nation (Mosse, 1976; 1990: chs. 1, 2). Such movements evinced a fervent religious character exalting the spiritual glories, physical beauties and heroic qualities of native history, language, literature and customs against the infernal corruptions of other cultures. Oaths of sacrifice to Kali (as 'national' goddess) in India; impassioned ceremonies of public testament to the born-again effects of adopting the Gaelic language in Ireland; commemorations of heroic battles and of fallen soldiers to inculcate the cult of sacrifice; and pilgrimages of the young German members of the early twentieth-century *Wandervogel* to battle fields, religious shrines and the birth place of famous artists – these public displays of commitment to certain behaviours and rejection of others bound diverse individuals to a distinctive moral community and to the institutions necessary to maintain it.

The effect was to form young people from the different sectors of the nation into a counter-cultural society in which status was gained by service to the nation, and one which was capable of resisting the norms of the dominant society. Although romantic revivalists were, in general, peaceful and reformist, conflict was seen as a necessary part of nationalism, for the young must overthrow the established order in order to regenerate the nation. Within existing national states the influence of such nationalism was usually diffuse. But where nationalists were confronted by a repressive (and also foreign) regime, the ideal of heroic sacrifice could organise young men into revolutionary brotherhoods.

National Revivalism and Social Transformation

This, however, was very much a minority enthusiasm of intellectuals dependent on an educated stratum. Since my previous chapter emphasised the power of ethnic and other traditional values and institutions and their capacity to mobilise opinion well into the modern period, how can we explain the capacity of such movements to become hegemonic? I shall briefly consider the long-term effects of the scientific revolutions beginning in the seventeenth century and the role of outsiders in initiating revivalism outside the developed world, and then the novel challenges faced by societies in the modern world and the strategies employed by revivalists to overcome them. I shall argue that although revivalism remained throughout a minority project, it took a wider, though limited, social hold first through a process of *moral innovation*, which presented populations with new maps of identity and political prescriptions at times of social polarisation when established traditions were shaken by modernisation. It also created a counter community knit by a cult of heroic sacrifice for the nation. Periodically, throughout the modern period political systems have been faced with extraordinary crises, at which points these counter communities became the launch pads of revolutionary action, generating myths that legitimised the hegemony of new governing elites and national state structures.

The long scientific revolution

As Anthony Smith (1971: ch. 10) has argued, modern nationalism is one response to the secularisation of the world that arose from the scientific revolutions of the seventeenth century. As the disenchanting scientific ethos has challenged religious cosmologies, this has given rise to a 'dual legitimation crisis', which is both cognitive and social. The problem is to combine the sense of rootedness provided by religious tradition with the idea of progress provided by science. This inspired three solutions: an outright secularism expressed in aspirations for a cosmopolitan political order; a neo-traditionalist solution using secular political mechanisms to reject secular ideals; and a religious reformism that tried to combine the best of religious tradition and science. Each allied with older ethnic traditions in order to mobilise the community.

Revivalism represented a variety of the third solution, and it drew its constituency from secular intellectuals, reform-minded clerics and the professional middle classes (as civil servants, lawyers, teachers and journalists) who, because of their education and professional training, were alienated from their traditional values by their secular education and imbued with new expectations of social and political mobility. Revivalist intellectuals identified with the nation out of a search for meaning that they sought to validate through 'scientific' scholarship. This search drew them first into heterodox religious belief systems and then to their concrete embodiment in a living nation whose 'truth' could be authenticated by historical research. Smith's model is plausible.

As we saw, many intellectuals came to nationalism via mystical religions such as theosophy, spiritualism and pantheism. Sir William Jones, although a Christian of deist tendencies, was attracted to Indian culture through his love of nature found in the *Sakuntala* and the mystical poetry of the *Gita Govinda*. Asia stood for the imagination and Europe for (Grecian) reason, and Jones saw his task as regenerating both by uniting them as complementary elements of an overarching world civilisation (Mukherjee, 1968: 120). George Petrie, the leader of the early nineteenth-century Irish revival, was initially drawn to an archaeological search for Ireland's ancient past by a Wordsworthian pantheist love of nature and the antiquities embedded in it (Stokes, 1868: 5–7). Convinced of the existence of an integrating national life force, these scholars saw it as their duty to discover the nation (its history, land and culture), to communicate the lost legacy to its members, and to dedicate their lives to its revival. An important part of their life's work was in establishing scientific societies to authoritatively document their research in the eyes of an international community of scholars. In many cases they established their discipline as a national profession.

Like Jones, Petrie saw himself as a revisionist rescuing his national history both from patriotic fantasists and also from foreign detractors. More than anyone else Petrie formalised archaeology as a scientific discipline, revitalising the Royal Irish Academy as a forum of scholarly debate and founding several archaeological societies. His archaeological papers established the physical evidence of a civilised society in Ireland in the early pagan era, and of a period of great artistic achievement in the early middle ages, just as Jones' and Colebrooke's work laid the basis of the scholarly study of ancient India. In short, the long term power of the revivalist claims came from their successfully documenting a historical record of multiple pasts of collective creativity.

Part of the authority of the intellectuals over this rationally trained intelligentsia was the apparent *scientific* standing of the nation. Certainly, this research resonated at times when a rising ethnic intelligentsia found itself blocked from power by established holders of power (whether foreign or native oligarchs). Nonetheless, such strata were not only concerned with power, but also (in the manner of all *arrivistes*) with roots and identity in a period of large-scale social change. They looked back, as Anthony Smith argues, to earlier historical periods, not just to legitimise their political strategies but also to find lessons for the present. They sought to reconnect with their society by leading it from backwardness. Certainly, there was wishful thinking involved – in Lonnrot's compilation of *Kalevala* from scattered folk verses into a unified epic – and, in moulding historical evidence to create national continuities, historians such as Michelet, Petrie and Palacky were myth-makers. But these 'findings' were not constructed after the fact to justify the claims of an already emergent class: they either preceded or accompanied the development of native intelligentsia, forming their identities, as is suggested by the gap between the 'rediscovery' of Aryan India and the rise of a significant Indian revivalist movement in the 1880s. The ideas of the intellectuals had different well-springs than the needs of their social constituencies.

What generated a sense of excitement among intellectuals and intelligentsia alike was the revelation of unanticipated sites, historical episodes, cultural treasures and populations that arose out of the drive to know the nation. The discovery of the Karelian region, of a Hellenic and a Vedic age, of the *Edda*, made such an impact because they revealed a formerly 'hidden' nation of extraordinary power. Their sudden reappearance was taken as a sign that a new historical destiny was about to unfold, by identifying with which young nationalists would change the world. So it was for the Irish poets W. B. Yeats and AE, newly converted by theosophical ideas, who believed their 'disclosure' of spiritual parallels in the Celtic legends of the peasantry of the West foreshadowed the coming of an Irish Avatar (Hutchinson, 1987: 236–9). Such discoveries, as we saw, could redefine the identity and direction of national movements.

The role of 'outsiders'

Nonetheless, the question remains, given that nationalism formed in many backward agrarian societies with low levels of urbanisation, industrialisation and education, how did revivalists obtain their initial impetus to mount a challenge to established social custodians and the state? The short answer is that the impulse often came from those groups who were in some way outside the traditional culture and who sought to understand or reconstitute it, or who 'discovered' alternative versions of the ethnic past. These groups included foreign scholars, modern imperial officials and religious missionaries, religious minorities and borderland or diaspora populations.

Foreign scholars, as we have seen in many countries played an important part in resuscitating and often reconstructing ancient ethnic cultures. They might have several motives: an interest in discovering the origins of their own cultures; a need in the case of imperial officials and religious missionaries to understand the customs, laws and languages of the peoples they conquered in the interests of better government and evangelism; and a sense of moral obligation to 'fallen' representatives of a once great missionary civilisation. We have cited the contribution of European philhellenic enlighteners and romantics to the Greek national revival. Members of the Baltic German gentry, fascination by the 'original' peoples who influenced their ancestors, pioneered the study of the ethnic folk customs of their 'somnolent' peasantries.

The British Orientalist scholars brought together by William Hastings to serve the administration of the East India Company had a profound effect on Indian nationalism, making Bengal the centre of language modernisation and literary revival. Convinced of their duty to rule India on 'national' lines, they set up Hindu College for the Calcutta elite, promoting a pride in the Indian heritage and social reform on Hindu lines in an attack of native customs such as *sati* (widow immolation). Christian missionaries played an important nationalising role. The Baptist William Carey, ally of the Orientalists, was the first publisher of the Indian vernacular languages. His aim was to undermine the Brahmin caste that claimed a monopoly of the Sanskrit scriptures by publishing them in Indian vernaculars (Kopf, 1969: ch. 5). In the Indian subcontinent the threat of Christian evangelism stimulated the rise of Hindu movements that revived an ancient indigenous heritage in their defence. In 1828 Rammohun Roy established Brahmo Samaj, appropriating the Orientalist conception of early Hinduism as rational and monotheistic to reform the religion and thus deflect Christian polemics against such practices as idol worship and *sati* (Van der Veer, 1999: 30). European missions in Africa and Asia, and American missions in the Middle East, transformed many oral languages into native standards, and set up schools in order to translate the scriptures and create an indigenous elite able to read them (Hastings, 1997: ch. 7).

Well-educated religious minorities were overrepresented in the early stages of many nationalisms – Protestants in Slovak, Irish and Korean, Copts in Egyptian and Maronite Christians in Lebanese – although those identifying with nationalism may themselves have been a minority of their minority. Their sense of marginality led them to find a secular ethnic past preceding and relativising the religious traditions of the majority that would give them a role in the political community. Such feelings were possibly increased by the gradual march of democracy that would undermine the status of the minority. Egyptian Copts, who perceived themselves to be the truest descendants of ancient Egypt, were active in asserting the claims of the Pharaonic era against the prestige of the later Arab-Islam period. Although they composed only between six per cent and 10 per cent of Egypt's population, they constituted about 40 per cent of Egyptologists between 1928–40, and some even adopted Pharaonic names. Western-educated upper and middle classes in the relatively cosmopolitan cities of Cairo and Alexandria identified with the relative secularism of the Wafd regime (Reid, 1997: 140). In similar fashion, Syrian Christians championed the Aramaeans as the original founders of their nation; Maronite Christians claimed the Phoenicians as ancestors of Lebanon to establish a national identity not linked with the Arab Muslim majority (Lewis, 1998: 74). Non-Arab and French-educated Christian and other religious minorities (the Druze and Alawis) founded a Pan-Arabism defined by language and history in Lebanon and Syria (Pfaff, 1993: 116–17).

Many nationalists came from diaspora or overseas populations. Some combined a sense of nostalgia for a homeland with a sense of shame at its backwardness compared with the free institutions and vigour of their host society. A Greek neo-classical nationalism formed in the late eighteenth century amongst scholars and merchants in the Balkans, many of whom were educated or travelled widely in Europe. Conscious of the backwardness of their homeland compared with Europe, and also of the philhellenic exaltation of classical Greece as the originator of European civilisation, they funded cultural societies, libraries and literary publications in order to regenerate their 'fallen' kinsmen (Jusdanis, 2001: 122–33). Pan-Africanism originated among the descendants of black slaves in the USA seeking roots and dignity, and developed a second base among African intellectuals in France. Other diasporas were radicalised by the spread of democratic principles that made their status increasingly precarious. Zionism was born in the Jewish diaspora of Western and Eastern Europe and was triggered by the rising tide of anti-Semitism from the mid-nineteenth century that in Western Europe eroded liberal hopes of assimilation offered by the Enlightenment, and that in Russia and Eastern Europe resulted in waves of pogroms.

Borderlands, where identity was problematic or threatened, were also sources of nationalism. During the 1930s the Germans in eastern borderlands were prominent in German racial nationalism, and likewise Russians in border zones were overrepresented in nationalism movements of the nineteenth century. Many nationalists were of mixed ethnic descent and conscious of this: Zia Gokalp, the philosopher of Turkish nationalism, was of Kurdish descent; Patrick Pearse was one of many Irish nationalists born to mixed English and Irish parentage; Thomas Masaryk, the Czech historian, was of Slovak birth; and Adam Mickiewicz was of Polish and Jewish descent.

All this indicates the transformational energies that came from 'outside' traditional society. Together such groups provided academic and financial resources, and autonomous communication networks through which heterodox versions of the collective past could be developed, legitimised and disseminated. Nonetheless, what gave them autonomy from the institutions of their target society also made them unrepresentative of it and provoked resistance. How was it that such radically different ideas were able to establish themselves within these societies and overcome the emotional, cognitive and institutional resistance of religious and landed elites? To what extent were they successful in replacing older identities?

Moral Innovators

What allowed national revivalism to challenge traditions, ethnic and otherwise, were the continuous and unpredictable external and internal shocks to the existing social order unleashed by secular modernisation and carried world wide by European imperialism. Although traditional autocratic regimes first in Central and Eastern Europe, then in the Middle East and Asia regarded with horror the liberal democratic legacy of the French Revolution, they realised the mobilising capacities (especially military) of the national model. They also confronted an unprecedented challenge. Even China, the greatest of the non-European states, faced destruction by the early twentieth century. The Opium Wars of the 1840s had forced the entry of China into the Western capitalist world system and over the next 50 years it was rocked by internal rebellions and foreign assaults, culminating in its defeat by Meiji Japan in 1895 and the threat of partition by European powers.

In response these regimes felt compelled to introduce limited reforms (expanding education, emancipating serfs, opening access to public offices and sponsoring technological innovation) to ensure their survival. As they reformed, conflicts erupted between traditionalists and modernisers. The traditionalists initially sought to block out 'the West' and the ideas of progress that threatened to destroy indigenous values. Modernisers in nineteenth-century Russia, China and India adopted a radical anti-traditionalism, many adopting the ideas of political nationalism, and argued that the only salvation of their society was to copy the models of the advanced West, if needs be abandoning the great traditions of Orthodoxy or Confucianism or Hinduism that doomed their peoples to backwardness and poverty. But such projects could result in intense social conflict as well as creating a sense of demoralisation *vis-à-vis* the external enemy.

National revivalism offered a third way, by preaching a modernisation from within. We find national revivalists regularly establishing formal institutions at times of conflict. They found an early constituency in religious reform movements. Both nationalists and reformists sought a solution to the internal conflict by evoking a national golden age and studying the experience of other countries.

For this reason I have described such nationalists as *moral innovators*, providing new directions at times of social crisis (Hutchinson, 1987, 1999). The golden age for such nationalists was a time when the nation was a dynamic high culture, harmonising all dimensions of human experience (religious, scientific, artistic, military), in active contact with the other great centres of culture, and making a permanent contribution to human civilisation. This evolutionary historical vision claimed to present an innovative solution that would reconcile the interests of traditionalists and modernisers, thereby redirecting energies away from destructive conflict into a co-operative reconstruction of the national community. The golden age was used to transform the accepted meanings of 'tradition' and 'modernity' so that in their 'authentic' national forms they were one and the same, and thereby persuade their adherents to ally in the national project. The aim was to reform ossified tradition and to articulate the options by which modernisation should be pursued.

To traditionalists, national revivalists argued that it was a misunderstanding to conceive of tradition as a passive repetition of custom. Traditionalists must recognise that tradition had continually to be renewed, sometimes by adapting the ideas of others, and its authentic expression was to be found in the golden age when the national community was a dynamic, modernising civilisation confidently exchanging ideas and technologies with other cultures. For example, Swami Vivekananda's neo-Vedantic movement, formed in the 1880s, sought to undermine the authority of Hindu tradition by evoking, as the authentic India, an Aryan civilisation that had allegedly instructed two of the great world centres of learning (Greece and Persia), and that denied there were inherent barriers between the sexes and castes, or between religious and secular learning. It rejected the religious taboos on contacts with foreigners and the caste hierarchies as later inventions of the Brahmin priesthood, which were deviations from this dynamic democratic civilisation (Heimsath, 1964: ch. 7). In effect, such movements were internalising as essential components of ethnic or ethnoreligious tradition the ideals and institutions of civil society and liberal democracy.

To modernisers who uncritically admired foreign models, revivalists argued that the greatest embodiment of a successful modernity was to be found in the golden age of their nation, which had instructed the then backward 'West'. Whatever the West now had was borrowed from their nation, and hence they should look to their own traditions for inspiration. Liang Qichao, one of the leaders of the Chinese reform movement, thus claimed that China was a primary world civilisation when the West was still barbarous, hence the West was once no better than the Chinese were now, and what was of value in the West had been taken from China. At other times he would argue that it was foolish to imitate blindly Western values, for its progress had arisen out of its own unique patterns of growth and decay. Indeed, the West was now in decay, for it had overdeveloped the material in relation to the spiritual and was now faced with internal dissolution. History had reserved a special mission for the Chinese, who had retained their ancient religious and aesthetic traditions and were well placed to lead the world, as they had in the past, to a new golden age in which the moral and the material would be integrated (Levenson, 1959: 93–4).

Such cultural nationalists began as reformers in conservative dress. They found an early constituency in religious reform movements that wished to revise dogmas, laicise teachings, develop vernacular languages, and 'scientific' agriculture in order to make (religious) tradition a living force in the community. The Grundtvig 'meeting movement' of Lutheran peasant intellectuals in Denmark, the Bernacacina movement of Slovak lower clergy in the early nineteenth-century, the Arya Samaj in late nineteenth-century India, and Protestant theosophical societies in late nineteenth-century Ireland were important allies and incubators of a cultural nationalism in their respective countries.

In China ethnic revivalism found its leaders in the social reform movement of the 1890s. Like his fellow Chinese reformers, Liang Qichao had begun in 1898 by allying with the Emperor and a small number of sympathetic officials, but, radicalised by the crushing of the movement and its exiling, he broke with an ethnocentric perspective of China as a unique Confucian civilisation. China was to be reconstructed as one among other nations of the world, from whose history one could learn.

Liang and his fellow nationalists directed their writings at a growing literate public, influenced by Social Darwinist ideas and aware of the foreign threat to China. In search of solutions, revivalists looked outward to world historical studies of polities, ancient and modern, that had disappeared from history, and analysed in journals contemporary anti-colonial movements (the Boer and Indian campaigns), the struggles of the Young Turks to modernise the Ottoman Empire, and the successes of the Meiji Reformers in Japan, especially after Japan's defeat of the Tsarist Russian Empire in 1905. The reformers disagreed in their analyses, some stressing the importance of a strong state, others the creation of a powerful ethnic consciousness, but by 1911 educated opinion had come to believe that the answer to the Chinese crisis was the transformation of a foreign-led (Manchu) dynastic Empire into a national state, led by a patriotic elite. Increasingly they saw China as leader of an Asian civilisation against the West (Karl, 2002: chs. 2, 4–6).

Although usually small in scale, revivalists established counter-culture movements, based on networks of independent institutions and international linkages, and the use of new circuits of communication (newspapers, academies and cultural societies). This gave them a social reach into the literate section of the populations. In colonial societies the nationalist intelligentsia of lawyers, officials and journalists had a power out of proportion to their numbers with respect to the British state and traditionalist leaders, because they uniquely combined a mastery of the languages and techniques of modernity (often as officals within state administrations) with the traditional discourses and networks of their indigenous societies. Their main constituency was, as we have seen, an educated middle class, but they sought to draw to the nation all its constituent elements, and might attract neo-traditionalist forces that aspired to more radical solutions, in using new political technologies in order to defend true religion.

Nonetheless, cultural nationalists were not so much inventors as mediators who, by attracting support from modernisers and traditionalists, imported conflicts within their movements over the balance to be struck between conserving distinctive traditions and the promotion of socio-economic progress. Revivalists have oscillated across a modernist–traditionalist continuum. They might inconsistently adopt opposing positions, or shift from one to the other, either for instrumental or affective reasons. In the early years of the twentieth century, the Gaelic revival had something of a modernising thrust, directed against the otherworldly passivity encouraged by the Catholic Church, that aimed to create a vigorous lay Irish Catholic middle-class culture. But, faced with the continued sway of English culture over urban Ireland and the eruption of class conflict across Britain and Ireland, by 1913 its lower-middle-class intelligentsia, many of rural origins, allied increasingly with fervent neo-traditionalist movements that sought to mobilise the urban poor and the peasantry to shore up a crumbling community from foreign temptations (Garvin, 1987: chs. 5, 6). In this regard, cultural nationalists have been neither outright modernists nor traditionalists, but ideological innovators. They articulate the shifting options for societies seeking to determine their path to modernisation, in a manner that balances their concern to preserve a distinctive identity with a drive for progress.

National Sacrifice and Mythic Overlaying

However, the revivalist strategy of inner reform had limitations. Revivalism might find allies in reforming state elites who saw nation-creation as the road to social modernisation. But in seeking to permeate powerful social institutions, they were often in danger of being co-opted by them. They could be suborned by religious and gentry interests that sought to retain their patriarchal hold over the people, and by states who might use them to obtain support for reform without empowering their peoples. By themselves they lacked the resources to gain majority support, especially against the state, that was able to diffuse its values through the education system, bureaucratic career structures and police power. As has often been noted, nationalist movements may be numerically small before they gain power.

How then did revivalism succeed in making national identities hegemonic in contexts where it faced resistance from dominant institutions? The answer lies in constructing a community of sacrifice with its separate mythos, capable of overriding established mythologies. Revivalism was creating a new religion of a deified people, whose heroic virtues were represented by an elite of martial intellectuals, who, in the manner of ancient warrior castes, challenged the status of priestly classes. Although for the most part revivalism promoted a peaceful permeation of the community, it created through its overlapping institutions (language associations, theatres, sporting associations) a counter-culture of young activists, imbued with a religious sense of mission to the nation and contemptuous of their degraded society. A switch to sacrificial struggle remained a strategic option to which nationalists could turn when the 'nation' seemed threatened by internal crisis or when the state was faced with a systemic crisis, such as war or social revolution.

The resonance of this worship of the people was in turn affected by the degree to which the population itself had been politically mobilised, above all in warfare. As the scale of war increased during the nineteenth century and the twentieth century, so the people and its blood sacrifices became the object of worship, increasingly displacing the conventional deities. A powerful romantic tradition expressed itself in the arts, notably Tolstoy's *War and Peace*, and national ceremonies and monuments in many countries. This came to a peak in the world wars, which generated huge mass commemorative ceremonies. Nationalists could tap such embedded memories of sacrifice against the state. Nonetheless, such cults could also be co-opted by official elites, as in Wilhelmine Germany (Hobsbawm, 1983b: 272–5), and might be weak in countries without large-scale wartime 'sacrifice'.

In such circumstances nationalists had to compensate by mythologising themselves as the authentic voice of the nation, destined to redeem it by their sacrifices and try to override existing traditions. The revolutionary potential within an otherwise pacific movement has erupted periodically during the past two centuries during times of unpredictable ideological revolts, great power struggles and class conflict that have recurrently generated millenarian expectations of a general overthrow of established structures. The French Revolution and the subsequent military resistance to French domination in the German territories and elsewhere institutionalised in nineteenth-century Europe the romantic mystique of a national hero, willing to sacrifice himself for the nation (Mosse, 1990: chs. 2, 3). Although the old order was restored in 1815, a sense of revolutionary possibility existed because of the social upheavals engendered by rapid industrialisation. Europe was hit by waves of national as well as social revolts in the 1820s, 1830s and in 1848. Although these failed, a tradition of 'martyrs' was established in countries such as Ireland, Poland and Italy, who embodied the willingness of each generation to sacrifice themselves for the nation. The apocalyptic world wars of the twentieth century resulted in a wave of nationalist revolutions in Central and Eastern Europe following the collapse of the Romanov, Habsburg and Ottoman Empires in 1918–19, and in Asia and Africa after 1945 following the defeat of the Imperial European powers.

Because of their sense of historical destiny, national revivalists were hardened to adversity and they viewed a large-scale crisis as a sign of a prospective rebirth of the nation. At such times, as alternatives to a failing system, they had a directive effect in a situation of increasing fluidity and confusion in several ways. They threw up leaders, sometimes endowed with a charismatic cultural authority, outside established structures and untainted by the past, and they energised demoralised populations by offering positive alternative social pathways. When this resulted in a revolutionary rising or a war of independence this collective experience became the basis of a new set of national legends that could legitimise the formation of a national social and political order. These legends were inscribed into popular consciousness through official national days, ceremonies of remembrance and large-scale indoctrination in state schools.

We can observe this process in modern Ireland, where through revolt and a war of independence a nationalist elite established a national mythology overriding existing ethnic traditions by a process of *mythic overlaying*. By overlaying I refer to the creation of fresh myths by the new nationalists embodied in extraordinary contemporary collective sacrifice against a traditional 'enemy' that can be presented as a renovation of a national continuum when the old myths have failed. In so doing, the new elites are able to legitimise themselves to the collectivity. But, as we shall see, the old mythic structures are not obliterated. Rather, they are pushed into a substratum, available to resume their hold on collective loyalties, should the new conceptions prove wanting.

The Easter Rising of 1916 was the fourth of a series of significant nationalist revolts (of 1798, 1848 and 1867) against British authority in Ireland, and exemplifies a pattern. The revolts of 1798, 1848 and 1867 ended a period of revivalism whose early ambitions had been a peaceful nationalisation of the competing communities in Ireland but which had switched to insurrection in an atmosphere of social and political instability. Wolfe Tone's failed 1798 rebellion erupted when Britain was at war with revolutionary France and hoped for French support; Thomas Davis's 1848 rebellion occurred in the desperation of the Irish famine, which appeared to threaten the destruction not only of nationalist hopes but the Irish nation. Although these failed, the Fenian Brotherhood (who rebelled in 1867), building on their memories, created a mystique of martyrdom and permanently institutionalised an underground revolutionary tradition.

The late nineteenth-century Irish revivalists had rejected physical force in advocating an Irish language and literary renaissance. Their goal was to replace dominant otherworldly Catholic conceptions of Ireland as a martyred nation that they claimed had weakened Irish resistance to the encroachment of secular British industrial values. Inspired by Celtic high cultural achievements in the early medieval ages, they sought to recreate Ireland as a rural but dynamic, Gaelic-speaking, democratic community that would take its part in modern Europe. After initial successes in mobilising a new Catholic educated middle class, the revival ran out of steam by 1914, outflanked by a neo-traditionalist Catholic resurgence in the countryside and by the continued 'anglicisation' of Irish society. At this point, a small group of Irish revivalists, led by Patrick Pearse and Thomas MacDonagh allied with the revolutionary movement, and developed a cult of the legendary Irish warrior hero Cúchulainn, but the majority of revivalists supported a constitutional nationalist campaign for a Home Rule parliament that they hoped would enact revivalist programmes. However, the outbreak of the First World War led to the British government shelving Home Rule and incorporating Ireland into the war effort, initially with popular support.

Despair at this co-option of Irish political and religious elites into the war effort (and hopes of German support) led to the Easter Rebellion in 1916. Patrick Pearse, one its leaders, created the canonical legend of the 'Rising' as a self-conscious act of religious sacrifice to redeem Irish sins, drawing parallels with Christ's crucifixion and Cúchulainn's triumphant death facing his enemies. The execution of the rebel leaders and the imposition of martial law by the British confirmed the myth, radicalised the population and inspired the subsequent successful war of liberation against Britain. The Easter Rebellion and the subsequent guerrilla war created the potent founding myth of the new national state in 1922 and of the new governing class, two-thirds of whom entered politics through the revivalist organisations. By creating new cultural icons (great writers such as Yeats, a heroic war generation and the Irish language) the revival had forged a new secular definition of Irish identity.

Here we find a clear example of the successful nationalist construction of myth based on collective sacrifice that overrode older ethnoreligious legitimations and justified a revivalist programme that supported the renaissance of the Irish language and the Irish-speaking west. Nonetheless, the national myth was an overlay, not a replacement. For the myth had itself fused national and religious symbolism (as in the choice of Easter), and the nationalists dramatised British atrocities in the course of a brutal guerrilla war as a continuation of the historic 'martyrdom' of a helpless Catholic nation. The secular linguistic nationalism of the new state proved to be elite-based and thin, as after independence Ireland found itself still confronted with economic and cultural competition from a powerful British neighbour. To reinforce its national character, the new state rooted itself in historic ethnocentric religious and rural sentiments. The Catholic Church was given official status, and the Irish state developed until recently a distinctive puritanical Catholic social policy, effectively prohibiting divorce, contraception and abortion (Hutchinson, 1987: ch. 9).

A comparable story can be told for contemporary Israel. Zionism was a secular nationalism that broke with the historic Jewish diaspora identity regulated by the rabbis in the ghettos. It arose from secularised Jews in Western Europe, many of whom, attracted by the liberal ideas of the European Enlightenment, hoped to overcome centuries of anti-Semitism by breaking with their enclosed religious life and assimilating to the values of their European national states. Zionism was born when a wave of pogroms in Russia in the late nineteenth century and growing anti-Semitism in Western Europe indicated that the assimilationist option would fail and that, to be secure, Jews must have a nation-state of their own. In the early twentieth century successive waves of Jews, swelling as anti-Semitism heightened in Europe, emigrated to their ancient homeland in Palestine (then under British mandate), establishing in 1920 the Histadrut (General Federation of Jewish Workers), which, in the name of a romantic nationalist socialist vision, sought to conquer and settle the land, reform the individual and achieve self-realisation (Sternhell, 1999: introduction).

Nonetheless, Zionism remained a minority option, denounced by Orthodox rabbis as blasphemous since the ingathering of Jews in Palestine could only await the return of the Messiah at the end of history. What achieved the triumph of a Zionist nationalism over its religious opponents were two factors. The first was the near destruction of European Jewry in the Holocaust, which demonstrated the vulnerability of the historic diaspora and the failure of traditional religious quietism to protect Jews. The second was the series of wars against the Arabs, culminating in the achievement in 1947 of the state of Israel, which created a pantheon of legends and heroes (Zerubavel, 1995: ch. 5). After independence the secular ideal of the proud Zionist warrior achieving national freedom against overwhelming odds, counter-posed to the passive religious victims of the Holocaust, legitimised the hegemony of nationalist over traditional religious identities, and also the hegemony of the Labour party drawn from the Histadrut. Nationalists resurrected as part of this indomitable ideal long-forgotten myths of Massada, which recalled a collective 'sacrifice' (suicide) of Jewish Zealots in their fight for freedom against the Roman Empire. The overwhelming victory of the 1967 Six Day War reinforced the prestige of the secular state.

Nonetheless, the older religious identities remained potent – increasingly so as disillusionment increased with the failures of secular Zionism. From the beginning, the centrality of the biblical heritage for all Jews compelled the state to accommodate religious Jews, by granting religious parties control of the education ministry, defining citizenship in religious terms and exempting religious students from conscription. To religious zealots the Six

Day War, bringing the capture of Jerusalem and the West Bank, foreshadowed the coming of a messianic age or at least justified the rapid settlement of recaptured biblical homelands. The failure of the Labour regime to undertake this, the near defeat of the state in 1973, and evidence of Labour corruption and economic failure, has led to resurgence of a religiously based nationalism that threatens civil discord between secular and Orthodox.

Conclusions

This analysis does suggest that the nation is indeed a modern construction. It is created by relatively small elites who see themselves as part of a dynamic world order in which their society must survive and participate. What makes it possible is a world of continuous innovation that makes traditional identities obsolete and regularly shakes even the most apparently powerful political structures.

But revivalism faces both ways, recognising that 'tradition' must be reconstituted – not destroyed – as the basis of political action and, at the same time, that societies must innovate. In this way nationalists effect change by mediating between the constituent identities of populations rather than by enforcing a vision from above. Moreover, although nationalists are able to achieve political hegemony and establish their own collective myths of legitimacy, they do so on an already layered past, which retains its potentiality for later reactivation.

Another aspect of the analysis worth observing is the unpredictability of nation-formation. We have noted how revivalism results in the discovery of unknown or forgotten pasts, cultural artefacts and heritages, communities and sacred sites that channel political action. National identity construction was shaped by the existence (or otherwise) of a heritage, and varied according to whether this heritage was living (as in Ireland or Finland) or documentary only (having disappeared from social memory, in the case of the Slovaks). Moreover, the communitarian strategies result in social groups being mobilised unexpectedly by the process of symbolic definition itself. This underlines the inappropriateness of speaking about 'invention' or even 'construction'. Nation-formation is frequently a long drawn-out process of trial and error or fierce contestation. In cases such as the Slovaks, where there was little sense of an earlier ethnic identity, nationalists seem to have more scope for invention, but their problem is that they have insufficient material with which to appeal to the apathetic masses. They themselves are unsure who they are, and Slovak nationalists have oscillated between advocating a Slovak, Pan-Slav, Czecho-Slovak, and now again a Slovak identity (Brock, 1976). We might suggest that where ethnic traditions are absent, the problem of nationalists is still more difficult: they have greater room for manoeuvre, but without the raw materials on which to build they are dependent on long periods of intergroup conflict in order to achieve a sense of collective identity.

This raises issues to be considered in the following chapters. On what grounds are specific historic pasts selected as emblematic of the nation where there are multiple heritages, and what are the consequences of cultural conflict between these heritages? Given that elite groups pioneer the national project, to what extent do national identities root themselves in the populations at large, by what processes, and how do they operate in the conduct of everyday life?

3

Cultural Wars

Introduction

A striking feature of the contemporary period has been the explosion of deep-seated cultural conflicts within many established national states. In the French presidential election of 2001 the Gaullist Jacques Chirac had to appeal to his socialist opponents for support in defending the republic against the neo-fascist demagogue Jean-Marie Le Pen. In the same year, in Greece Archbishop Christodoulos rallied millions of Greeks against a secularising campaign of the Socialist PASOK government to detach the nation from its Orthodox heritage (by the removal of religious affiliation from citizens' identity cards). In China, a Mandarin-speaking northern concept of the nation, dominated by a rural xenophobic peasant and autarchic vision, has been contested by a Southern decentralised liberal-democratic ideal centred on the coastal trading regions and their distinctive languages and cultures, which is oriented to the Chinese ecumene of the diaspora and a global economy (Friedman, 1995).

To some postmodernists this eruption of difference marks the end of the unitary identities characteristic of the modern period that provided the necessary cement of mature industrial societies. It foreshadows a shift to a new postnational world of multiple attachments. Postmodernists, however, have failed to explore the significance of competition over the *longue durée* between repertoires of development. Such disputes are not something novel, nor are they the transitional problems of relatively new national projects. Ethnic heritages, we have observed, are not singular but layered, and, just as ethnic revivalists in the premodern period have clashed over different pasts, so too have nationalists in the modern period.

In this chapter, then, I will examine a third site of conflict, between compeing conceptions of the nation, often of a quasi-ethnic nature, that develop into long-running cultural wars. By 'cultural wars' I do not mean clashes between classes, regions and religions and other ideologies that periodically erupt within nations. These will be discussed in the next chapter. Rather I wish to focus on differences that seem to be systemic, that organise symbolic and political projects round two or three rival conceptions of the national past, taking on a quasi-ethnic form, and that articulate a diverse and changing set of issues and grievances. These differences usually take the form of cultural *clusters*, rather than of 'church-like' organisations that impose a high degree of control and uniformity. In reality, individuals adopt a range of heterogeneous positions and, as we shall see, shift between them. Nonetheless, they represent important reference points that have social consequences. With a few exceptions (Hosking and Schopflin, 1997; Smith, 1984; Young, 1993), the significance of persisting differences has been neglected because of the widespread assumption that nations are an embodiment of a long-term trend to cultural homogenisation in the modern world. Such cultural wars, however, are important in determining how societies modernise.

After giving examples of such conflict, I will consider the following questions:

1. How do we explain the origins of such conflicts and their evolving nature?
2. Are such conflicts positive in their effects by institutionalising a sense of cultural pluralism, or negative, in polarising societies and instigating civil strife?
3. What prevents such conflicts from resulting in national fission?
4. What explains the survival of such repertoires in spite of the immense social changes of the modern period?

Although these conflicts are the result of deep historical cleavages, they in turn have had directive effects on the ways that societies modernise, for better and for worse.

Cultural Wars in Modern Nations

Let me begin by giving a snap shot of five long-running disputes within French, Russian, Greek, English and Irish nationalisms. I shall later refer in passing to several other cases: the struggle between Catholic and Hussite traditions in the Czech lands; between supporters of *Nynorsk* and *Riksmål* language cultures in Norway; and between Western liberal and Eastern 'organic' nationalists in Germany.

In France, the major divide was triggered by the Revolution of 1789 against the *ancien régime* of monarchy, church and aristocracy. The experience of the Revolution produced three quite distinct versions of the French nation. Although republican myth endowed France with a European and, indeed, universal mission to free humanity from monarchical and social oppression, it also articulated French history as the struggle between two enemy peoples – between a Frankish nobility and a Gallo-Roman third estate who had preserved much of the heritage (including the republican traditions) of ancient Rome (Geary, 2002: 20–2).

During the revolutionary period Gallic symbols (the cock) were raised to prominence alongside Roman neo-classical models (Pastoureau, 1998: 417). Republicanism entailed the defence of the one and indivisible nation against provincial separatisms, clerical superstition (particularly in education) and social inequality. The counter-revolutionary myth presented France as having an ancient and providential mission through its alliance of Crown, altar and nobility to defend the cause of Christian civilisation in Europe. A third and lesser tradition was of Bonapartist Empire, invoking Napoleon Bonaparte as the national saviour who, transcending the divisions of republicanism and monarchism, established French leadership of the European nations, in the manner of a modern Charlemagne. These competing projects dominated the modern history of France, obtaining a variety of social constituencies and producing recurring political instabilities. They produced the First Republic (1792–1804), Napoleon's Empire (1804–14), the Bourbon restoration (1815–30), constitutional monarchy (1830–48), the Second Republic (1848–51), the Second Empire (1852–70), the Third Republic (1871–1940), Vichy (1941–45), the Fourth Republic (1945–58) and de Gaulle's Fifth Republic (1958–).

The Napoleonic invasion of Russia was the catalyst of a modern Russian nationalism emerging within and outside the Imperial regime, which divided into two tendencies. One was 'Westerner', which demanded that Russia be raised from Asiatic backwardness by developing according to norms of Western Europe. An early manifestation was the Decembrist military officers who, influenced by contemporary European ideas, rebelled in 1825 to demand a constitutional government. The other was 'Russianist' or Slavophile, which in the late 1830s rejected Western statism in favour of reviving a rural social order based on Orthodox religious values and a harmonious co-operation between Tsar, aristocracy and peasantry. The Slavophile–Westerner debates occured first within the gentry but widened with the extension of education (Neumann, 1996: ch. 2). During the nineteenth century the Tsarist autocratic state, claiming to stand for the defence of the Christian *ancien régime* of Europe and yet deeply fearful of the revolutionary forces developing, sought to co-opt these movements, at times allying with Slavophiles and Pan-Slavists to defend the traditional social order and promote a Russification of the Empire, and at other times (under Alexander II) promoting limited liberal reforms (the emancipation of the serfs) in order to modernise the economy and army. By the 1890s, as Russia underwent rapid industrialisation, the regime was also confronted by two varieties of revolutionary socialist movements – one rural populist (and Russianist), the other urban and influenced by European Marxism – and faced unrest among the non-Russian nationalities. Defeat at the hands of Japan triggered the 1905 revolution, which the regime survived, but catastrophic defeat in the First World War resulted in the Bolshevik seizure of power in 1917.

In the Soviet regime Westerner–Slavophile divisions opened up between Trotsky, who argued that communism could be sustained in the USSR only by achieving revolution in Europe, and Stalin who advocated socialism in one country. Stalin triumphed. Although suspicious of nationalism *per se*, the regime invoked traditional Orthodox Russian ideals at times of crisis, to mobilise the defence of the USSR against Hitler and to sustain the state after Khrushchev's repudiation of the Stalinist record eroded the legitimacy of Marxist-Leninism (Popielovsky, 1989). Under Gorbachev, although there was a renewed swing to Western liberal models, familiar Westerner–Slavophile divisions re-emerged among dissidents such as Sakharov and Solzhenitsyn. Debates continued to alter the balance between the two in the Yeltsin and Putin eras, with communists often siding with neo-Slavophile nationalists in attacking Western liberals, but there has been a continuous shifting across the spectrum by liberals and Russianists (Neumann 2002: 204–5).

Throughout the nineteenth century tensions existed within Greek nationalism between secular republican and Orthodox ideals. The first looked to Athens as the capital of a revived Hellas, and was strongest in a mercantile diaspora influenced by Western European philhellenism; the second, held by the peasantry, clergy and the notables of the Aegean, dreamed of the regaining of Constantinople from the Ottoman Empire and the reconstitution of the Byzantine Empire (Herzfeld, 1982: ch. 1). Inspired by Koraes and Rhigas, Greek secular nationalists sought Greece's readmission to the forefront of Western Europe by overthrowing not just the Oriental Ottoman yoke but also the religious obscurantism of Orthodoxy. Nonetheless, when conflict broke out in 1821, ethnoreligious fervour amongst the peasantry and lower clergy was a driving force of the independence struggle in spite of the attempts of the upper clergy to control it (Frazee, 1969: chs 2, 3). A secular, monarchical Greek state was established, but was weakened by these divisions and by the fact that a large majority of Greeks remained outside it. Struggles persisted even over self-designation – whether to call members of the nation 'Hellenes', 'Romioi' (after the Roman Byzantine Empire) or 'Graikoi' (an early Christian name rejecting the pagan appellation of Hellenes) (Tsoukalas, 2002: 38).

Such divisions were resolved by the development of the 'Great Idea' (*Megali*) of Kolettis, who declared that the Greek state had a sacred mission to destroy the Ottoman Empire and reunite all Greeks in a single state that would establish a revived Byzantine Empire in Eastern Europe, based in Constantinople. Its destiny would be to enlighten the East by its rise, just as it had done for Europe by its fall (Augustinos, 1977: ch. 1). Intellectuals worked to reconcile the classical heritage with the medieval religious character of the Byzantine state, but one of the divisive issues was of language – whether to employ the archaic language of classical times (*katharevousa*) or the demotic as a literary medium. This was a continuously divisive issue, for in spite of *katharevousa* becoming the language of state and the official class, the demotic remained entrenched in everyday life, and the linguistic divide militated against a modernisation from above. Only in the 1980s was the language conflict settled when the PASOK government decided in favour of the demotic.

In these battles the (foreign-born) Greek monarchy participated, largely in favour of the nationalist 'Great Idea'. This state-based ethnic identity came under attack mainly from figures and forces in the diaspora and from the rise of ethnic nationalisms amongst the other Orthodox peoples, which threatened the idea of Greek expansion and unification. Greece was dragged into a disastrous war by a revolt in Crete, which dealt a shattering blow to irredentist dreams. A sense of national crisis between 1897 and 1921 evoked a cultural nationalist critique of official Greece that encompassed the monarchy, parliament, army, language and the educational system. It advocated less reliance on Europe as the standard, and more emphasis on the Greek world (Augustinos, 1977: ch. 2).

The tensions between a European-oriented and an ethnoreligious nationalism merely took new forms in 1914 when the king, espousing neutralism, clashed with the liberal and reformist prime minister Venizelos, who wished to support the Allies against the Triple Alliance. After defeat against the Turks and a mass transfer of populations in 1922 between Turkey and Greece ended the Byzantine dream, the split between republican Venizelists and royalists dominated the interwar period. The monarchy, discredited by 1922, was replaced by a republic from 1924, during which there was an attempt to engineer a shift from an ethnic to a civic nation built on modern political institutions. This, however, was destabilised periodically by military interventions, and in 1935 the monarchy was restored by a military dictatorship under General Metaxas that claimed to embody a third Hellenic Civilisation (combining Hellenism and Byzantium). This created intense social divisions, which continued when Greece was invaded and occupied by Germany and into the post-war period, as communist and anti-communist resistance movements clashed with each other and with royalists collaborators. The defeat of the communists led to the triumph of a rightwing authoritarian nationalism that culminated in the dictatorship of the Colonels between 1967 and 1974. This, though claiming to offer a Hellenic-Christian synthesis, isolated Greece from Europe. After its overthrow there was a return to democratic rivalry between pro-Western conservatives, who took Greece into the EU in 1981, and a neutralist socialist party suspicious of NATO and the USA, and oriented to the Balkan region. Since then the socialist PASOK has swung in support of the EU (Koksalakis and Psimmenos, 2003).

A 'little English' nationalism, using the discourse of Anglo-Saxon and Protestant liberties, has long existed in tension with an Imperial Anglo-British identity based on the crown, after England became the core nationality of a British state following the union of Scottish and English parliaments in 1707. The Saxon myth came in two varieties, Whig and Radical. The Whig version, expressed in the myth of the Glorious Revolution of 1688, presented the enlightened aristocracy as the defenders of Parliament against the Crown. The radical version legitimised a mid-eighteenth-century English nationalism that emerged among middle classes during the 'second hundred years war' with France. They demanded parliamentary representation and the end of the exclusion from public office of Protestants who refused to conform to the established Church of England. Their target was the 1689 settlement between Crown and aristocracy, which established the control of parliament by a landed oligarchy. In support of their goals they invoked the Anglo-Saxon period as a golden age of democratic liberties destroyed by the (French) Norman conquest as a weapon against the political corruption of Francophile Whig landed classes (Newman, 1987: 183–91). But the outbreak of war with revolutionary France made this radicalism suspect, and this nationalism was soon driven underground and subsumed within a conservative *British* nationalism oriented round King, Protestantism and Empire (Colley, 1992: chs 4, 5).

After the defeat of Napoleon, the Anglo-Saxon myth was re-invoked by Chartist radicals, feeding off social and economic discontents of early industrialisation, who demanded universal suffrage and annual parliaments. As the modern party system formed, the Tories (later the Conservatives) mobilised in defence of Crown, Established Church and the landed interest, while the Whigs (later the Liberals) became the voice of moderate parliamentary reform, Protestant nonconformity and the industrial interests. In response to popular unrest the landed classes extended the franchise by stages, and the battleground began to shift to the privileges enjoyed by the landed establishment, notably their inherited wealth and their political power maintained through the House of Lords. The Conservatives under Disraeli, evoking an idealised 'Gothic' middle ages, formulated a 'One Nation' ideal of a union of all classes led by a patriotic aristocracy under an Imperial British Crown. After the rapid expansion of empire from 1870, the sense of ethnic and religious election given by Anglo-Saxonism was co-opted by Tory Imperialists, who proclaimed the racial mission of Anglo-Saxon peoples to rule the lesser peoples and spread English liberties (Curtis, 1968: ch. 1). The Liberals, suspicious of Empire as a potential threat to national liberties, drew on old nonconformist radicalism in their struggle against the Anglican landlord establishment and its supporters in the House of Lords, which culminated in the curbing of the powers of the House of Lords. By the beginning of the twentieth century the new Labour Party evoked the more radical ideologies of the Civil War (of the underground Levellers and Diggers) to justify socialist programmes that would abolish the House of Lords, reject Empire and, for some, establish a republic. This campaign and the defence of monarchy continues to this day, as does the appeal to Anglo-Saxonism and Civil War ideologies by left and right.

In Ireland there was a cultural battle between Anglo-Irish and Irish Gaelic protagonists to define the Irish nation during the nineteenth and early twentieth centuries. The first had its constituency among the Protestant minority who were descendants of the English conquest of the seventeenth century, whereas the second developed among the dispossessed Catholic and Gaelic majority. The Anglo-Irish ideal formed as a cultural project during the late eighteenth century following a political campaign among the Protestant Ascendancy, resentful of the Imperial claims of the British over the Irish parliament, who protested the separate rights of the Irish kingdom. Very much a minority project even among Protestants, it aimed at the construction of a new Irish nation, uniting Catholics and Protestants, by infusing components from the Gaelic past (particularly pagan eras) into the dominant English culture (Hutchinson, 1987: ch. 2). When the failed rebellion of the Protestant-led United Irishmen against Britain in 1798 revealed the hatred of the Catholic peasantry for the

Protestant Ascendancy, the Protestant minority, aware that its privileges were dependent on the protection of the British state, switched (with a few significant exceptions) to a self-consciously British identity and supported, in 1801, a union of Irish and British parliaments (Boyce, 1982: chs 4, 5).

In the early nineteenth century an Irish nationalism revived under the leadership of Daniel O'Connell, who campaigned first for Catholic Emancipation (the right of Catholics to hold public office without 'apostasy'), which was achieved in 1829, and then for the return of the Irish parliament. This was a constitutional Catholic middle-class nationalism that, like the earlier Protestant movements, cited Anglo-Norman legal traditions, but its popular base was the peasantry, fired by Gaelic Catholic and millenarian traditions (Garvin, 1981: ch. 3). This crusade was shattered by the Great Famine of the 1840s. From the mid nineteenth century cultural differences between the two national traditions became manifest, intensified by the re-emergence in the 1870s of constitutional nationalist politics that allied with Land League struggles against Protestant landlordism.

A Protestant minority revived an Anglo-Irish aspiration of a new synthetic nation expressed first in George Petrie's and Samuel Ferguson's work and later in Yeats's Anglo-Irish literary revival. A Gaelic revival, by contrast, envisaged a culturally distinct Ireland, whose golden age was in the early middle ages, and one separated from English culture by an Irish language culture dominated by Catholic values. This found its base in the new educated generation of Catholics with secondary and university qualifications (Hutchinson, 1987: ch. 8). Many of these Gaelic revivalists also supported the political campaigns for Home Rule, but their movement was in tension with both the anglicising Catholic mainstream and the Anglo-Irish project, which they viewed as an elitist attempt to foist an exotic English romantic conception on the Irish people (Lyons, 1979: chs 2, 3).

The Gaelic revival trained the revolutionary elite who staged the Easter Rising of 1916, led the War of Independence and dominated the newly independent state. After independence a struggle continued, with Anglo-Irish proponents resisting unsuccessfully the drive of Gaelic revivalist to define the independent nation as Irish-speaking, rural and Catholic in its ethos and social policies. However, by the 1930s the Anglo-Irish revival as a project had collapsed (and most Irish Protestants had emigrated) (Lyons, 1979: ch. 6). During the postwar period it was clear that the Gaelic ideal had ossified, with the Irish language in continuous retreat and English (or American) cultural influences dominant. From the 1970s it was being challenged by those looking to secular models of European liberal democracies.

The roots of conflict

How does one explain such deep-seated and long-running conflicts, and over what questions do societies divide? Can we explain the eruption of different historical mythologies in the modern world by class, regional or religious-secular cleavages? Or do we have to acknowledge the independent power of divergent deep-seated historical memories?

In a fascinating analysis of competing myth-complexes Anthony Smith distinguishes between genealogical and ideological myths. The former are conservative and couched in the idiom of biology, custom and continuity, whereas the latter are radical, claiming spiritual affinity with a remote but 'authentic' past whose restoration would overthrow the present corrupt order (1984: 95–6) Examples of the latter are Greek nationalists' 'rediscovery' of Hellas, repudiating the Orthodox Church's subservience to the Oriental Turks, and secular Zionists' location of the golden age in the biblical Davidic kingdoms, effectively rejecting the 2000-year diaspora experience and the rabbinical leadership (see also Zerubavel, 1995: ch. 2).

This, of course, might suggest that these mythic contests express a battle between established and rising social groups who find or invent myths which justify revolutionary change. Could not modernist scholars argue that the formation of these rival repertoires from the late eighteenth century is linked to the rise of competing interest groups in the novel contexts of state activism, democratisation and industrialisation (see Hobsbawm, 1983)?

Class and Regional Tensions

My description suggests there was a class dimension to many of these struggles. In France, Krzysztof Pomian argues, the identification of Franks with the nobility and of the Gauls with commoners furnished an ideology that articulated and justified conflict, and from the early eighteenth century through to the period of the Second Empire provided a way of thinking about the confrontations between first the nobility and the third estate, and then the aristocracy and the bourgeoisie (Pomian, 1996: 74–6). In similar fashion the revival of the Anglo-Saxon myth from mid-eighteenth-century England expressed a strong class and religious resentment of English middle-class nonconformists at their political exclusion by the Francophile (Norman) Anglican aristocracy. It was accompanied by the valorisation of native writers (such as Shakespeare) against foreign models, a cult of simplicity of character and a romantic turn to the language of the people, and a conversion to the evangelical enthusiasm of Methodism against an effete Anglicanism (Newman, 1987: ch. 6). In Russia, the Slavophiles were drawn from leading Muscovite landowning families for whom St Petersburg court and society represented the divorce of the Tsarist regime from a partnership with the Russian nation based on the land (Lieven, 2000: 207; Riasonovsky, 1952: 29–30).

These contests also expressed regional rivalries, intensified by the growing power of a centralising state. In France support for the Catholic Church and monarchism was strong in the West (particularly the Vendée region) and the Midi, resentful of an overweening Paris (Gildea, 1994: 171). In Norway the long-running battle over the rival claims of *Landsmål* (later to be known as *Nynorsk*) and *Bokmål* (later to become *Riksmål*) to be the national language was related to divisions of region and class. The former was built on oral dialects of peasant communities in the West and Midland regions, whereas the latter was close to Danish standard, spoken by the Oslo political and social elites, and dominant in the East and North, and these regions had long been separated. Politically, *Bokmål* was championed by the Conservative party (*Høyre*) while *Landsmål* was championed by the nationalist-democratic Liberal party (*Venstre*), and later by Marxist organisations, as part of a struggle by peripheral peasant communities against a centralising state whose governing classes viewed them with disdain (Haugland, 1980: 26–8). In the contemporary Ukraine there are cultural schisms between a Western region, promoting the Ukrainian language, a European orientation and a radical dichotomization with Russia, and an Eastern part, conscious of a common Eurasian Orthodox heritage with Russia (Smith et al., 1998, ch. 2).

However, a cursory analysis demonstrates that interests alone cannot explain why these cultural divisions should act as reference and mobilising points for very different social and political projects. The Slavophile and Westerner divisions in Russia originated among the liberal gentry in the 1830s, but as the educated stratum expanded and became more socially diverse, so the alternatives they posed articulated rival visions of socialism. In the late nineteenth century, revolutionary Populists opposed the introduction of industrial capitalism – sponsored by the regime to preserve Russia's great power status – arguing that Russia could pioneer a unique pathway to communism based on the institution of *mir* (village commune). Marxists, however, looking to the experience of Western Europe, supported the industrialisation of Russia (and hence the rise of an urban proletariat) as a necessary condition for the development of socialism. The later split within Marxism between Mensheviks and Bolsheviks over the question of whether a socialist revolution in 'backward' Russia was possible without a prior revolution in an advanced European capitalist society was another version of this division.

In Ireland Gaelic and Anglo-Irish conceptions became reference points for very different social and religious projects. The former gave expression to conservative religious movements, designed to preserve clerical leadership of Catholics threatened by the influx of secular materialist values from England, to modernist programmes of D. P. Moran and Arthur Griffith to create a self-reliant industrial middle class Ireland, and to socialists such as W. P. Ryan and James Connolly, who presented Gaelic Ireland as a democratic communalist society before the introduction of Anglo-Normans (Boyce, 1982: ch. 8 and 310–14). The Anglo-Irish revival gained support in the late eighteenth and early nineteenth centuries from upper-middle-class Protestant professionals and clergy who formed the bulk of the membership of the Royal Irish Academy. It also appealed, however, to sections of the Protestant lower middle class and even working classes, who became active in theosophical circles, Sir Horace Plunkett's Agricultural Co-operative and the arts and crafts movement (Lyons, 1979: ch. 3).

In France the French Revolution inspired very different political programmes during the nineteenth and twentieth centuries, with constitutional monarchists, liberals and radical republicans, socialists and communists claiming ideological descent from its different phases (Hobsbawm, 1962: ch. 6). During the late nineteenth century, although a working-class mobilisation threatened both bourgeois republicanism and traditionalist monarchism, the mass mobilisation of the electorate was articulated in terms of the old divisions, with the socialist left inspired by the radical wing of the Revolution and an authoritarian right (Action Française) employing anti-Semitism in order to mobilise the working classes against what they perceived to be a corrupt capitalist Third Republic.

What this indicates is that these rival symbolic repertoires, in appealing to multiple class and status groups, do not so much express sectional struggles as different visions of the nation. But why are such visions justified by reference to descent? Does this suggest the power of historical memory to affect the ways groups define the options for their societies? As we know, what people choose to remember and forget is selective: 'memories' become significant when they appear to provide guidance at times of social disorder, and those 'memories' are particularly potent when associated with traumatic events.

The Trauma of History

We can understand these divisions, I suggest, as arising out of powerful collective experiences such as state-religious schisms; revolutions or civil wars; wars and colonisations; and religio-national conflicts, whose consequences have been formative and memories of which have been carried by social institutions. Round such 'memories' rival repertoires develop as mobilisers of collective action.

In Russia, the Westerner and Slavophile division has roots in a older cultural cleavage within Russia, dating from Tsar Peter the Great (1682–1725) who sought to introduce on a large scale Western European techniques, customs and personnel in order to transform Russia from relative weakness into a European great power. He subverted traditional Russia by taking the pagan Roman title of 'imperator', subordinating the Orthodox church to the state, moving his capital westwards from 'holy' Moscow to a new 'European' city of St Petersburg (and thus shaking Russian messianic pretensions to be the Third Rome), creating a civil bureaucracy staffed by foreigners, notably Germans, and by enforcing 'European' dress and customs on the nobility. His legacy, continued by Catherine II (1762–96), made hegemonic Western cultural influences (including the French language) among the upper classes. But it provoked opposition. Peter's assault on the heritage of Holy Mother Orthodoxy, continuing Tsar Alexei's reforms, reinforced the alienation of a large section of Russian society from the state and the transfer of the Russian messianic idea, carried by millions of Old Believers, from the state to the Russian people (Hosking, 1997).

By the late eighteenth century the Russian Tendency emerged within official circles (with support of the military and intellectuals), led by Admiral Shishkov, President of the Russian Academy. Rejecting French influences among the elite, this defined Russia not in terms of Tsar and bureaucracy but of the cultural practices of the people, notably the Russian language. The debates that followed focused on the proper bases of the Russian language (Church Slavonic or the demotic) and on the place of Russia in European history, with protagonists viewing Russia as either the Christian saviour of an increasingly Godless Europe or as an embarrassing Asiatic outsider. This was the setting of the later debates that examined the degree to which Russia could pioneer a new path to progress based on its unique Orthodox heritage and communal institutions such as the *mir*, or whether it must engage in a large-scale adoption of ideas and institutions from the advanced Western European societies (Seton-Watson, 1977: 82–5). These debates remained among the gentry for a long time, but by the late nineteenth century the intellectual class broadened to include educated members of the peasantry, among whom the messianic ideas of Russia as the Third Rome still persisted.

The competing Anglo-Irish and Irish nationalisms of the nineteenth century derived from the memories and consequences of the seventeenth-century English conquest of Ireland. Ireland had earlier become a separate kingdom under the English Crown, with its local parliament in Dublin, after a large-scale settlement of Anglo-Normans (or Old English) in the twelfth century. The Old English, however, had never controlled the island. What triggered the full conquest was the conversion of England to Protestantism. An English government, fearful of the loyalty of Catholic Ireland in a period of religio-dynastic wars, colonised Ireland with English and Scottish Protestants who replaced the native Gaelic and Old English social order and reduced Ireland's Irish-language (Gaelic) culture to the status of a peasant demotic.

The new Protestant minority developed a local patriotism in the mid-eighteenth century in appropriating the parliamentary institutions and the historical arguments of the Old English against their subordination to Britain. But Anglo-Irish nationalism was always ambivalent: the Protestants remained fundamentally English and then British in orientation, committed to maintaining their social and landed Ascendancy over the native Catholics, and aware of their status as conquerors. Although a minority of the Protestant community sought to unite with the native community in creating a new hybrid Irish nation they could only do this by finding a distant pagan past that sought to bypass the poisonous memories of conquest (Beckett, 1976: 102–10, 143–7).

In contrast, the conquest resulted in the formation of a new Catholic nation, forging the Gaelic Irish with the Anglo-Norman or Old English settlers in a common ruin. When an Irish nationalism developed in the nineteenth century under the leadership of a Catholic middle class, demanding the return of an Irish parliament, this was articulated in the language of Anglo-Norman constitutional rights under the Crown. This nationalism, however, fed off the sentiments of a vengeful peasantry wishing to restore a Gaelic landed community, which were formed by seventeenth- and eighteenth-century Jacobite traditions, the memory of land confiscations expressed in ballads and oral tradition and, above all, by the Catholic Church which presented itself as the defender of a martyred people (O'Farrell, 1976). With the diffusion of secondary education from the 1870s a radical intelligentsia arose from the peasantry and lower middle classes steeped in this culture, drawn to the separatist vision of Gaelic revival and intensely hostile to the Anglo-Irish revival, which it saw as a surrogate for Protestant Ascendancy (Garvin, 1987: ch. 3).

Modern English conflicts found their reference point in the English Civil War. This was not just a struggle between Crown and Parliament over the rights of the king to tax and rule his subjects through the royal prerogative. It was also a battle between long-established Saxon and British 'national' myths.

Common lawyers were the primary bearers of the Anglo-Saxon myths from the sixteenth century onwards. They 'revived' a golden age of parliamentary liberties and of a pure (Protestant) Christianity that had been corrupted by Romish continental tyrannies. The idea of ethnic exceptionalism fused with radical Puritanism to make England a Chosen People (MacDougall, 1982: 63). The (Scottish) Stuart dynasty, which after the union of the English and Scottish Crowns in 1603 succeeded to the British throne, was attacked as foreign, overly sympathetic to Catholic France and Spain, and suspected of wishing to introduce a continental despotism. The Stuarts rejected Anglo-Saxon ideologies, claiming their rights to the British monarchy as descendents of the (legendary) British King Arthur (Hill, 1968: 68).

Although parliament overthrew and executed King Charles I in 1649, the struggle was unresolved and the memories of the bloody divisions shaped later British politics. The conflict generated millenarian sects such as the Levellers and Diggers who used Saxon myths to justify socially radical and socialist ideas that conservative parliamentarians crushed, but which inspired later working-class movements. Social hierarchy was restored with the Stuart monarchy in 1660, only for James II, suspected of trying to overthrow parliament and the established Protestant Anglican Church, to be ousted in the Glorious Revolution of 1688 that brought William of Orange to England. The divisions within the landed classes between Tory (Jacobite) monarchists and Whig defenders of the 1689 settlement continued into the late eighteenth century. Although overlaid by the formation of an Anglo-British state which rapidly developed an imperial identity in the eighteenth century, the Anglo-Saxon myth resonated in the nineteenth century, given a racial imperial character by Conservatives, but countered by liberal and socialist versions.

How far can the alternative projects of French nationalists be related to older divisions? It hardly seems plausible to view the battle of republicans and their opponents as a modern struggle of Gauls against Franks! The Gauls only emerged as mythic forebears in the fifteenth century as a result of humanist scholarship, and at this point Franks and Gauls were depicted as one family. But the increasing conflicts between monarchy, nobility and the third estate during the seventeenth century were viewed though the lens of the classical and post-classical world. With the rise of royal absolutism, Louis, XIII and Louis XIV distanced themselves from medieval Christian in favour of classical (Imperial) models in presenting France as the new Rome (Burke, 1994: 194–5). Aristocratic opponents, such as Count Boulainvilliers, who sought to restore the rights of provincial parlements, attacked what they saw as an alliance of Crown and Third Estate against their estate in ethnic terms. The *noblesse d'epée* were descendants of the Frankish warrior bands who had overthrown the Romans and conquered the Gauls, and they denounced the re-Romanisation of the state under the Capetian monarchy and the destruction of the free society of the Franks based on an elective kingship and regular aristocratic assemblies. This appeal to Frankish descent was also a claim to aristocratic caste rights over the third estate and provoked a counter middle-class nationalism that, although drawn to republican Roman and Spartan models of virtue, also turned to an ancient 'French' period not tainted with nobility or monarchy – that of the Gauls (Bell, 2001: 151–3).

It was, of course, the profound experiences of the Revolutionary period that instituted the long-lasting battle of cultures in France. On the one side, there were the heroic liberation myths of the storming of the Bastille, the rallying of the people to defend the republic against a perfidious monarchy and aristocracy allied to foreign monarchies, the establishment of a national citizenship and the triumphs of French arms and ideas in Europe. Royalist and Catholic supporters remembered the 'blasphemous' execution of the king, the Terror, the assault on the secular and religious rights of the clergy and the violent crushing of the Vendée in 1794. But the violence of the revolutionary project itself sprang from a total repudiation of the long heritage of the *ancien régime* as an unnatural and foreign (Frankish) yoke on the people. This was expressed in a new Revolutionary calendar that presented the Revolution as beginning a new era of human history, the ahistorical evocation of classical models and the rediscovery of the Gauls, who were to be led to freedom after over a thousand years of servitude.

It may seem more problematic to relate Greek conflicts to any memories of historical schism between Hellenes and Orthodox, since the Hellenic populations of the Peleponnese were swamped by Teutonic, Gothic and Slavic migrations from the third to the seventh centuries AD, and the population of mainland Greece was absorbed into the thousand-year Orthodox Roman Empire in the East. The Greek trauma was the fall of the holy city of Constantinople in 1453 and the subjection of the people of God to the Muslim yoke, an event commemorated in song and legend down the centuries. Indeed, in some ways the Ottoman overthrow of the Byzantine Empire reinforced the sway of Orthodoxy over the Greek largely peasant-based population. The collapse of the Empire was blamed on the treachery of the Latin West that intensified in a largely illiterate population hostility to the European Christendom that had betrayed the people of God. The *millet* system strengthened the power of the Constantinople Patriarchy, since it exercised secular as well as religious power over the Orthodox community, and the Greek Phanariot class obtained a privileged position in the Imperial administration. Among the clergy a millenarian tradition persisted that Constantinople would rise again (Campbell and Sherrard, 1968: ch. 1).

Yet Hellenism had never been entirely suppressed. Byzantines had always maintained a tradition of Hellenic culture (language and literature), Hellenising tendencies surfaced from the eleventh century, and when Byzantium faced destruction in the late fifteenth century at the hands of the Muslim Turks, a movement of neo-Platonic intellectuals led by Pletho envisaged a Hellenic nation in the Peloponnese (Jusdanis, 2001: 130). A bifurcation gradually developed within the Greek population after the conquest of Byzantium. From the fifteenth century a Greek diaspora of merchant colonies formed in all the major European cities, and Greeks, allowed to dominate the Ottoman internal and external trade, were active in the Balkans. Theirs was a different Greece, a vision of human perfection developed and transmitted by European humanist circles, and one encountered by Greeks who were educated in European academies, notably Venetia's Padua University, from the fifteenth to the eighteenth centuries. Within this tradition invidious comparisons were regularly drawn between the virtuous Greeks of antiquity and their present decadence. During the eighteenth century when philhellenism promoted the republican models of Greek antiquity as the means to regenerate contemporary Europe, this contrast intensified a conflict between the rationalist perfection of ancient Greeks and the corruption of the Orthodox legacy that had cut Greeks from their authentic past. One must not overdo this contrast. As well as secular intellectuals and merchants, many clerics sponsored the revival of Greek learning and the wave of publications that poured into mainland Greece from the diaspora. Nonetheless, Hellenic nationalists saw Greece's revival as dependent on rejoining the West; their Orthodox equivalents looked East to their co-religionists in the Balkans and Russia, hoping to reconquer the Byzantine Empire (Campbell and Sherrard, 1968: ch. 1). What is important is that Hellenism, as a project of European modernisation, had virtually no ideological or institutional roots in a clientelist and village-based society, and had symbolic rather than substantive functions.

Because of this there was a rift between the secular republican ideology of the political class and the embedded Orthodox realities on the ground.

There are many other examples that could be cited. A recent study of Czech nationalism identifies rival Catholic and Hussite conceptions of the national history, focused on the formative moment of the defeat of the Czech Protestant nobility at White Mountain in 1620 and the incorporation of the Czech lands into the Catholic Habsburg Empire. The Catholic conception has at its core St Wenceslas, the symbolic 'founder' of the Czech *state* in the tenth century and unifier of the Bohemian peoples, who became a rallying figure in the nineteenth century for a revived Czech state. Although a religious (and barely tolerated) minority, Protestants provided the mainspring of the Czech nationalist movements. Their symbol was Jan Hus, an early Catholic fifteenth-century reformer, supported by the Czech nobility, who was burned as a heretic. Hus represented the spiritual greatness of the Czech *nation*, its language and culture and its resistance to German dominance. Although Wenceslas was an unproblematic symbol as long as Czech demands were for autonomy within the Habsburg Empire, as the drive for independence grew in the late nineteenth century, Hus became symbolically dominant, given the close association between the Catholic Church and the Habsburg monarchy. On the achievement of independence in 1918, one million followers and about 300 priests renounced Catholicism under the banner of freedom from Rome (Holy, 1996: 34–40).

What this suggests is that cultural wars are shaped by powerful collective experiences such as state-religious schisms (Russia); revolutions and/or civil wars (France and England); wars and colonisations (Ireland); or religio-national conflicts (Czech lands), the memories of which are carried by various social strata and institutions (legal, religious, literary and political). Round these mythic memories rival repertoires develop as mobilisers of collective action. We shall see that these repertoires have internal and external dimensions. They offer different perspectives about the nature of politics, the status of social groups, relations between regions, the country-side and the city, economic and social policies and also foreign policy. It is notable that not all these projects were of similar weight. The 'memories' of ancient Greece were not substantiated in a living culture as were their Orthodox equivalents; the same might be said too of the Irish Protestant idealisation of a pagan Gaelic Ireland compared to the embedded Catholic social order of priests and people bound together by common experiences of confiscation and persecution.

Significance and Consequences

What then are the significance and consequences of these divisions? Does their persistence indicate that they provide necessary options for societies? Or do they constrict alternatives by polarising and possibly anachronising debate, thereby preventing the full exploration of different possibilities? Given that they express at times diametrically opposed views of the nation and may use as reference points periods of civil or ethnic warfare, what prevents societies disintegrating into civil conflict?

No ethnic community or modern nation would long survive unless it contained a plurality of traditions. But what of those cases where the consciousness of having a differentiated past does not feed in a diffuse manner into national debates but configures antithetic competition, as, for instance, in France and Russia? Even in these extreme cases, I will suggest we can find evidence of patterns of alternation between rival movements that mobilise different social energies by which to overcome crises, thereby strengthening the nation as it navigates the many challenges (political, economic, military and ideological) of the modern world.

In France republicanism has been the dominant tradition, but has had to compete with right-wing religious nationalist and Bonapartist alternatives, each of which puts forward a vision of France as a society and defines a European mission.

Republicanism defines France as a nation one and indivisible, as the guarantor of the democratic liberties of its citizens and, because of its revolutionary heritage, the bearer of a world mission to spread enlightenment and modernity. It sacralises France as the primary nation of modernity, destined to lead and regenerate European civilisation. It has produced a Parisian-dominated and centralist state, suspicious of regional and religious liberties as covers for political reaction (Gildea, 1994: 169). Anti-republican opponents, whose core institution has been the Catholic Church, have articulated a strongly patriarchal, religious and rural vision of a France of provincial liberties, rooted in a golden medieval age, that stands against the moral and social chaos of secular modernity. It gives weight to France as an ancient, virtually primordial European community, descended from Clovis, and to its great legacy as a builder and defender of European Christendom as leader of the Crusades, as a creator of canonical vernacular styles such as Gothic architecture, as a model of culture to the European courts through the prestige of its language, and also as the great military power of the continent. Catholic France has retained powerful support in the West and Midi regions (Johnson, 1993: 53–4). The third, Bonapartist, tradition looks to a charismatic hero like Napoleon who, in alliance with the Church, restored social order and France's military glories, and, drawing on the legacy of Charlemagne, established France as the imperial ruler of Europe, though one that professed to respect the liberties of nations (Fontana, 2002).

The persistence of these traditions indicates co-existence of at least three Frances, each of which at various crises has become hegemonic. Although the First Republic dissolved in chaos, Napoleon used its missionary enlightenment ideology to justify his imperial expansion, and at home he made a Concordat with the Church and established his Civil Code. But as a usurper, raised by his genius in arms, he was undone by military defeat. The return of the Bourbon monarchy that followed preserved the existence of France as a great power within a restored European balance of power system. But the traditional *Ancien Régime* could not be restored, and after the revolutions of 1830 and 1848, a Second Republic was declared. Social breakdown justified Napoleon III's seizure of power in 1851, just as it had his uncle's, and he promised to restore order and revitalise France's mission to Europe as the defender of the liberties of oppressed nations. French intervention was instrumental in the national unification of Italy. However, just as military defeat had destroyed Napoleon I, so humiliation at the hands of Bismarck shattered the prestige of his nephew in 1870, bringing back a (Third) Republic that restored a middle-class democracy.

Determined to regenerate France, republicans sought to nationalise the people (transform 'peasants into Frenchmen') by mass patriotic secondary education, military conscription and the economic unification of the territory (Weber, 1976). The extension of secular state education led to prolonged conflict with the Church in the late nineteenth century, and the Republic was tested by financial scandals and economic depression. On the left, it was challenged by class-based socialist and syndicalist movements. Counter-revolutionaries, with many sympathisers in the army, contrasted French *gloire* under the *ancien régime* with French national weakness in the face of a rising Germany. Splits occurred within the right between monarchists and proto-fascists, who favoured a racial, hierarchical, Catholic nation and attempted to co-opt socialist support of the lower middle and working classes by tapping traditional anti-Semitic and anti-capitalist prejudices (Gildea, 1994: chs 6, 7).

Although victory in the First World War vindicated the republic, which was able to rally both the right and the left, during the postwar period depression and mass unemployment eroded republican morale in the face of a mobilisation of the extreme left and the right. The humiliating collapse of France in 1940 led to its effective partition, and in the 'autonomous' zone Marshall Pétain's Vichy regime obtained strong Church and popular support in repudiating secular republicanism and promising a national regeneration based on Catholic piety, respect for social hierarchy and the superior life of the land. The Allied liberation of France, however, resulted once again in the marginalisation of the Right, the triumphant return of the charismatic de Gaulle and the establishment of a Fourth Republic. But this regime was discredited by a return to the internal divisions of earlier republics, humiliating losses of Empire in Asia and Africa, and finally the prospect of defeat in Algeria. Once again, in alliance with the French army, de Gaulle returned to power, marrying Bonapartist with republican traditions in establishing a Fifth Republic based on a presidential democracy that would restore France's great power status and its leadership of Europe.

There is a comparable pattern of alternation in Russia during the nineteenth and twentieth centuries, as a despotic Imperial state sought to co-opt at different times Slavophile and Westerner projects in defining Russian development and its external relations, above all with Europe. Iver Neumann (1996: ch. 1) argues that three main positions developed in the nineteenth century. The first was the state's legitimism that viewed Russia as the protector of a European Christian *ancien régime* threatened by secular revolution and was suspicious of nationalism, but the state was forced to create an official nationalism by the late nineteenth century to broaden its dynastic appeal. The second was a romantic Slavophile nationalism, which argued that there was a distinctive Russian character drawn from Orthodox Christianity and its rural communal institutions that must provide the model first of Russian and then European development. This sought to strengthen a Russian society against the erosion of European secular ideas, would look to countries like Britain as successful conservative models that promoted a social progress led by Crown and the (Tory) landed order (Pipes, 1977: 268; Riasonovsky, 1952: 104–5). It would veer from a rejection of dynastic great power adventures to visions of leading a league of Slavic nations (Lieven, 2000: 219, 247). The third was Westerner in so far as it argued that, for a backward and Asiatic society to progress, Russia must tap the advanced technologies of Western Europe and adapt them to Russian conditions, if needs be by revolution.

Reacting against the Russian enlightenment sponsored by Catherine the Great, the Russian Tendency had emerged in the late eighteenth century, rejecting French influences among the elite and defining Russia by the cultural practices of the people. It was defeated when in 1815 the Tsar, after the overthrow of Napoleonic France, presented the idea of a Holy Alliance of European Christian monarchs. A fear of European-wide revolutions renewed this conservative nationalism in the 1820s and 1830s. On the other side, Decembrist officers, influenced by their encounter in France with Enlightenment ideas, rebelled unsuccessfully in 1825 after the state suppressed debate about democracy and constitutional government.

The state's reaction, shaped by the revolutionary waves in Europe in the early nineteenth century, was to isolate Russia and try to re-arm it against European ideas, embodied in the principles of Count Uvarov, the Minister of Education, of autocracy, orthodoxy and nationality. During the 1830s a Russian cultural nationalism, inspired by German idealism, presented Russia as spiritually ahead of Europe and attacked representative government as bureaucratic and mercantile, threatening the landed order. Although the Slavophiles argued for the moral superiority of Russia and demanded that the upper classes abandon European fashions and return to the people, they also attacked the gap between Tsar and the land (and people) introduced by Peter the Great's state bureaucratisation and continued by later administrations. For Westerners, Peter was a hero, and westernisation was to be encouraged, especially the development of a middle class. During the 1830s and 1840s debate raged between the Slavophiles and Westerners, both of which were suppressed by the state as a threat to its authority (Neumann, 1996: ch. 3).

In response to the 1848 revolutions the regime intervened to save the Habsburgs and moved to co-opt Slavophiles' cult of Holy Russia, while Westerners were shaken by the failure of liberal movements in Western Europe. However, the regime's attachment to Slavophiles ended with the Crimean War, which exposed Russia's military inferiority to European powers. Under Tsar Alexander II there was a switch to Westerner policies from 1861 to advance the modernisation of Russian society, including the abolition of serfdom, opening of educational opportunities to the middle classes, limited political freedoms and industrialisation. But no specific political space was allowed to a civil society, and Westerners went into opposition, first dividing into liberal and socialist wings, while a Russian Populism formed that rejected industrialisation in favour of a rural socialist society based on the *mir*. The assassination of Tsar Alexander II in 1881 was carried out by Populists in despair at state-sponsored industrialisation. Slavophiles, initially demoralised by the Crimean defeat, swung from spiritual introspection during the 1880s into an aggressive Pan-Slavist foreign policy, but this was not taken up by Alexander III, who continued earlier official nationality and Russification policies together with political repression (Neumann, 1996: ch. 5; Pipes, 1977: 269–78).

Defeat in war with Japan triggered a liberal revolution in 1905, which the Tsar neutralised, and the period to 1914 was marked by battles on the left between a Menshevik Marxism looking to Western models and patterns and a Bolshevik Marxism which asserted Russia's capacity as a catalyst of world revolution. The collapse of the state during the First World War brought the latter to power, and after Lenin's death, the Bolsheviks themselves divided between Stalin's advocacy of Socialism in One Country and Trotsky's failed advocacy of World Revolution. A Eurasian alternative developed in the 1920s, arguing that Russia was neither European nor Asiatic but both. In practice, the Bolshevik regime married Russian messianic ideas to communist utopianism, and although a Russian nationalism and the Orthodox Church were anathematised, a national Bolshevism survived, and at times of crises such as the Nazi invasion in 1941, Stalin invoked these latter themes to mobilise support for the regime.

As disillusion with the regime intensified in the postwar period under Brezhnev, so a popular neo-Slavophile cultural movement developed, rejecting Marxism as a western imposition on Russia, but this was accompanied by dissident movements of liberal Westerners (Popielovsky, 1989). Under Gorbachev, Boris Yeltsin was able to tap both currents, and his period of government was marked by a full-scale revival of the debates between neo-Slavophile nationalists defending Orthodoxy and liberal Westerners who sought constitutional freedoms and a liberal capitalism.

In summary, the examples indicate that these rival traditions offered repertoire for states and sections of a developing civil society that articulated alternative strategies to master changing external and internal challenges. Failure in warfare resulted in a switching between options, as the formerly excluded took up the baton of saving the nation; alienated social classes were recruited by different national factions and their energies mobilised for the national cause; and debates about opposing visions sharpened an understanding of the characteristics of the nation and the policies most appropriate to them.

Polarisation

Nonetheless, is it not arguable that the dominance and institutionalisation of such competing concepts of national origins distorted social development by presenting options as antitheses? The case for polarisation is that such disputes produced a simplified view of the national past that obliterated alternative readings in favour of an anachronising dichotomisation. Arguably, they obscured the synthetic characteristics of national cultures and hence possible productive accommodations were overlooked. They also imparted a bitterness and hardness to ideological differences by presenting them in terms of a fundamental quasi-biological divide that made it difficult for opponents to adopt common ground. In short, such conflicts produced not cultural pluralism but rather, pathological hostilities that permanently weakened the national community.

Certainly, the tone of debates in Russia was marked by extremism. The Slavophile 'revival' of the late 1830s was triggered by the famous letter of Peter Chaadaev who, deeply affected by Catholic thought, argued that alone of the major nations Russia had contributed nothing to civilisation because it had been cut off from European Christendom by the polluted source of Byzantium. In response, Slavophiles denounced Russian ills as derived entirely from the bureaucratic despotism of Peter the Great, and constructed an idealised pre-Petrine Russia that bore no relation to historical reality. Westerners, in reply, valorised Peter and the Russian state as the lone agents of rescuing Russia from its Asiatic backwardness (Pipes, 1977: 266–9; Riasonovsky, 1985: ch. 2). McDaniel (1996) has argued that a combination of Russian messianism and a cult of state-driven modernisation from above produced a solipsistic extremism, which has prevented Russia developing a distinctive and viable modern society. The Slavophiles exaggerated Russian virtues and the importance of the spiritual against the technicism of the West, thereby reinforcing a conservative authoritarianism and irrationalism, whereas Westerners, by aggressively repudiating the Russian heritage, legitimised an ideological extremism and violence against established customs. The result in each case has been to lurch from one form of fanaticism to another, which left Russia open to despotic government and utopian thinking. A liberal culture could not develop, nor could traditions of pragmatic reform.

It is also arguable that the intensity of the French schism between supporters of the indivisible republic and of an *ancien régime* of regional liberties has resulted not only in extremities of violence against ideological opponents but also an overcentralisation of French society, with a top-heavy Paris and weak local government (Gildea, 1994: ch. 4). In its revulsion against the mess of local and resistant traditions in *ancien régime* France, the Republic imposed a rationalist administration on the regions stripping them of much of their power. The disloyalty of regions in the West and Midi during the revolutionary wars raised fears that calls for regional decentralisation were part of a counter-revolutionary plot. From the 1860s there were strong pressures in regions such as Franche-Comté and Flanders and in provincial cities for greater autonomy which were supported by local groups across the political spectrum. This was resisted as a threat to the unity of the Republic. Indeed, the inability of the French right to win a national election after 1871 confirmed a suspicion of autonomist pressures. Moreover, a law was passed in 1938 criminalising any attempts to undermine the territorial integrity of France (Gildea, 1994: 170, 178, 184). Only in 1981 was a measure of devolution conceded to the regions, in part to 'buy off' ethnic threats from Bretons, Corsicans and Basques.

The bitterness between left and right undoubtedly weakened French unity against external enemies in the revolutionary period and in the Second World War against the German enemy. The memory of the 'Godless' assault on Catholic institutions during the Revolution, the imposition of a dogmatic secularism in education and the powerful anti-democratic ethos of the 1930s created a venomous anti-republican subculture and contributed to the ease with which the Republic was replaced by the Vichy regime in 1940. Under the slogan of 'Work, Family and Fatherland', its leader, Marshall Pétain, with the support of the army and Church, attributed the national catastrophe to the sins of the Republic (Burrin, 1996)

In Ireland the Gaelic-linguistic and Anglo-Irish literary nationalist 'revivals' appeared to intensify the cultural hostility between Protestants and Catholics, in spite of the nonsectarian and integrative aims of their founders. During the guerilla war against Britain and the still more virulent civil war between supporters and opponents of the Treaty with Britain, republican nationalists targeted the great houses of the Protestant gentry. After independence there was a large-scale emigration of the Protestant minority, perceived as 'England's garrison in Ireland', who found their position increasingly untenable. Although Protestant intellectuals such as Yeats remained, he and his allies, who had been the mainstays of a syncretic Anglo-Irish vision, found themselves isolated in the face of an officially sponsored Gaelic Catholic culture, commitment to which became a unifying project for Catholic elites in the aftermath of the bitter civil war. The great public heritage of the golden age of Irish Protestantism, the neo-classical and Georgian buildings of eighteenth-century Dublin, were pulled down or deliberately allowed to decay: symbols of an oppressive English urban Ascendancy that represented an affront to a Gaelic rural and populist culture (Lowenthal, 1985: 334–5).

This last example demonstrates how these conflicts did not stay at the political level, but could become embedded in the culture and lives of their societies. The disputes raged over the content of national education, street names and architecture, ceremonies and commemorations, the forms of national language, literature and history. In Norway, Einar Haugen argues, the language struggle between *Landsmål* and *Bokmål* resulted in a schizoglossia – a personality split that left many Norwegians linguistically divided and uncertain. The struggle of the former to become the national language did not succeed and has set up two cultural camps. In the field of literature the books in one language often are not reviewed in the press of the other side; there are two inadequately funded national theatres; in education two nearly identical standard languages are taught and government documents have to be published in both languages (Haugen, 1966: 280–1).

The bitter struggles between republicans and their opponents in France resulted in a 'statuomania' in urban spaces. In Paris a monumental split developed between liberal, secular republican East Paris (site of the Pantheon and Bastille) and military, imperial West Paris (Place Vendôme, Étoile, Invalides) (Agulhon, 1998: 535). In villages from 1860 to 1910 combined town hall/school buildings were built opposite churches, and in the cities government buildings and statues of Marianne and republican heroes confronted churches and representations of the Virgin (Langlois, 1996: 125). Even the fallen soldiers fought this iconographical war, as republican neo-classical heroic images vied with symbols of Christian suffering in the cemeteries.

At times, hostilities between rival national projects erupted into civil war and even into attempts at ethnic fission. The French Revolution was a civil war, and at times of national strife and crisis the Vendée region, loyal to Clergy and Crown, revolted in 1815, 1832 and 1870, and there was civil strife in the West and Midi in 1830 and 1848 (Gildea, 1994: 27–30). Susan-Mary Grant (1997) argues that the American Civil War was in fact a war of two nationalisms that had originated shortly after the Revolution in rival northern and southern conceptions of the meaning of the Declaration of Independence and the Constitution. By the mid-nineteenth century the sense of division between an expansive industrial North and a conservative agrarian South had generated competing myths of origins, with Southerners claiming descent from Cavalier stock and to defend the original Constitution against the Northern 'Roundheads'.

Elie Kedourie (1960: ch. 6) maintains that such civic and ethnic wars are no surprise. Because nations are essentially subjective entities, national symbols are selected out of a range of possibilities by opportunistic nationalist elites, and the expectations engendered in the followers are utopian. Because the nation is for its adherents 'a family', such civil conflicts are marked by greater fanaticism than wars against a foreign oppressor, and there is also the possibility of separate nations being formed by them.

But is extremist conflict in these settings the responsibility of nationalism or of older social and political traditions? Were not the responsible

101

factors in (pre-Revolutionary) France and Russia the traditions of state despotism that prevented a proper testing of social alternatives and encouraged a utopian dimension to social thinking and a doctrinaire root and branch politics? The violence of the assault on the Church and aristocracy in France resulted, in turn, in an equally total repudiation of the principles and practices of the revolution. The absence of a liberal civil society was even more apparent in Russia and encouraged a winner-takes-all stance to state power. By and large despotic states have sought to co-opt and manipulate the opposing traditions, and thereby discredited each tradition in the eyes of the other. Moreover, geopolitical considerations ingrained in the historical memory may override ideology. The overcentralisation of France is not just an effect of the republican tradition, since in practice supporters of the *ancien régime* when in office made no attempt to return authority to regions. 'France' historically had 'grown' from the expansion of the Ile-de-Paris, adding provinces by dynastic marriage, treaty and conquest, with the outer provinces being incorporated in 'recent' memory – Flanders and Franche-Comté (1678), Lorraine (1761), Corsica (1768). Invading armies of the European *ancien régime* had as one of their pretexts the defence of the provincial liberties of Flanders, Alsace and Brittany. The historic exposure of France to invasions produced an overcentralised state, reluctant to cede autonomies, particularly to border regions, traditionally antagonistic to the overweening claims of Paris.

The spiralling of national differences into civil war is more likely at times of great instability, political or economic. The French Revolution was triggered by famine and economic crisis and its radicalisation followed a worsening military situation. Pétain's Vichy's regime, tainted by its record of collaboration, was a target of the French Resistance's struggle against German occupation. The Irish civil war (1922–23) erupted after the success of the revolutionary rising of Easter 1916 had discredited constitutional politics, and after a period in which militarised elites (from 1918) had been operating in a guerrilla war of independence, beyond popular control or accountability. The national struggle between the Chinese Communists and Chiang Kai-shek's Kuomintang in the 1930s was intensified by the war against the Japanese invader, and after the war the Communists justified their successful campaign by the latter's failure against the foreign enemy.

The Chinese example may suggest that the presence of a threatening 'other' is insufficient by itself to unify the warring parties, though there are many cases where national protagonists put aside their differences to fight a foreign enemy (for example Norway during the Second World War). What is instructive is how few descend into civil war under stable conditions and how rarely cultural differences lead to the fission of populations into two separate nationalities. We might suggest that it is easier for societies to recover from civil conflict because of the existence of acknowledged common founding myths. Both sides in the American and Irish civil wars claimed to be the true custodians of their national liberation myths, respectively the American War of Independence, and the Easter Rising and subsequent war of independence. This surely was a factor in the relatively speedy restoration of national unity after the bloody conflicts.

The Elaboration of a National Identity

This last point implies that the protagonists in these cultural wars may share (perhaps unwittingly) many assumptions, and that, where there is a common ethnic substratum, ideological competition defines and elaborates a national identity. W. J. Argyle shows how competitive claims between different but intermingled or adjoining ethnic categories in central Europe crystallised national identities, when intellectuals, in order to authenticate their group *vis-à-vis* another, were driven to research their geographies, cultural heritages, histories and political institutions (Argyle, 1976). A similar process occurs in the debates *within* nations, when rivals validate their vision by reference to an authentic past. The effects are to define, codify and elaborate the characteristics of the nation. Out of the debates about the authenticity of certain figures or practices, an internalisation of national values takes place; there is a battle to 'own' certain symbols and one finds groups at times of crisis often switching between rival repertoires.

In modern France the competing visions turned to a medieval golden age and, in particular, the figure of Joan of Arc to gain popular legitimacy. In his *History of France* (1841), the romantic historian Jules Michelet introduced her as a woman of the people and pious Catholic, betrayed by Church and Monarchy to the English who burnt her as a heretic. His aim was to ground the Revolution, discredited by the Jacobin dictatorship, as a historical outgrowth of the French people. Joan embodied the democratic spirit of France, crushed by the *ancien régime*. Catholic apologists responded in different ways. Some, in exclusive terms, presented Joan as saving France in order to save the Catholic Church, of which France was the eldest daughter; others hoped to build bridges to republicans, particularly after the advent of a mass socialist movement in the 1890s. After the outbreak of the First World War representatives of the extreme right, such as Charles Maurras, joined with republicans to establish great festivals devoted to Joan that

103

united the nation in the desperate struggle with Germany. A national festival in 1921 after her canonisation seemed to establish an official cult uniting all French, but the struggle over her memory resumed in the interwar period when groups from the left and right challenged the bourgeois Republic. Action Française monarchists sought to reclaim her for the extreme right, while communists in the late 1930s attempted to win Catholic working-class support for the Popular Front by depicting her as a member of the proletariat betrayed by the ruling classes. Vichy fought in vain to monopolise her cult. These battles have continued into the contemporary period, with Le Pen's Front National evoking her campaign to expel foreign invaders from French soil as inspiration for their anti-immigrant agenda (Gildea, 1994: 154–65; Winock, 1998).

Robert Gildea argues that such intense and persistent struggles demonstrate that the divided nature of the French past means there are few symbols that can elicit a set of values on which a final French consensus can be built (1994: 154–65). The only common denominator, he suggests, is a sense of *gloire* (great power) to which monarchists, republicans and Bonapartists can lay claim, by conveniently ignoring disasters. But his analysis of the myth of St Joan shows how ethnic symbols act as a common reference point for competing groups and as a nationalising agent for new entrants into the political process. Such symbols offer a shared language through which differences are expressed and elaborated. By appealing to them as legitimising devices, groups imply the existence of a larger and enfolding national entity in which they all participate and which, in turn, they acknowledge as exercising a coercive power over them.

In addition, the more they articulate ideological differences through battles about the purity of this version of the language (in the Norwegian case) or the meaning of this particular historical actor, the more such battles seem to have the character of a family quarrel, one that is intensely felt but one that marks off the disputants from those outside this cultural tradition (other nationalities) to whom these issues are inscrutable. In practice, Republicans and their conservative opponents did find a pragmatic middle ground most of the time. Most French men and women found no contradiction between being Catholic and republican. Republicans understood the value of the Catholic faith as a buttress of social stability when they were challenged by the rise of radical socialism during the nineteenth century.

Similar points can be made of the Russian debate between supporters of the autocracy, Slavophiles and Westerners who turned to the past in order to justify their views of the relationships of Russia to Europe and to Asia, of people to ruler and the status of different classes.

Slavophiles and Westerners found in Peter the Great a common reference point. For the former Russia had preserved a unique Orthodox civilisation based on the communal spirit (*sobornost*) in the Russian lands for a thousand years against Asian hordes and from western invasions. But Peter the Great had weakened the solidarity of Russia by assimilating it to the rationalist and legalist ethos of a Latin Christian Europe that produced a state founded on violence and separated from the people. They based their historical interpretation on ancient chronicles that presented a conciliar relationship between people and ruler. Russia had been a patriarchal, not a patrimonial state, and this had been shattered by Peter. Russia had since followed a bureaucratic rationalist path foreign to its nature, producing alienation between social groups. They viewed Westerner demands for a constitution and social order on European lines as continuing Peter's work (Riasonovsky, 1985: ch. 2).

Westerner historians attacked the Slavophile golden age, by showing that the peasant commune (*mir*) was a recent construct of the state in order to gather taxes and that the Russian state had never engaged in a partnership with society but had crushed it. They used European history as the norm of human development, arguing like Belinsky that humanity went through historical stages, from natural immediacy, to abstract universalism, to national reality. Orthodoxy, in separating Russia from the classical universalism of Catholic Europe, had weakened the nation, which fell under the Tatar yoke. Only Peter the Great's actions had rescued Russia from being stuck like Asia in an unconscious stage. The role of Westerners was to advance a process already happening, including the development of a bourgeoisie (Pipes, 1977: 268–9; Rabow-Edling, 2001: ch. 2).

In these debates protagonists differed profoundly over many issues, but the debates reinforced a belief in Russian difference, for better or for worse. Debates over Russian history formed a consensus of what Russia's distinctive institutions were – Orthodoxy, the autocracy, the *mir* – as well as what it lacked – for example, a commercial middle class. It established that Russian characteristics were formed by Mongol and other invasions from the Asian steppes, by influences from Byzantium, invasions and cultural influences from the West, and that many of these influences and pressures continued into the present. This consensus, however, inspired different projects of social reform. Both Slavophiles and Westerners saw themselves involved in a project of Russian enlightenment and engaged in a social transformation that pitted them at different times against the autocratic state (Rabow-Edling, 2001: chs 3, 4). The debates also encouraged a codification of rival cultural heroes and villains that extended across the entire range of Russian culture and, finally, an elaboration of rival social projects of national reform that defined what Russia's role was to be *viv-à-vis* Europe and Asia and Byzantium/Balkans, whether that of imitator, creative assimilator, moral leader or redeemer.

A self-conscious and evolving tradition of social thinking developed from which the participants would draw in order to diagnose how to meet the new circumstances of the present and to address the problems of new social classes as they became mobilised by agrarian and industrial changes. It would be misleading to reify individuals under simple labels, and even to the extent that camps did form, there were debates within them. An internalisation of the ideas of the 'other' resulted as proponents used the arguments of their opponent against them and borrowed ideas from the other in the process of arguments with their allies. Westerners resident in Europe experienced a sense of their Russian 'otherness' whereas Slavophiles in their critique of autocratic tradition looked outward to how conservatives in Europe had successfully managed to combine tradition and innovation (e.g. the Slavophiles' admiration of English Tory landed democracy). By the 1860s a new wing of conservative nationalists, 'enthusiasts of the soil', associated with the journals of the Dostoevsky brothers, repudiated the dogmatism of earlier Slavophiles, agreeing with the more 'realistic' Westerners of the need for a greater liberalism (freedom of thought) in Russian society, and the need to reach out to the people among whom education and literacy had to be promoted (Thaden, 1964: 59–63).

For this reason, we see figures switching positions as they come to understand the strength of the other side. The Westerner Alexander Herzen – uneasy at wholesale importation of European ideas, especially after the failure of the liberal European revolutions in 1848 – declared that Westerners would be cut off from the people as long as they ignored the questions posed by the Slavophiles (Neumann, 1996: 170). In similar vein, Dostoevsky, advocate of Russia's Orthodox mission and its Eastern destiny, reveals the ambivalence of neo-Slavophiles: 'In Europe we were Asiatics, whereas in Asia we too are Europeans ... We shall go to Asia as masters' (cited in Neumann, 1996: 64). These visions have alternated in power both at the level of state and of 'educated society', with groups at times switching positions, in part affected by the sense of place and security of the national territory.

In the case of Greece, a degree of consensus developed early, facilitated by the important role played by Orthodox clerics in promoting the Hellenic ideal, and by the fact that on independence the large majority of the Greek-speaking population still resided outside the Greek state and within the Ottoman Empire. The Hellenic–Orthodox divisions were bridged in the 1840s by the irredentist 'Great Idea' to liberate all Greeks within a state that, in effect, would be a reconstituted Byzantine Empire and that would operate as a bridge between 'West' and 'East'. The Greek example indicates that the development of a common project is not of itself a good thing. In yoking Hellenism to Byzantinism, the early modernising drive of a European-inspired elite was subordinated to the ethnocentric ethos of a rural, religious and backward society, suspicious of the Latin West and European statecraft. The irredentist preoccupation led to a neglect of Greece's economic and social development and to top-heavy state and weak civil society traditions (Pepelassis, 1958).

At first sight the Irish debate between Gaelic and Anglo-Irish revivalists marks an exception to these patterns of mutual accommodation. The determination of Gaelic revivalists to establish their hegemony over the newly independent Ireland froze the country into a sterile official culture since it resulted in the actual or psychological emigration of the Protestant minority, and with them a section of society that had sought to build a national culture that recognised the cross-cultural realities of modern Ireland. The apparent failure to find a common Irish heritage is explained by the nature of the historical divide between the two, based on a 'foreign' conquest that created two different ethnicities, one profoundly anti-Protestant and the other, at best ambivalently Irish, and for the most part identifying themselves as British.

The late nineteenth-century Gaelic and Anglo-Irish revivals both saw anglicisation as the common enemy, and the former at first viewed the Anglo-Irish literary movement as a means to promote the forgotten glories of the Gaelic heritage to English-speaking Ireland. Yeats, for his part, approved the Gaelic Irish-language revival as a means of preserving the literary traditions of the pagan eras. They both defended the Irish-speaking West of Ireland as Ireland's spiritual heartland and inspired reform movements – on the Protestant side Plunkett's agricultural co-operative society modelled on Denmark, and on the Catholic side a series of temperance and educational societies. But Anglo-Irish nationalists and reformers represented only a small minority within the Protestant population, and the Anglo-Irish emphasis on a golden age of warrior pagan aristocratic heroes came into conflict with the Gaelic League's populist vision of a mobilised rural peasantry allied to a missionary Catholic Church. Increasingly, the Anglo-Irish were attacked as exotics seeking covertly to re-establish a Protestant Ascendancy by redefining the authentic Irish nation as aristocratic and pagan and hence subverting the dreams of the Catholic majority to rule their country. In short, the cultural struggle intensified the sense of distance between the two groups and the antithetical nature of their national visions.

Persisting Differences

If these competing repertoires often arise out of climatic historical events, why should they persist even if they are carried by major institutions? After all, we have observed that ethnic and national identities are layered and that new collective experiences may override or at least add other elements to the established mix. Given that national societies encounter unpredictable and catastrophic shocks in the modern world, should one not expect these repertoires to be replaced by others more relevant to new circumstances? Might not circumstances dictate the emphatic triumph of one side over another? Or alternatively, in more peaceful and stable democratic societies, will the process of debate not result in the forming of common ground which results in a fading of intensities?

Novel processes of various kinds may seem to make older debates irrelevant. At first sight, the formation of a British state resulted in the subsuming of English national identity into a British Imperialism in which the Crown was a central unifying symbol, and this was followed by the rise of an industrial society. As we saw, the democratic thrust of Anglo-Saxonism was co-opted during the second half of the nineteenth century into a racial imperialism that sang the unique governing mission of the English people. The conflation of Englishness and Britishness has resulted arguably in an identity confusion that is only now becoming explicit. The loss of Empire, the devolution of power and the rise of the Scottish and Welsh nationalisms are raising questions about what Englishness is (see Langlands, 1999: 63–4; McCrone, 1998: ch. 2). Even in Ireland history moves on. The eruption of a brutal civil war between supporters and opponents of the Treaty with Britain after the electoral defeat of the latter, and the 'emigration' from the new state of Protestants in the decade after Irish independence, foreshadowed a new era. In current historiography the major issue of twentieth-century Irish nationalism is not ethnocultural (the rivalry between Anglo-Irish and Gaelic ideals) but political (the struggle for legitimacy between constitutional and revolutionary traditions of nationalism). This gains credibility from the organisation of the Irish democratic system round the divisions of the Irish civil war. The two dominant parties remain *Fianna Fail* and *Fine Gael*, representing the anti-Treaty and pro-Treaty legacy respectively.

Alternatively, traumatic historical events may appear to 'decide' in favour of a particular vision. We saw how Greece's catastrophic defeat of 1922 at the hands of the new Turkish national state and the subsequent exchange of populations ended the external mission to recover Byzantine glories, leading to an unstable era of liberal governments of a republican stance. The German case, too, is instructive. Here, nationalism had swung from the beginning between liberal enlighteners, who saw Germany as part of Western European democracies, and 'Easterner' and authoritarian conceptions that viewed Germany as a leader of the Central and Eastern European peoples. In the nineteenth century constitutional liberalism was co-opted by Bismarck to a Prussian autocratic militarism, and during the First World War the German Reich developed plans for a *Mitteleuropa* extending deeply into the Ukraine. Defeat resulted in the liberal Weimar Republic, but this was overthrown by revolutionary conservatives (Nazis), whose goal was an enormous racial empire extending to the Ukraine. The battle of visions, however, seemed to be ended by the collapse of Nazi *Ostpolitik* and Germany's partition in 1945. Postwar Germans have re-emphasised Western Germany's commitment to liberal democratic traditions exemplified in its support for the European Union, and rejected Prussian statist traditions in favour of a constitution decentralising substantial powers to the regional *ländler* based on nineteenth-century models of German confederation.

Matters, however, are not so simple since one finds the apparently old debates reappearing. In England, an Imperial Britain always evoked fears (registered in Gibbon's *Decline and Fall*) of the potential corruption of parliamentary liberties by an unconstrained executive government; the Victorian period was marked by a Gothic revival, glorifying public buildings and monuments such as Westminster Abbey (site of the coronation of the last Saxon king, Harold); and in the late nineteenth century an English cultural nationalism promoting a general vernacular revival rejected Imperial temptations and sought a return to the world of the shire. Anglo-Saxon liberties and their legacy (the seventeenth-century assault of the Crown) continue to be evoked on the right and left, in defence of English parliamentary liberties against a 'despotic' European Union or of 'the people' against a political establishment.

In Germany the problems of national identity have been repressed rather than addressed, and Adenauer's shift to the West was qualified by Willy Brandt's opening the West German state to its eastern neighbours, including the GDR, as means of keeping open the possibility of eventual national re-unification. German re-unification, the tearing down of the iron curtain and the prospects of eastern extension of the European Union has revised older questions about Germany's place in Europe, now that its change of capital from Bonn to Berlin re-orients it to the east. Its foreign policy of unilateral recognition of Slovenian and Croatian independence in the Balkans demonstrates a reassertion of distinctive German interests.

In Greece, too, the division between a European-oriented and insular ethnoreligious nationalism muffled by the Great Idea merely took new forms in battles during the interwar period between liberal republicans, monarchists allied to the army and a utopian populist socialism. The territorial settlement and exchange of populations after 1922 meant that Greece became one of the most (ethno-) religiously homogeneous populations in Europe, with 97 per cent claiming to be Orthodox, which all parties had to acknowledge. The debates have continued into the modern period in struggles between Church and State, particularly under socialist governments. Although Greeks retain a strong commitment to membership of the EU, which guarantees its borders against the more populous Turkey, its sympathy with Serbia as a fellow Orthodox people opposed by Muslim Albanians has created strains with its partners in the European Union and NATO during the recent war over Kosovo.

The Irish case demonstrates how the 'objective' issues raised by the historical legacies remain even if one of the parties dies. As we saw, the Anglo-Irish heritage came under assault after Irish independence, particularly after de Valera's determination to cement a Gaelic Catholic hegemony during the economic war with Britain in the 1930s. But if the great architectural legacy of the Anglo-Irish was allowed to fall into neglect, the institutions they founded – the Royal Irish Academy, Trinity College, Dublin and the Abbey Theatre – remained. Yeats and his associates had developed models of how a sense of Irishness was to be articulated using the genres of modern culture and through the medium of the real national language: an English inflected with Irish idioms. Although the Abbey Theatre was originally to be aristocratic and symbolist, it explored various genres, from Synge's satirical drama, Lennox Robinson's realist depictions of peasant life and Sean O'Casey's socialist working-class drama. As the failure of the Gaelic revival to develop a modern Irish language culture became apparent, so too did the importance of the minority legacy for an Ireland that continues to be cross-cultural in character. Indeed, it may be easier in this case to resume the search for a distinctive Irish culture in English without the Anglo-Irish presence reminding Catholics of the association of Gaelicism with humiliation and of Englishness with Ascendancy. The evolution of the Irish republic into a European liberal democracy and member of the EU, and recognition of the problems of (Protestant) Unionist and (Catholic) Nationalist divisions in (British-ruled) Northern Ireland, has been accompanied by the sympathetic reincorporation into the history of Ireland of the national contribution of the largely vanished Protestants (see Foster, 1988; Kiberd, 1996).

What this indicates is that these rival visions have staying power since they reflect the diverse heritages of populations whose territorial location continues to expose them to unpredictable impacts from several directions. The nation is not simply a space but a geographical milieu and subject to recurring and multiple influences from peoples, north, south, east and west. It is also situated in time with a layered past, and its different pasts are brought into play to cope with shifting challenges. There can be no final definition of a national identity.

In recognition of this many nations have declared a special position as mediator between different culture zones, one that implies a creative role as synthesiser and that also 'protects' them from being absorbed into dominant surrounding cultures. It often expresses hopes that the nation will not continue to be a battleground between opposing states or blocs. Kolettis presented the Greeks as the bridge between Europe and the East. The nineteenth-century Czech historian, Palacky, declared Czechs to be the bridge between the powerful Germans and the Slavs (including Russia). Today Czech intellectuals such as Milan Kundera perceive themselves to be in the centre of Europe, wishing to 'rejoin' the West after suffering the Eastern yoke, without succumbing to its technicism and materialism (Holy, 1996: ch. 6). In similar fashion, Finnish intellectuals in the nineteenth and twentieth centuries sought a mediating role, balancing between Finland's 'Western heritage' represented by its Swedish legacy and the Russian 'East'. At first Fennoman nationalists were Russophile, and rejected the industrialising programmes of liberal Westerners in seeking to liberate their country from Swedish social and cultural influence. But as Russifying pressures grew from the late nineteenth century, so they made common cause with the Westerners (Meinander, 2002: 149–54).

Even powerful countries such as Russia have taken on a role as mediator and synthesiser between civilisational blocs. The emergence in the twentieth century of a Eurasian conception acknowledges that modern Russia has been shaped by interaction with Western and Central Europe, Byzantium and the Asian steppes, and that Westerners and Slavophiles represent complementary not antithetical visions.

The eastern–western oscillations of German identity are a product of the radically expanding and contracting character of its population settlements and borders over centuries. The Norwegian language divisions persist because of the power of the two ideals within national life. On the one hand, there is a need to feel distinctive and linked to an Old Norse heritage and the distinctive world of its peasant communities in the west. On the other hand, much of its high culture (including the writings of Ibsen and Bjornson) testifies to a sense of connection to other Scandinavian cultures (notably Denmark) and also to Germany. England is torn between an inward insular identity of 'yeoman' liberties in peaceful shires and a pride in its global British mission as a world power (still with a permanent seat on the Security Council of the United Nations). In France, although politically subordinate to republican tradition in the modern era, Catholicism and its medieval Gothicism evokes a sense of historical depth of a great European culture. Its vitality, together with that of the political right, reflects a scepticism about the 'shallowness' of enlightened modernity, a resentment at Parisian arrogance with respect to the regions, and a rooted ethnocentrism that has its voice at times of perceived crisis (such as high immigration) when an oligarchic political system seems unresponsive.

Conclusions

This chapter shows that the dynamic character of many nationalisms owes much to persisting differences that are legitimised by myths of descent. Conflicts between rival visions shape the ways societies perceive the problems that they face as well as the strategies they might use to overcome them. This internal diversity is not just an arbitrary play of difference; rather the selection of options is 'historically' weighted. Although ethnicity is compatible with pluralism, it is a constrained pluralism. Where we find such contestation it is not necessarily benign – it does by definition offer choice and possibly a regenerating alternation, as previously excluded energies, social groups and institutions are 'made' available to the nation. But it can produce a polarisation of options, a 'diversion' of public energies into symbolic issues (e.g. language) that might have gone into enhancing economic and social development, and at worst into a destructive conflict and even violence. Nor does it mean that the options selected out of this contestation are the 'correct' or most 'rational'. Repertoires survive to the extent that the ideas and sentiments they represent are ingrained in particular domains of life and appear to be justified by 'objective' factors.

Fredrik Barth, in particular, drew attention to the internal diversity of ethnic groups, but such internal difference was masked and perhaps made possible by processes of differentiation against external others. Such diversity by itself does not motivate the development of alternatives unless driven by some commitment, in this case historical. Nor is an external 'other' (e.g. an invading power) a guarantor of a broader in-group consensus. What keeps such contestation in check is, in the final analysis, a sense of common values, a consciousness of which may arise out of the cultural debates themselves.

4

Hot and Banal Nationalisms

Introduction

So far we have looked at the processes of nation-formation from the point of nationalist elites, notably national revivalists. From their perspective the nation was an autonomous and distinctive self-realising community that asserted the primacy of the spiritual over the material. Revivalism gave rise to a flowering of the arts: everywhere schools of national literature, drama, music, painting, architecture, arts and crafts, sports and recreations formed to create a community of heroes prepared to sacrifice themselves for the nation. In many countries nationalist movements, often with rival ideals, crystallised periodically against existing elites at times of social conflict in order to regenerate the nation. In spite of their communitarian ideals, we saw that they could only achieve their goals by nationalising the state and using it to make the nation.

What is striking is the apparent contrast between the early ideals of national romantics and the mass nations that emerged: between, on the one hand, a sacred community of sacrifice, knit by a worship of the golden age, the virtues of rural life and the arts; and, on the other, the profane realities of urbanised industrial-technological societies, integrated by economic growth, mass media and popular culture. In the everyday life of citizens a sense of nationality is expressed by such activities as visits to industrial exhibitions, membership of national heritage societies, weekend tours to picturesque national sites and attendance at international sporting occasions. For this reason many suggest that there are stages of nation-formation – in the early phase of the intellectuals give rise to the national idea, but their romantic ideals fall into the background as political and economic processes incorporate ever-larger sections of the population (Hroch, 1985). The dominant modernist tendency is to view national formation in linear – even teleological – terms in which there is a shift from an ideological nationalism of elites to the routinised identities of sovereign national states as rival class, regional and religious identities are incorporated from above into solidary mass nations. There is, in other words, a shift from the ideological programmes of nationalist elites to the banal identities of settled national states.

In this chapter I will explore the relations between mass national identities and other collective identities such as class, religion, region and gender, which have often been characterised by conflicts. I shall reject as mythical the modernist account of the national state as a late nineteenth-century institution, constructed from above by the progressive integration of the masses into a national state that is unitary and sovereign. Throughout the modern period nations and national states have been beset by class, regional and religious conflicts, and national states have never been sovereign actors. Although nations have increasingly taken on a mass character in most European countries (though not in many countries outside Europe), national identities arise from civil society rather than state, they co-exist with other identities, and the salience of national identities may vary from country to country and may also fluctuate over time. I suggest the co-formation of two types of nationalism – the 'sacred' transformational movement produced by a sense of crisis, and the 'profane' or banal nationalism that people unselfconsciously consume as part of giving meaning to the experiences of everyday life. In seeking to explain fluctuations in the salience of national identities this chapter will identify unpredictable factors such as warfare, famines and large-scale migrations of populations in triggering movements from below for and against the nation and national state.

The Rise of the Mass Nation

For many scholars the realities of a modern world of powerful secular states, dependent for their survival within a competitive interstate system on harnessing the capacities of industrialisation, explain a shift from elite to mass nationalisms. Michael Mann rightly argues (1993) that states are crucial for modern nations because they organise their military defence, supply the necessary infrastructure (law, education and communications) of capitalism, are the site of political democracy, guarantee social welfare rights and engage in the macroeconomic planning that sustains economic and social life (Mann, 1993: 314). He is one of many who have charted the rise of the modern national state as a consequence of ideological, administrative, economic and military transformations.

First, as the secular enlightenment, undermined the cognitive claims and organisational power of religion in favour of a project of emancipation, so it authorised politics as the means of human improvement. Inevitably, political rulers had increasingly to legitimise themselves as representative of the general will, and during the nineteenth century states offered a career open to talent by extending education (previously monopolised by the clergy) to broader sections of the population. With the spread of a political consciousness through education, excluded social classes organised to demand citizenship and thereby participate in the state. The extension of citizenship in its various forms, civil, social and political, served to bind the mass of the population to the state. Andreas Wimmer (2002: ch. 3) argues that the nationalisation of the working classes is a consequence of the provision of social welfare (social citizenship) that drives them to construct boundaries against foreign workers whose migration threatens to dilute their new rights. The national state became the engine of modernity, the means by which individuals were to improve their life chances.

Secondly, the administrative reach of the state over its territory and population was intensified by revolutions in communications that enabled regular censuses and surveys, improved monitoring, taxing, policing and the provision of social welfare. The national state is, in Anthony Giddens' words, 'a bounded power container'. As the expanding state and society became ever more intermeshed so the former required the psychological bond supplied by nationalism (Giddens, 1985: 116–21).

Thirdly, the state was an important enabler of industrial capitalism through its legal protection of property, regulation of internal and international trade, supervision of the money supply and financial institutions, supportive tax structures and, later, macroeconomic policies to facilitate 'full employment'. The rise of territorial currencies in Europe, North America and Japan from the mid-nineteenth century, made possible by new industrial techniques to produce standardised currencies (notes and coins) in mass quantities, increased the capacity of states to create national collectives (Helleiner, 2003: chs 3, 5). By 1914 only a few independent countries such as China, the Ottoman Empire and some countries in the Middle East and Latin America lacked state-managed fiduciary coinages (Helleiner, 2003: 34). Nationalist imagery suffused daily economic exchange when carried on coins and notes. By becoming a common medium of communication, currencies economically integrated regionally separated populations, and differentiated them from national neighbours. Common interest rates and taxation policies came to harmonise populations into a single economic cycle, bolstering their sense of being members of a national community that shared a common fate. Where the currency was managed in accordance with popular values it reinforced a sense of identification with the state as a protector of common sovereignty, even suggesting a mystical bond between people and national state when it was managed in a stable manner (Helleiner, 2003: 11).

Finally, revolutions in armaments and military organisation entailed the rise of large, efficient and culturally homogeneous national states capable of maintaining permanent standing armies and taxing and mobilising their populations in defence of the territory. Many of these innovations, for example the rise of standing armies composed of trained infantry, had developed in the seventeenth and eighteenth centuries (Howard, 1976: ch. 4). But their impact was intensified by the patriotic *levée en masse* of the French Revolution. State expenditures exploded from the late eighteenth century. Whereas in earlier centuries they consumed about three per cent of gross national product in peace and five per cent in war, by the 1760s these figures were respectively 10 per cent and 20 per cent, and during the Napoleonic Wars they reached between 30 per cent and 40 per cent (Mann, 1993: 214–15). Posen (1995) argues that the two key institutions of the mass nation in the nineteenth century were universal military conscription and primary education. European states competing with each other required a mass army, which was now larger than before, ideologically mobilised and more lethal. They promoted education in order to create a motivated population, capable of entering as recruits, being quickly trained for battle and willing for economic sacrifice.

Many scholars date the rise of the mass nation in Western Europe to the late nineteenth and early twentieth centuries when state centralisation and industrialisation integrated populations into a common economic and political space (Connor, 1990; Hobsbawm, 1983, 1990). Charles Tilly (1995: 196–7) argues that the European states, faced with intensified military competition from their neighbours, needed to extract ever-greater resources (including their military sacrifice) from reluctant populations. This led to policies of *circumscription* (the control over contiguous and sharply defined boundaries) and *centralisation* as rulers substituted direct top-to-bottom government for the indirect rule of tribute-bearing intermediaries, allying with the bourgeoisie to promote a national solidarity and cultural homogenisation.

This interpretation has gained support from Eugene Weber's *Peasants into Frenchmen* (1976), which examines the formation of the exemplary modern nation. In this study Weber argues that even in 1870, decades after the Revolution, much of France was regional rather than national in its consciousness, speaking local patois rather than French. Nor was it economically integrated: with the partial exception of northern and northeastern France the communication system linked localities vertically to Paris, rather than horizontally to each other. A French nation formed only after the humiliating defeat by the Prussian-led German Confederation, when the Third Republic (1871–1914) instituted a national secondary education system that inculcated a patriotic historical consciousness, military conscription, networks of communications connecting the regions to the centre and a territory-wide economy. In short the rise of the nation as a mass phenomenon came late, and indeed, for much of Europe, formed during the First World War, which put the whole population onto a war footing.

All this suggests the formed nation was very different from that envisaged by early intellectual elites – one that reflected the sentiments and desires of militarised industrial and consumer societies. From the mid nineteenth century great industrial fairs such as the Crystal Palace Exhibition of 1851 became celebrations of the vitality, wealth and ingenuity of the nation. Hobsbawm (1983) observes the permeation of the expanded public space by national imagery of flags and stamps in the late nineteenth century, which occurs at the same time as the elaboration of working and middle-class cultures based on sports and other leisure pastimes. As such national states become the units of a world community, so an era of competitive sports, organised on national lines in arenas such as the Olympics, further reinforced and activated mass national sentiments.

Statist pressures from above, however, cannot explain by themselves why large sections of the population came to identify with a given state as a national state. Tilly (who puts forward an explicitly coercive interpretation) admits that such pressures produced not just state-led but state-seeking nationalisms of minorities. This highlights the neglect by these scholars of ethnicity as an active factor in the formation of mass national identities, particularly in multi-ethnic states. In Europe, the period 1870–1914 was one of intensifying nationalisms of minorities against a state homogenisation that was perceived to be driven by the interests of dominant nationalities. Even the liberal activism of the British state in Ireland, in expanding higher education, opening the Civil Service to Catholics and extending welfare (including old age pensions) gave rise to separatist as well as constitutional wings of Irish nationalism (Hutchinson, 1987: chs 5, 8).

In the field of military planning Cynthia Enloe has shown how ethnic considerations shaped the recruitment of states. State elites have been often wary of conscription because of the uncertain loyalties of their minorities, preferring to rely on professional armies. Conscription did not necessarily mould populations into a common nationality, and indeed it was viewed as a last resort by military planners, who mobilised the most costly and least reliable last and demobilised them first. Russian Imperial armies in the nineteenth century tended to be drafted from fellow Slavs in the west and only rarely from Asia (Enloe, 1980: 65). Conscription often resulted in national differentiation rather than national state unity, especially when minorities would join in the expectation that their participation in war would give them greater political rights. The toll on Bretons, whose poor peasantry was recruited in disproportionate numbers during the First World War, was a cause of nationalist resentment (Enloe, 1980: 53).

Moreover, the rise of state-territorial currencies and the bringing together of populations into a common economic space does not necessarily establish social solidarities. Exchange and interest rates, trade policies and taxes have always had an uneven impact on regional economies and where such disparities are long term and are overlaid on ethnic differences, they can excite ethnic autonomist campaigns to control their own economic destiny. Economic nationalism surfaced from the mid-nineteenth century in Ireland, and perceptions of being 'internal colonies' of the national state has fuelled post-1945 Scottish, Welsh, Breton and Basque nationalisms (Hechter, 1975).

But what of the situation in state-led nationalism of the dominant ethnie? Here again, if we examine the late nineteenth and early twentieth centuries, when we are supposed to witness the formation of the solidary mass nation, we find many states subject to intense resistance from anti-imperial, religious, regional and class interests.

The new German national state, unified from above in war in 1871, was hobbled from the start by Bismarck's attempt to use nationalism to preserve from social revolution an Imperial Prussian, aristocratic and Lutheran ascendancy in a rapidly industrialising country. Unification had been preceded by a prolonged conflict with Catholic Austria in the 1860s over leadership of the German states, won militarily by Prussia, though at the cost of excluding large numbers of German-speakers from the future *kleindeutsch* Germany. Between 1870 and 1880 Bismarck waged a cultural war with Catholic Germans opposed to Prussian Lutheran dominance, expelling the Jesuits, dissolving religious orders and driving bishops into exile. Although relations with the Papacy were restored, the Catholic minority in the southern German states felt marginalised. A Marxian Social Democratic subculture had also formed amongst the German working class, hostile to the German Reich and unchecked by the combination of government repression of socialist activities and the introduction of welfare policies (Roberts, 1967: 73, 203–7).

In France the republican-dominated Third Republic was wracked by fundamental religious, socialist, counter-revolutionary and regional challenges. The secular republican onslaught on the Church, ranging through educational policy to marriage laws, culminated in the sweeping away of Napoleon's Concordat and the separation of Church and State in 1905. During this period, the Dreyfus trial pitched republicans against Royalists, Catholics and the army. The defeated right wing regrouped round Action Française (1899), which explicitly rejected the republic in favour of an integral nationalism, based on a restored monarchy. On the left, anti-regime socialist ideologies took root among the urban working class, including the Second International, which refused to participate in bourgeois republican institutions, and a revolutionary Syndicalism, which advocated revolution through a general strike. In the late nineteenth century the nationalising drive of republican centralists fanned resistance, articulated by diverse figures such as Barrès, Maurras and Mistral, in defence of the regional languages and cultures, Catholic traditions and 'lost' autonomies of Alsace, Brittany, French Flanders, Provence and Languedoc (Gildea, 1994: 177–211).

In Britain an Anglo-British Imperial and Protestant ideal was confronted by radical political and social movements that, in alliance with Irish nationalism, resulted in near civil war. Conservative governments dominated much of the period 1870–1914, seeking to defend the Crown, traditional landed order and the Anglican Church in an urbanising and democratising society. But a rising national sentiment in Wales, Scotland and, above all, Ireland led to the disestablishment of the Anglican Church in Wales and Ireland and pressures for Home Rule in Ireland. A radicalised Liberal government, in alliance with an emerging Labour party (from 1906) and Irish nationalists, threatened the powers of the House of Lords, perceived by Conservatives as the constitutional defender of the landed interest and Anglican Church. By 1914 Britain seemed to be on the verge of constitutional breakdown.

If this suggests that the unified mass nation is something of a myth, and that there are always multiple and competing allegiances, so too is the related idea of the national state as sovereign power container, capable of circumscribing its populations, militarily able and economically autonomous. During the nineteenth century the national state in Western Europe clearly lacked sovereignty according to many benchmarks. The era of nationalism and national state formation was also one of the expansion of transnational capitalism. International trade increased ninefold between 1820 and 1880 (Woodruff, 1973: 658 n.1), and the permeability of the frontiers of European national states to the movement of goods, capital and people in the period 1870–1914 was not surpassed until after the Second World War (Milward, 1997: 11). Foreign commodity trade rose steadily between 1825 and 1910 as a percentage of gross domestic product: in Britain from about 25 per cent to 50 per cent, in France from 10 per cent to 33 per cent; and in Germany over a third of such trade was foreign by 1910 (Mann, 1993: 283). International specialisation resulted in a dramatic shrinking of agricultural sectors in many countries, a loss of self-sufficiency in food production and rural depopulation. The era of national states was accompanied by the largest period of emigration in European history of some 40 million people between 1851 and 1920, many from the most powerful states such as Britain and Germany (Woodruff, 1973: 700–1). In military affairs, too, national states could not afford to act autonomously: this was the period of accelerating power competition that forced together into alliances Britain and France and Imperial Russia, and Germany and the Habsburg and Ottoman Empires. In the cultural sphere, there were intense challenges to national authority in many countries from the Catholic Church. Bismarck, as we saw, failed in his attempts to cow the Catholic Church in Bavaria and elsewhere, and the new state of Italy was weakened by the rejection of the state's legitimacy by the Papacy because of the nationalist seizure of Papal territories.

But what of the First World War: does this not demonstrate that when the chips were down the European peoples set aside their sectional interests and rallied to the national flag and defence of the homeland? This does seem to be the case (though the war intensified tensions with national minorities). All countries, however, were bedevilled by social unrest – in Britain notably in the mining areas of the minority nations, Wales and Scotland, and increasing hardship and prospects of defeat in Germany resulted in the socialist November revolution of 1919 that overthrew the Kaiser and brought into being the democratic Weimar Republic. After the war participant states, both victors and defeated, were haunted by the fear that their social order would be swept away by an international communist revolution inspired by the Bolshevik coup in 1917. Britain fended off this threat, but not the secession of Ireland from the UK, nor indeed, in 1926, the General Strike that polarised the country. In France, although the parties united during the First World War, divisions resumed in the postwar period, intensified by the Depression. Movements for regional autonomy emerged in the regained (strongly Catholic) provinces of Alsace and Lorraine, in French Flanders, Brittany and Corsica. The economic crisis radicalised opponents of the republic on the right and left, manifested in the formation of working-class communist movements with loyalties to the Moscow-based Comintern and the cause of the international proletariat rather than the national state. In Germany the democratic Weimar Republic struggled to achieve legitimacy, perceived by the right as the product of a Jewish socialist conspiracy against Germany's national interest and by the left as a bourgeois front against the coming proletarian revolution. It was engulfed from the start by uprisings from the extremes before it was overthrown by the National Socialists.

In short it is difficult to see a movement towards the absorption of different social groups and sectors into a unitary national society during the period 1870–1939. Indeed, the rise of nationalism may have resulted in the hardening of boundaries against certain groups. Feminist scholars have claimed that nationalism was a masculinist ideology and played a crucial role in 'gendering' the emerging division in modern societies between a public and private sphere (Hunt, 1992; Landes, 1988: 2–7). During the defining period of nationalism in revolutionary France, the 'body politic' was reserved for the male attributes of rationality and control of the emotions, whereas women represented the world of the sentiment with their proper domain the nurturing of children. Republican ideology linked citizenship to a willingness to fight for the nation. Further elaborated by Michelet and Mazzini during the nineteenth century, this cult of military sacrifice in defence of the *patria* allocated to men the rights of active subjects. Women became mere objects to be defended, symbols of the purity of the nation and active only as biological producers and educators (Sluga, 1998).

It is equally difficult to identify the European national state as a sovereign actor in this later period. The economic and partial military-command integration of the Allied Powers (Britain, France and USA) in later stages of the First World War foreshadowed, W.H. McNeill (1984: 343–4) argues, transnational forms of war management that were realised in the Second World War. The interwar period, although one of national protectionism as a response to economic instabilities and the Depression, also witnessed the rise of formidable challenges to the liberal national state in the form of Nazism and Bolshevism, each of which sought to overthrow the current national state system – the former in order to construct a racial Empire, the latter to create a socialist international.

Nationalism From Below

Is then the growth of national sentiment during the nineteenth century something of an illusion? Rather the opposite, it would seem. In many countries, both with respect to dominant and minority nationalities, we find communitarian cultural nationalisms recurrently emerging at times of conflict, often provoked by state-inspired modernisation, in order to unify the nation by a return to an authentic national past.

In England a pre-romantic nationalism developed in the mid- to late eighteenth century, idealising the Lake District in poetry (e.g. Wordsworth) and painting (e.g. Turner) as mountain republics that preserved a primordial 'Celtic' life of freedom and moral independence (Darby, 2000: ch. 2). In the first half of the nineteenth century vigorous battles took place between the proponents of urban industrial progress and rural romantics, amidst a widespread mood of violence and social crisis in the countryside. The Great (International) Exhibition at Crystal Palace in 1851 was hailed as confirming England as the Workshop of the World. But the Exhibition was itself housed in a Gothic court designed by Augustus Pugin, who, like Disraeli's Young England circles and the contemporary Pre-Raphaelite movement, celebrated medieval England as the authentic England of Christian spirituality, aesthetic harmony and social order (Auerbach, 1999: 170–2). This Gothic revival looked to the village community as the link with a more stable past. Increasingly, as the North and the Midlands underwent industrialisation the real England was perceived to be in the South, particularly the 'Home Counties', site of conservative and Anglican rural values.

After the 1870s the Gothic revival was succeeded by a more broadly based vernacular movement that revived the whole heritage of England between the later middle ages to the Hanoverian period. The context was a exodus from the land because of the collapse of agricultural markets and the huge expansion of London, and the rise of urban working-class culture. In the late nineteenth and twentieth centuries an English cultural nationalism formed in defence of the 'traditional' orientations to countryside and shire, against a cosmopolitanism and materialism centred in the London megalopolis. But if part of this movement was a revulsion against a militarist drive for World Empire, all parties – imperialists, liberals and socialists – could cite the rural past as a justification of their goals. Conservatives found in the countryside the country houses that bred the officers and gentry and deferential folk who formed the core of the Empire; liberals and radicals such as C. F. Masterman and G. K. Chesterton viewed the country as representing the fount of ancient English democratic liberties that were being sacrificed in the drive for Empire; and socialists like William Morris located in late medieval English society a model for the future communitarian socialist ideal (Wiener, 1981: 59–60).

In the early nineteenth century a German cultural nationalism from below commemorated the 1813 War of Liberation, was suspicious of Prussian authoritarianism and was allied to campaigns for a united liberal-democratic German national state. Based in the towns, patriotic middle-class groups formed into gymnastic associations, choral societies and 'sharp shooting' clubs, and organised festivals round monuments to the fallen and pilgrimages to sacred places, using traditional emblems such as oak leaves (Mosse, 1975). After German unification the imperial state sought to co-opt these forces, and from 1888 Wilhelm II implemented an official cultural nationalism based on gigantic monument building (in the style of the *Hermannsdenkmal* in the Teutoberg forest) and a neo-Romanesque architectural revival. But the federal constitution left cultural policy in the hands of the states, provinces and cities, and after the fall of Bismarck, the charismatic founder of the new national state, a new wave of initiatives from below struggled to create a stronger emotional bond to the nation, and, in some cases, nationalise the Imperial state.

This could take various forms, but they each expressed a disillusionment with the official nationalism of the German state and a dissatisfaction with the borders of Germany that excluded German-speakers in Austria and the East. The *Wandervogel*, a middle-class youth movement 'returning' to rural and local communities and chivalric medieval German culture, was pacific and libertarian; not so, the nationalist pressure groups (Pan-Germans, Navy League, Colonial Society, Eastern Marches Society) that demanded German territorial expansion (Eley, 1986: 78–9). One of the culturally significant was the *Heimatschutz* whose goal was the historical preservation of homelands, nature conservation, 'life reform' and industrial design directed against the pressures of industrial and commercial development. Much of the impetus came from Protestant middle-class activists who evoked the glories of the burgher past, using Gothic and baroque vocabularies. A leading proponent, Georg Dehio, portrayed this in nationalist terms, arguing that the destruction of ancient monuments emanated from a French enlightenment hatred of history. This was a multicentred crusade that combined national and local patriotism (Koshar, 1998: 20–64).

Impending defeat and social desperation in the First World War led to the overthrow of the Imperial regime in a social revolution, but the 'unjust' Versailles Treaty led to a nationalist backlash that undermined the leftist pacific governments of the Weimar Republic. Before the First World War the chief proponents of *Heimatschutz* were upper- and middle-class professionals and industrialists, but this now broadened as a movement. War commemoration and preservationism, however, were co-opted by Nazi and extreme nationalists who tied this to the betrayal of 1918 and the return of German territories, and also to a campaign against the cultural modernism of Weimar.

If these were cultural nationalisms of a dominant nationality against the state, the Irish cultural nationalist movements of the nineteenth century – the Anglo-Irish and the Gaelic revival – expressed a revulsion not just against an interventionist British state but also against what they saw as the anglicised and oligarchic character of Irish political nationalist movements, based in Dublin. Reviving both the glories of the pagan aristocratic Celtic culture and also the Christian early medieval period, these movements by the early twentieth century had developed a constituency among young educated Catholic middle and lower-middle classes that sought a grassroots revival of Irish society based on the regions and localities. They mobilised all those excluded by the established political parties, including religious reform movements, temperance leagues, industrial associations and agricultural co-operative organisations (Hutchinson, 1987). As we saw earlier, the Gaelic revival provided much of the governing class of independent Ireland and was strongly oriented to a rural populist ethos that saw the Western *gaeltacht* as its spiritual heartland.

This suggests that the increasing activism of the state does not so much consolidate national identities as intensify historic rivalries. Such internal national conflicts often derive from perceptions that the state has historically been the possession of a particular colonising region, class or religion which has used the state to impose its values, cultural practices and extractive demands on the rest of the population. The political and economic centre of France has been the region of the Ile de France; London and the Home Counties in England, and Dublin in Ireland, have long been seen by the rest of their respective countries as appropriating the rights of the nation. Such animosities take on a new dimension in the modern world because of the enhanced power of the central state and its tendencies to continually invade social spheres in the name of modernisation, which provokes countervailing romantic conceptions of community as a site of multiple diversities. Historic differences are thus in part articulated through the competition between cultural nationalists emphasising the role of inner traditions, often historically suppressed by an 'alien' state, and promoting decentralisation or regional liberties, and political or civic nationalists, inspired often by external models which seek to modernise the society from a central site.

Nonetheless, these communitarian nationalist revivals were minority projects. What is interesting is the degree to which national symbols and genres were eagerly consumed by an educated public: increasingly they pervaded public life and were inscribed into the domestic life of the people. As a new secular urban civil society formed oriented to mass consumption, so its public building, from parliaments to railway stations, its commercial architecture and housing, its leisure activities, ranging from tourism to gardening, assumed a national character.

In England national emblems were of long standing. The greenwood and its outlaws had long been a defiant symbol of English liberties against Norman despotism, represented most famously in the legend of Robin Hood, and from Stuart times the fate of English oak forests from which the navy was built became a preoccupation of poets (Schama, 1995: ch. 3). This had broadened by the mid-eighteenth century to a middle-class cult of native landscape, particularly the Lake District, formed by guidebooks and better road communications. In part it expressed a hostility to a Gallophile aristocracy associated with foreign travels, and by the early nineteenth century proximity to the industrial Midlands had made the Lake District a popular area of tourism (Darby, 2000: 58–60, 77–88). Battles to protect this region from industry and mass tourism and to define it as a *national* park highlighted the changing status of the countryside from economic resource to place of leisure and regeneration (Darby, 2000: ch. 5). As we noted, the Gothic revival took off just as, by 1851, a majority of the English population was becoming urban. A thirst for historical pedigrees took over even in the cities. Cathedral cities portrayed themselves as refuges from the present and the industrialising cities competed to assert their ancient origins (Briggs, 1968: 380–91). Gothic styles triumphed, pervading both the public and private architecture of the Victorian era, from the rebuilt Houses of Parliament and Manchester Town Hall to shops and public houses.

During the second half of the century the recurring distress of agricultural and industrial depressions reinforced the conviction of many that the real England was in the countryside and, indeed, a 'garden' (Lowenthal, 1994: 22). The vernacular revival inspired the development of new middle-class garden suburbs from the late nineteenth century, such as Bedford Park and Hampstead, and public housing estates in the interwar period reflect a medieval nostalgia. In the fields of design William Morris's arts and crafts movement evoked a late fourteenth-century England of village communities (Wiener, 1981: 29–66). Everything from suburban gardens to domestic wallpaper was given an English vernacular character.

In Ireland the national revival of the early nineteenth century considerably expanded the stock of national symbols as the round tower, Celtic cross, Ardagh chalice and Royal Tara Brooch, Hiberno-Romanesque styles of architecture, the illustrative manuscripts of the *Book of Kells* and many sacred sites (for example the monasteries of Clonmacnois, Monasterboice and Aran) were added to the traditional symbols of shamrock, harp and wolfhound. Several of the leading Irish revivalists made their living as topographical artists, and the picturesque scenes in numerous guidebooks catered to a burgeoning tourist industry, facilitated by improvements in literacy and in communications, including sea travel, the expansion of railways to the remoter regions and, later in the century, by the introduction of the bicycle. Industries arose in the cities and the regions to provide souvenirs (including Celtic designs in jewellery and wood) for the mass tourist market (Sheehy, 1980: ch. 5).

National symbols were deployed from the 1840s by the Catholic Church and the Established (Anglican) Church of Ireland as they competed to claim the status of being the true heirs of St Patrick, the national saint. In the building expansion that followed both churches adopted Hiberno-Romanesque styles, including round towers and Celtic crosses, to evoke Ireland's golden age of Christianity. In funerary sculptures too, Celtic designs were prominent. The dominant traditions in secular public architecture remained Georgian, but round towers and Celtic crosses mushroomed in unexpected places, including the façades of public houses in the cities (Sheehy, 1980: ch. 4). Celtic design and iconography, popularised in major industrial exhibitions of the 1850s, also implanted itself in the developing domestic sphere of middle-class Ireland. New furniture establishments in Dublin, Belfast and the Irish towns, in producing artefacts for the drawing room and boudoir in native wood, particularly bog oak, employed Celtic iconography, as did makers of porcelain and glass (Sheehy, 1980: ch. 5).

In Germany, too, a national past was eagerly consumed by aspirant middle classes in the form of tourism, photography and postcards (Koshar, 1998: 20–64). Among the cherished monuments were medieval castles and churches and urban fortifications and residential structures. Local patriotisms competed: the Rhenish Association for the Preservation of Historic Sites argued for its pre-eminence as a participant in the cultural war with France not simply because of its wealth of monuments but also because of its strategic location between France and the rest of Germany. After the First World War the sense of loss generated new democratic rituals and organisations similar to those in Britain and France, and Germans saturated public buildings with crosses, plaques and insignia on church bells. Germans travelled not just to war graves, but also, in response to the extreme political instabilities, engaged in unprecedented numbers in cultural tourism to historic sites, especially in the Rhineland (Koshar, 1998: 138–41).

War supplied for all major countries a mass of romantic legends, heroes such as Nelson, the glorious sacrifice of the Light Cavalry in the Crimea, and the triumphs of Empire. By the end of the nineteenth century this created a nationalistic popular culture, and spawned patriotic youth organisations such as the Boy Scouts in Britain (Paris, 2000: ch. 1). The huge losses of the First World War and then the Second World War resulted in new ceremonies and symbols of a democratic nation – the Tomb of the Unknown Soldier, the annual ceremonies of remembrance, the creation of official war cemeteries (Winter, 1995: ch. 4). The postwar pilgrimages to battle sites and war graves, the formation of returned servicemen leagues to commemorate the dead and serve the interests of the survivors, and later, the mythisation of the war experience in literature and films embedded a sense of national identity (Mosse, 1990: chs 3, 5).

This discussion demonstrates that a national consciousness measured by the popularity of traditional myths and symbols such as Robin Hood, the English and German oak and the shamrock long predated the late nineteenth century. Although national myths and symbols may have been produced or redeveloped initially by elites and used instrumentally by states, they were appropriated and consumed during the nineteenth and twentieth centuries by new social groups. The analysis suggests that there are at least two types of nationalism at work in national identity formation. One is the 'hot' didactic and transformative nationalism, analysed in Chapter 2, that aims to instil the idea of the nation as a sacred and transcendent object of worship for which people must make sacrifices. This emerges in waves as a project that is self-conscious, systematic and prescriptive, providing exemplary forms of conduct in order to unify all the components (of class, region, religion and gender) of the purported nation. Revivalists find allies (and rivals) in political ideologues who use cultural nationalism to construct political communities, demarcated from others by multiple boundaries. The other is the informal or 'banal' nationalism of populations who 'consume' nationalism in a relatively unselfconscious manner as a guide to the conduct of everyday life as expressed in popular songs, political posters, stamps, banknotes, coinage and brand names of staple products (see Yoshino, 1999). It seems to be a continuous phenomenon in the modern period.

This raises three issues. First, is a collective national consciousness a channeller or a product of political mobilisation? Second, what are the factors that trigger these waves of nationalist mobilisation? And third, what is the relationship between 'hot' and 'banal' nationalism, and how is the emergence of a national civil society compatible with the persistence of religious, class and regional identities and with the problematic nature of national sovereignty?

Patterns of Mass Identification with the Nation

How do we explain the formation of the mass nations that we know today? Are they shaped in their formation by earlier ethnic traditions? Or is the development of an inclusive and solidary national society the product of political mobilisation?

Michael Mann has no problem explaining the rise of mass national identities when states are riven by conflicts; in fact the two are directly related (Mann, 1993: esp. chs 7, 16). The diffusion of nationalism results from two factors: the emergence of commercial capitalism and its universal social classes, and the formation of the modern state and its professional armed forces and administrators. Fiscal and military pressures resulting from geopolitical rivalry produced the politics of representation and, in turn, an identification with the territorial state. State expenditures exploded from the late eighteenth century (see above). This forced states not only to enhance their extractive capacities but also to promote the economic and social development of their territories, including education. In turn, the increasing fiscal and military demands mobilised ever-broader sections of the populations who demanded political representation as a price of taxation. States responded in various ways. In Britain, Belgium and France liberal elites pursued strategies of incorporation, by extending the vote and seeking to negotiate with reformist socialists. Older rural elites, fearful of urban mass society and the loss of religious legitimations sought to deploy a nationalism from above: Imperial Germany and the Habsburg Empire tried a semi-authoritarian route, seeking to enfold the middle classes and exclude the socialists within an only partially parliamentary government; and the Russian Empire went in an autocratic militarist direction. In spite of these differences, class struggles for representation increased their identification with the territorial state as the site in which group conflict was harmonised or decided.

This interpretation provides a powerful rationale for why citizenship entrenches a sense of identification on the part of the dominant nationality with the national state. By itself, however, it is overly political because of its focus on the constitution of the state rather than on the national community and its definition. Indeed, Mann admits that what he might be describing could be dubbed 'statism' rather than nationalism (Mann, 1993: 587). As we have noted, nationalist movements could arise either to reform a given state or to secede from it. Mann's interpretation underplays the degree to which *cohesive states could only be founded on older ethnic legitimations* and also the extent to which *class mobilisation itself was shaped by prior ethnic visions*. To explain the gradual nationalisation of the masses one has to understand the appeal of nationalism as a constructor of meaning that was able to trump without eradicating previous attachments to family, region, class, region and religion.

Underlying the rise of nationalism, we noted earlier, was a secular revolution that enabled it to decentre previously hegemonic religious ideologies and to present the nation as the necessary base of a competitive and innovative modern culture. State modernisation and economic development were undoubtedly crucial in making available secular education, a meritocratic career structure and a prosperous consumer society. But their effects were as much indirect, in helping engender a crisis of legitimation as the new educated middle and later working classes experienced entry to a society in transformation from rural to urban, from religious to secular and from oral to literate. It was in the first place aspiring educated groups who 'consumed' nationalism as a historicist and integrative vision of life that combined a notion of human progress together with a sense of rootedness enabling them to confront a world that was in profound transformation and unprecedented social conflict. This search for roots took two forms: one was an attempt to preserve links with an ancient past (castles, medieval churches, village and city squares) that was in danger of being eroded by modern development; the other was to invest with authenticity a novel public and private life by pervading it with 'ancient national symbols'.

Cultural nationalism provided a repertoire of images and styles for the proliferating and often competing institutions of a society becoming increasingly urbanised, literate and secular. Such national identities were not constructed from above but consumed from below by a civil society formed by the press, voluntary societies, religious organisations, reading societies, tourism, trade unions and political organisations. What is interesting is that such a repertoire, although finding a first constituency among the upper and educated middle classes, could be adopted across the political and class spectrum as education and aspirations spread.

Nonetheless, the capacity of these national identities to suborn other loyalties depended on whether or not they could attach themselves to a distinctive and earlier ethnocultural heritage that regulated identities of family, class and religion. The nature of these national identities varied as to whether or not it was oriented towards or against the culture and the rituals of the state. In the case of England and France there was a strong orientation to the state and its long-established ethno-historical core that for centuries were targets of aspiring individuals. Official England was based in the southern regions of London (centre of the royal court and parliament), Canterbury (site of the Church of England) and the ancient universities of Oxford and Cambridge. By the fifteenth century the London dialect became the King's English (in part because of the embryonic bureaucracy, the clerks of Chancery), and London was the site of the canonical works of national culture – Chaucer's *Canterbury Tales*, Shakespeare's plays and the King James Bible. Paris and its hinterland of cathedral cities, such as Reims, was still more important, from the thirteenth century dominating by virtue of its administration, universities, law courts and (later) royal court in defining the language and culture (Grillo, 1989: ch. 8).

These centres were challenged as a result of industrialisation and democratisation, which led the nonconformist north of England in cities like Manchester to reject culturally and politically the dominance of the effete south, home of the landowning classes and the Anglican Church. In France there were regional revolts against the dominance of Paris in the late nineteenth century in defence of local patois and customs, often supported by Catholic clergy: in 1882 the Archbishop of Cambrai, in reaction against the secularising thrust of Parisian nationalism, declared Flemish the 'language of heaven'. Charles Maurras rediscovered his Provençal roots living in 'anonymous' Paris where he learnt the Provençal language (Gildea, 1994: 179–83).

Nonetheless, London and Paris prevailed because for centuries they had been the sacred centres for aspiring individuals, and their high literary culture was the social norm. In the modern period their power increased, as they became the apex of education, the centres of mass media and the gateways to the vastly expanded career opportunities in government bureaucracies, the professions and businesses. As new classes from the provinces entered this new environment, conscious of being dislocated from traditions, they were drawn to established symbols of identity. In England the successful northern and Midlands businessmen sent their sons to the proliferating public schools in the 'Home Counties' surrounding London, train them for Oxbridge, Empire or the professions. The new world of metropolitan-dominated print culture of newspapers, novels and self-help literature of all kinds can be seen as conduct manuals. They instructed insecure individuals in national norms regulating large areas of life, including proper speech, required reading, sense of dress, the taking of holidays or leisure to national sites, national sports and the organisation of the suburban garden (see Mercer, 1992).

132

The problem faced by regionalists in France was that with a few exceptions, such as Brittany, they lacked historic centres that stood for traditions of political and cultural autonomy – the Occitanie of Mistral was united only by a negative memory of the Albigensian crusades. Long traditions of co-option by Paris of provincial leaders of an alternative civil society, and the inability to find powerful myths of origin, capable of defining a separate community with its own political mission, led to a failure of this regionalism to transform itself into a nation-threatening movement. As in the late nineteenth-century cultural nationalist reaction against London and Imperial centralisation that idealised the nation as the land, they were for the most part movements supporting a communitarian conception of nation based on local particularities to rebalance the power of the state.

To a greater extent German nationalism, reflecting a more diffuse ethnicity based on common language and cultural traditions, was expressed through loyalties to provinces and local cities. Still more, an Irish nationalism expressed itself successfully in resistance to an increasing intrusive British state in defence of a distinctive ethnoreligious community. This alliance of Catholic Church and Irish people, as we saw in Chapter 3, was forged during the English conquest and subsequent era of the Penal Laws that threatened the property rights of Catholics and excluded them from political power. The Catholic Church, representing itself as the bulwark of Irish identity, succeeded in 'colonising' the state educational system initially established to create a Catholic middle class loyal to the British Empire, and school teachers provided the cadres of later revivalist movements. The powerful nationalist movements from the 1830s onwards fed off a rapidly developing print culture of newspapers, pamphlets and popular histories that overlaid a much older oral culture laden with ethnic grievances. Although the national organisations were Dublin-based and their leadership was heavily drawn from Dublin lawyers, businessmen and journalists, theirs was a populist nationalism oriented to the preservation of a rural Ireland based in the West.

Class incorporation into the nation was also shaped by ethnicity. Hroch's famous study of stateless nations (1985) indicates that it is too mechanical to explain an identification of social classes with the territorial polity by state pressures and countervailing struggles for political representation. Rather, the political and social struggles of modernity were articulated and legitimised by reference to older idioms, in some cases local and religious but in others ethnonational. We observed how in France the struggle between the French bourgeoisie and the nobility was expressed in ethnic terms as a battle between Gauls and Franks. In England the drive for class power in the era of nationalism was formulated and legitimised through older ethnic traditions. The campaign of nonconformist middle classes for representation was justified by an Anglo-Saxonist Gallophobia against the national 'betrayal' by a Gallic Whig aristocracy when the nation was engaged in a long series of wars against France. Similarly, E. P. Thompson has shown how radical journalists such as William Cobbett activated English workers into a separate class consciousness, citing the rights of free-born Englishmen under the 'ancient constitution' to demand parliamentary reform and a purge of the corruptions of the 'great wen' of the London court and aristocracy to demand parliamentary reform (Thompson, 1968: ch. 4).

In Ireland a mass nationalism developed early in the nineteenth century when the peasantry were politically mobilised by much older ethnoreligious memories of dispossession against an English Protestant and landed Ascendancy. Although nationalist movements were led by a liberal constitutionalist middle class, this conservative peasant ethnocentrism provided the dynamism of the movement and shaped the populist character of the modern Irish state in which socialist working-class ideologies have been marginalised (Garvin, 1981: ch. 11). Where, as in Poland and many parts of Eastern Europe, the nobility differentiated themselves in ethnic terms from the peasantry (to legitimise serfdom), the development of a mass nation could prove problematic. Kristof has suggested that a gradual nationalisation occurred in Poland as a result of the downward social mobility of the disproportionately large nobility which, as it fell into impoverishment in the nineteenth century, penetrated virtually all social classes (Kristof, 1994: 225–6). Others have argued that the Polish peasantry became nationalised during the late nineteenth and early twentieth centuries when organised by their Catholic clergy against Germanising policies of (Lutheran) Prussia (Prizel, 1998: 50–4).

The problems of constructing a national identity capable of regulating class, religious and regional loyalties without an ethnic base are evident in the case of Italy, united in a national state in 1860. Although the state used the revolutionary struggle of the Risorgimento as a legitimating myth, having no ethnic core it failed to create an effective national community. In comparison, a German nation, for all its regional rivalries, could be built on a German language consciousness, Lutheran Protestantism and memories of the Holy Roman Empire.

From the fall of the Roman Empire, Italy lacked a strong centre, other than a religious institution, the Papacy; there was no common language, and the urban population identified with their warring city-states. Although during the Renaissance humanist intellectuals wrote of uniting an Italy subject to invasions by warring French kings and the Habsburgs, nothing came of this. An Italian nationalism developed in the nineteenth century, particularly in the north, but it was socially thin and riven by regional divisions. Like Germany, Italy was united from above, by Piedmont in alliance with Napoleon III's France. It was weakened by having as its capital Rome, which was also the seat of the transnational Catholic Church with which the national state collided, resulting in a State–Church schism until Mussolini's Concordat in 1929. The (Tuscan) national language was spoken by a tiny minority of the population, and there were intense regional divisions, especially between the backward south and the north. From the start the regions regarded the national state and its capital Rome almost as a foreign institution, governed by a clientelist class of notables (Hastings, 1997: 116–17; Llobera, 1994: 63–7). Italy has been torn by a strong North–South split which has continued to this day, seen recently in the project of the League of the North (based in the rich Lombardy region) to break with an Italy dominated by 'corrupt Southerners'.

Fluctuating Identities

The nation has become a surrogate religion, its iconography pervading the public and private sphere. The degree to which there are older ethnic repertoires that regulate a wide range of social behaviours affects the capacity of the nation and national state to engage with novel class, religious and regional tensions without these necessarily being a threat to its cohesion. Nonetheless, nationalism expresses a form of belonging rather than a defined philosophy of existence and it can be combined with many different ideologies. National identities co-exist sometimes harmoniously, sometimes in tension with the many other forms of identification individuals possess (familial, occupational, local, religious and other allegiances), and nationalists, I will argue, are generally selective in their choice of what must be explicitly regulated by national norms.

That said, the above analysis might suggest that the national mobilisation of groups is an evolutionary process, whereas, as we saw, nationalism as an ideological movement is episodic, triggered by a sense of crisis that the nation is in decline or under threat. Under such circumstances, nationalists seek to expand (and sometimes totalise) the sectors of life regulated by national norms as a means of redirecting all energies to the defence of the collectivity and insulating it from pollution and destruction. These resurgences are triggered by sudden threats to those primary goals identified by

Smith, namely the *autonomy, identity and territorial integrity* of the nation. The rise and subsidence cannot be charted in linear terms because such threats are unpredictable. The nation in Connor's words is a process, and a non-linear one, that is reversible (Connor, 1990).

In this section I will explore what these triggers are. I wish to examine the response of populations from below, namely how they construct national identities as a way of attributing meaning and finding direction in confronting difficult circumstances, rather than assume they are formed in groups from above. It is important therefore not to confuse an identification with the nation with that of the national state. In fact, obtaining statehood, though desirable for the reasons already specified, can erode identification with the nation. After independence the focus of the political elites on constructing state institutions, and having them recognised by the interstate order, tends to distance them from the nation as community. Many national states are multinational, and in the interests of political stability governing elites will occasionally subordinate the interests of the dominant nationality to those of the state. Even in those infrequent cases where state and ethnic boundaries entirely correspond there are recurrent tensions between nation and state. Although states are important protectors of the nation in a world of competing states, they also can be denationalising forces since, in the pursuit of economic and social efficiency, they adopt the successful strategies of their rivals, intervening to restructure social institutions and exposing their populations to international tastes and perspectives. As national identities become blurred with the interests of the state, so they lose the capacity to energise populations in the practice of their daily life in the spheres of family, occupation, and leisure activities.

In fact one might propose that economic success and stability make national ossification the norm, and that mass nationalist mobilisation depends on a sense of crisis. What then are relevant catalysts? We find a clue in the connection, observed above, between a nationalisation of emerging classes with foreign threat and a sense of betrayal by a class establishment. As I argued in Chapter 1, although states can be powerful engines of change, nations, whether or not they possess states, are regularly challenged by changing military balances, new technologies, religious movements and changes in demography and migration. In short, nations and national states are far from being autonomous and when these challenges cannot be managed, they have stimulated a mass mobilisation to nationalise the social world, especially to the extent that these crises evoke older ethnic stereotypes present in the collective memory. Although a collective national fervour fades after the crisis, the resultant collective experiences deposit new memories, agents and institutions that provide resources for the future. The effects, we shall see, are not always one way: national identities may be attenuated by these experiences or be profoundly modified as a consequence.

Warfare and military mobilisation

As we noted in Chapter 1, warfare has been one of the most potent agents of ethnic crystallisation. In the modern period (particularly in the Napoleonic era and the world wars) it has resulted in a continuous redefinition of populations with respect to each other. An ethnic nationalism has been fanned as a result of the invasion, overthrow and rise of states, the shifting of states into new geopolitical spaces, the turning of dominant groups into national minorities and vice versa, and large-scale transfers of population.

In examining modern interstate warfare, many scholars (Howard, 1976; McNeill, 1984; Mann, 1993; Tilly, 1995) have concentrated not so much on national identities as on mass integration into the national state: how state mobilisation produced pressures which led to the extension of citizenship (civil, political and social) to formerly low status groups such as the working classes, women and ethnic minorities. But the extension of citizenship by itself is not a gauge of national identities, since ethnic minorities can use it to organise against the territorial state.

I wish to examine the relationship between warfare and the perception of the nation as a community of sacrifice. George Mosse (1990) relates the rise of nationalism to the quasi-religious cult of the fallen soldier at the time of the French Revolution, as celebrated through heroic poetry, commemorative ceremonies, sacred sites, including special military burial fields, and the development of returned servicemen's leagues. This cult was linked to the idea of the soldier as 'volunteer-citizen' rather than peasant conscript and of a *willed* sacrifice for the nation (Cf. Marvin and Ingle, 1999: ch. 2). The resistance in German territories to Napoleon mythified by such (initially middle-class) cults was inspired by appeals to ethnic myths of descent from Arminius and other 'ancient' German heroes, and directed also against the existing German state structures. In turn, the experiences of warfare became the material of heroic myth, forming a continuity with older ethnic sacrifice.

Arguably, guerilla wars of liberation, rather than interstate wars, have been more community-forming. These, although usually conducted by small minorities, are dependent on grassroots support, giving them a demotic character that results in a greater penetration of nationalist sentiments – the Vietnamese liberation struggle against the French and then (sponsored by

137

the North Vietnamese state) against the USA; and the Irish war of independence against the British. Much of the nationalising effect of the French revolutionary wars came from the myths of resistance of peoples (in Spain and Russia) engaged in guerilla warfare against the French invaders. Such memories, deeply institutionalised in popular culture, are even more the possession of communities, out of reach of the state and difficult to change.

This is not to discount the profound nationalising effects of the statist wars in early nineteenth-century Europe, the Franco-Prussian war and the twentieth-century world wars. Michael Howard (1976: ch. 6) rightly argues that by the time of the Franco-Prussian war national identifications were undoubtedly heightened and extended by the scale and intensity of modern warfare. Its impact on populations was much greater since a greater proportion of the population was fighting; the rise of the mass media enabled the 'home front' to know and identify more directly with the fate of the fighting men; and the increasing importance of technology as societies became industrialised required ever more members of the collectivity to be mobilised and organised for the war effort. During the total wars of the last century the whole population became in turn targets of military planners through blockades and bombing, and states regulated every aspect of life for national purposes, conscripting labour for economic purposes, determining diet and alcohol use, and so forth.

Nonetheless the diffusion of such identities was not so much a result of conscriptive processes but from the reaction of populations themselves turning to ethnic and national identities in support of a threat to their national autonomy, and often reacting against the impotence and failure of the state. The endurance of national states depended on their being able to maintain the morale of their populations through all the deprivations. In invaded countries state conflict was accompanied (especially on the Eastern Front of the Second World War) by a guerilla war of peoples. From the early nineteenth century popular fervour was inspired by ethnic stereotypes: older images of France as the Catholic enemy of England were deployed in the wars against the Revolution and Napoleon. In turn, the legends and heroes of these wars (Nelson, Blücher and Napoleon) added to the deposit of national memories.

Whereas victory is likely to enhance the status of the national state, defeat will focus more attention on regenerating the nation. Smith (1981) has argued that great power nations, where the national identity is bound up with military glory, are more threatened by defeat, whereas small nations, particularly those who identify with an otherworldly religious mission may, on the other hand, see their sufferings as a confirmation of a higher destiny and as a stimulus for moral renewal to regain God's favour. The classic example of the former is Wilhelmine Germany, created from above by the Prussian state, victorious in war and yet identified with an Imperial Jünker elite and hence undermined by defeat in 1918. In contrast, the traumatic effect of the loss of Schleswig-Holstein on Denmark at the hands of Prussia in 1865 triggered an inner mobilisation round the slogan 'What has been lost externally will be regained internally' and a programme of land reclamation and intensive cultivation (Yahil, 1992). Likewise, the nationalisation of the French population after the defeat of 1870 was not just a product of the didactic patriotism of the Third Republic in schools and the mass army. Rather, the defeat elicited a large-scale popular response across the political spectrum to campaign for a national regeneration and the recovery of the lost provinces of Alsace and Lorraine. The old ethnic conflict between Gauls and Franks previously deployed internally was used to characterise an eternal struggle between French and Germans. A children's story, *Le Tour de la France par deux enfants*, of a 'voyage' through the land of France told through the eyes of two young boys escaping in 1871 from Lorraine, captured the national imagination and became a canonical pedagogic text, selling three million copies within ten years (Ozouf and Ozouf, 1997: 125–6).

Warfare, however, does not necessarily enhance the mass internalisation of national identities. It can produce a return to religious identities in the face of individual and collective destruction, and this can reinforce or undermine national identities. Defeat in war is threatening where national identities, lacking an ethnic past, are *perceived* to be an imposition, for example in the Middle East where in the minds of many Muslims the nation is regarded as a secular Western invention devised to divide the *umma* (religious community). Disillusion with the economic and social performance of a secular Arab elites, combined with defeat in the Six Day War and the loss of holy places to Israel, supported a radical Muslim critique of secular nationalism as a Western ideology, contrasting it with the glories of the older and authentic Islamic past (Hutchinson, 1994: ch. 3). Zionist socialist nationalism in Israel was apparently vindicated in 1967 but perceived to be increasingly corrupt and alienated from the people because of its oligarchic-bureaucratic character. When Israel only narrowly escaped military disaster in 1973, religious zealots seized on this as a divine repudiation of the secular materialism of the state, in this case taking the form of a religious settler nationalism.

Protracted warfare producing exhaustion and a threat to normal civil society has the potential of creating a popular disillusionment with national identities, reflected in the development of cynical stereotypes that express a scorn of the official ideals of sacrifices. The long French wars of the early nineteenth century produced a mythical figure, Chauvin, the typical peasant soldier, a dupe of authority and sexual opportunist (Puymège 1997), and the First World War contributed Hasek's *The Good Soldier Svejk*, a patriotic 'fool' who manipulated the system. The collapse into famine of Russia under Kerensky during a national war against Germany enabled the triumph of Bolshevik revolutionaries who won power on a programme of peace and land for the peasantry. The association between nationalism and war in the twentieth century, combined with the clear threat of *scientific* warfare to the physical and social survival of peoples, has undoubtedly resulted in a periodic weakening of identification with the national state. In much of Europe such disillusion was reflected after the First World War in anti-war and pacifist literature, memoirs and films, and after the Second World War in the rise of the European Union. The demand of many French families after 1919 for the return of the bodies of their sons from national battle sites might be regarded as an assertion of family over nation (Winter, 1995: ch. 2).

This disillusionment, however, is more directed against the governing elites of the national state than at the nation itself. As George Mosse (1990: ch. 4) has argued, even here the need of individuals to find meaning in their terrible experiences produces its own transforming myths (of the comradeship of the trenches). After the First World War the annual commemorations and the large-scale pilgrimages to the shrines to the dead, although expressing a horror of the mass death, reinforced the nation by commemorating the nobility of the sacrifice. The memory of sacrifice was carried in peacetime by permanent social institutions such as the British Legion. The experiences of common sacrifice and heroism, invoked in political oratory or the arts, have provided a repertoire of myths and images to evoke collective action in the present. The willingness to view satirical stereotypes such as *Svejk* as emblematic represents not a repudiation of the nation but an admiration for the survival instincts of the 'little man' in the face of authority.

To the extent that members of the nation claim a commitment or mission to universal civilised values, collusion in war crimes can, even more than defeat, delegitimise national identities. Since 1945 neither the Germans nor Japanese have been able to sustain a 'normal' national state and have altered their constitutions to forbid foreign military involvement. The genocide of the Nazi heritage eroded the national identities of (West) Germans and, in response, Germans have claimed a wider 'European' identity and rejected grand national narratives in favour of a concern with local and regional histories (Fulbrook, 1999: chs 6, 7). More than the Germans, the Japanese have pursued a strategy of amnesia with respect to their wartime atrocities. The brutalities of the failed Vietnam War eroded for a time national confidence in the USA and Australia and resulted in large-scale disaffection with nationalism in the young. How permanent such effects are is debatable. It might be argued that shame led merely to a displacement of national energies in postwar Germany and Japan from the political and military into the economic spheres, and being 'good Europeans' did not slow the German rush to national re-unification, in spite of arousing anxieties in their neighbours. There have been attempts in Japan and Germany to normalise their nationhood, by claiming a share in the status of victims: the Japanese as the first population subject to nuclear weapons, and the Germans because of the atrocities German minorities suffered in fleeing Eastern Europe towards the end of the Second World War. Nonetheless, the problems remain: because of the stigma attached to the war, these nations are unable to come to terms with their huge losses by officially mourning the military dead.

The aftermaths of warfare have been a factor in the (re-) nationalisation of populations. The Versailles Treaty resulted in the 'untidy' redrawing of boundaries, leaving sections of formerly dominant groups under the power of newly independent nations determined thoroughly to nationalise their state and wreak revenge for previous injustices. A dynamic triangular pattern of interaction formed in Eastern and Central Europe in which new nationalising-states with unwelcome minorities, the politicised ethnic minorities within them, and the 'homeland' states of these minorities had to redefine the nature and scope of their nationality claims (Brubaker, 1996: ch. 3). The resentments of once dominant minorities after Versailles, including Germans in new states such as Czechoslovakia and Poland, and Hungarians, one third of whom found themselves outside their national state in Romania, Czechoslovakia and the Ukraine, generated an irredentist nationalism that contributed to the outbreak of war in 1939 (Pearson, 1996; Sharp, 1996).

Economic dislocations

Waves of economic revolutions and dislocations have periodically instigated nationalist resurgences, particularly when they re-ignite older ethnic antagonisms. As Gellner argued, the feature of economic innovation is that it is uneven, emerging strongly in particular centres, and it has historically caused large-scale migrations from the countryside into the cities. In much of Eastern Europe cities were 'alien' citadels of the imperial (German) nationality who dominated business and the professions, and they were also disproportionately Jewish. Such migrations, therefore, created intense competition on ethnic lines. Budapest, which changed from being 75 per cent German to 80 per cent Magyar-speaking between 1848 and 1900, and Prague, where Czech migration had reduced the German population to 14 per cent by 1880, were centres of nationalist conflict. This was exacerbated by the growth of education and the consequent production of a mass newly qualified intelligentsia among the subordinate nationality seeking advancement (Pearson, 1983: 31–6).

In late nineteenth-century Europe international financial speculations contributed to the large-scale economic crisis in traditional national sectors and provoked a racial anti-Semitic nationalism that blamed Jews, prominent in banking and traditional ethnic scapegoats. Commodity prices collapsed as competition intensified in the emerging world agrarian market (made possible by speedier communications), and this shook the European landed order, symbolically central to national identity, and caused mass migration from the country to the cities. Reinforced by the large-scale flight of Jews from Russia and Eastern Europe into cities such as Vienna, this social dislocation fanned a racial nationalism of both the right and the left. In 1911 two-thirds of German voters in the Austrian elections voted for anti-Semitic parties (Roberts, 1967: 67).

Because industrial progress was increasingly integral to military strength, changes in economic performance could upset the power of states *vis-à-vis* each other and hence the nations they 'protected'. Prussia's deployment of railways in its crushing defeat of France in 1871, and German leadership of the 'second industrial revolution' of iron and steel seemed to presage the rise of a new hegemony in Europe. This intensified nationalist rivalries in the early twentieth century with France and also with Britain, which feared its traditional naval superiority was threatened by Tirpitz's development of a armoured battleship fleet. In Germany a mass of nationalist organisations (see above) obtaining a constituency amongst the middle and lower middle classes gave momentum to German drives for world empire and military expansion.

Economic depressions, notably the Great Depression of the 1930s, encouraged both nationalist protectionism and the spread of internationalist socialist ideologies among the working classes, for whom the world nature of the capitalist crises demonstrated the irrelevance of national solutions. More recently, national states justify themselves to their populations by citing league tables of economic performance and the strengths of their exchange rates. Crises affecting industrial performance, 'national champions', or the currency have often encouraged programmes of economic nationalism not just from governments but also from the mass media, industrialists and trade unions.

'Natural disturbances'

Unexpected natural changes – shifts in population balances, famines, diseases, ecological disturbances – largely beyond the control of states have destabilised relations between populations, heightening national tensions and conflict.

In Eastern Europe a century-long population explosion had by the late nineteenth century outstripped agricultural and industrial development, leading to unprecedented competition for land (McNeill, 1984: 310–12). Pearson argues that such increases were highest amongst less developed nations, causing the nationalist mobilisation of the more developed Poles, Magyars and Czechs to claim territory and independence before they were overhauled by their minorities (Pearson, 1983: 28). Social Darwinist doctrines combined with a heritage of medieval colonisation to justify the German drive for 'living space' in the East. Changes in birth rates relative to 'significant others' have regularly created anxieties about the future of the nation and heightened tensions between rival states (between France and Germany) and between ethnic populations within states (as between Russians and the Central Asian peoples in the former USSR).

Although emigration in huge numbers to the USA was looked upon as a safety valve, this was in part illusory. Individuals departed for the USA, in the expectation of returning, formed diaspora national communities in the New World that campaigned for the freedom of their nationality, and did in fact return in sizeable numbers (Pearson, 1983: 96–101). Famine and disease might provide another 'solution' that also, for a time, could shatter 'primordial' attachments to the homeland and lead to an inner religious retreat. To many Irish contemporaries, the Great Famine was a judgement of God, and very land seemed 'cursed', and an hysterical exodus followed to North America, Britain and the Antipodes, institutionalising large-scale emigration from the 1840s until the present. In the period immediately afterwards constitutional nationalist organisations collapsed and a powerful religious revival led by the Catholic Church followed. However, nationalists regrouped, and legends of Protestant missionaries offering soup to starving Catholics contributed to interpretations of the Famine as a genocidal British conspiracy rather than as a providential disaster, which powerfully reinforced Irish nationalism (Beckett, 1966: 344).

A racial nationalism in the European imperial states in the early twentieth century was fuelled by fears of demographic decline in the face of the superior fertility of the 'yellow races'. Demographic decline, in modern times, the result of falling birth rates that accompanies rising affluence, may appear to threaten the survival of the nation, especially if accompanied by emigration from culturally dissimilar groups. Improved communications has enhanced the impact of political persecutions in far distant countries on prosperous states. The Tsarist pogroms against the Jews from the 1880s compelled a mass flight of Jews from the Pale and provoked nationalist struggles to control immigration, in Britain leading to the Aliens Act of 1905. In postwar Europe there have been recurring xenophobic campaigns to control immigration from former European colonies.

Ideological threats

Finally, competing ideological movements arising from the heritage of the Enlightenment and religious counter-challenges, transmitted through transnational institutions such as churches, revolutionary internationals, diaspora groups and printed media have fed nationalist antagonisms. Many ethnic and national identities defined themselves as custodians of distinctive religious principles, differentiating themselves against infidel neighbours.

A popular English national Protestantism had long viewed Catholic France as the threatening other, and this interpreted the radical republicanism of the French Revolution as just another attempt to subvert national values, leading to the powerful nationalist evangelical revival focused on the Crown (Colley, 1992: 216–20). In similar fashion, British government attempts to introduce a secular education in Ireland in the 1840s were resisted by the Catholic Church and Irish nationalists as a another (Protestant) means to undermine the alliance between Church and nation. Polish Catholic clergy were to the forefront in resisting the Germanisation of the peasantry in Prussian Poland in the 1890s, which they feared would lead to secularism and socialism (Eley, 1986: 216–18). Papal 'ultramontane' rejection of secular nationalist principles, culminating in the Syllabus of Errors (1863) and the declaration of the doctrine of Infallibility (1870), sparked Protestant nationalist reactions in England and Germany and mobilised secular nationalists in France and Italy.

The Bolshevik revolution created a nationalist panic in Western and Eastern Europe, particularly among conservative middle-class groups, fearful not just of a large external enemy but also of an internal enemy in the form of an internationalist working class. Pilsudski sought to provide the new Polish state with a national mission, reviving its heritage as an *antemurale Christianitas*, this time not against Russian Orthodoxy but against godless Communism. The Russian Revolution provoked a xenophobic response in the USA, since the Bolsheviks – in claiming to represent the vanguard of history – threatened to usurp America's universal democratic mission (Pfaff, 1993: 185). The growing power of the USA after 1945, and particularly since the Cold War, has in turn provoked a culture war with France, as possessor of its own universal mission and protector of European civilisation against American cultural imperialism (Cauthen, 2004).

Outside Europe, the onslaught of Christian missions on native religions has stimulated indigenous nationalisms. The attack of British evangelical groups, protected by British authorities, on the religious foundations of Indian civilisation provoked a Hindu revivalist resistance, in the form of Vivekananda's neo-Vedantic movement and Dayananda's Arya Samaj. These movements created a Hindu public and, in advocating the protection of the Mother Cow from British and Indian butchers, incited mass participation in the public arena (van der Veer, 1999: 32–8). Arab nationalists viewed first European expansion into the Middle East, then the establishment of Israel, as a continuation of the Christian crusades against Islam, and their leaders from Nasser to Arafat have assumed the mantle of Saladin.

This brief discussion illustrates the episodic nature of the modern challenges that result in the periodic expansion and *contraction* of national identities, both in the spheres they regulate and also the social classes they penetrate. From time to time national loyalties are challenged by religious, class or familial loyalties; at other times they are reinforced by them. We can also observe that these processes or factors, though distinct, also interconnect. Indeed, they are sometimes mutually reinforcing but also sometimes may cut across each other. Krejci and Velimski (1981: ch. 5) argue that the effect of the two world wars and their peace settlements has been to dramatically increase through boundary changes, population transfers and ethnic cleansing the correspondence between ethnic and governmental boundaries in Europe. The population of ethnic nations without states or self-government decreased from 26 per cent in 1910, to seven per cent in 1930, to three per cent in 1950. But this has been partially countered by the entry into post-1945 Europe of large numbers of migrants from Turkey, North Africa and former European colonies.

The legacy of ideological nationalism

The reactions to these episodic challenges are shaped in part by older ethnic memories and images that are triggered into life. These periods of nationalist mobilisation, sometimes prolonged, in turn deposit further layers of 'experience' into collective memory.

Warfare has left a legacy of inspirational leaders and military heroes, villainous others, climatic battles and memories of collective endurance, sacred sites in the mass war graves, and institutions such as commemorative ceremonies and returned servicemen's leagues. Economic mobilisation has created myths of group discrimination by ethnic others, images of cheap foreign competition and swamping immigrants, and subcultures of conspiracy myths (notably anti-Semitic), many of which have been institutionalised in trade union and labour organisations as well as the conservative right. Demographic pressures have also reinforced group antagonisms, as have fears of national decline in emigrant nations, and famines and natural disasters have generated myths of the cruel indifference or malignity of others. Ideological struggles have sustained a sense of ethnic election on the part of custodians of religious or secular values, as well as images of enemies within, and these have been institutionalised by churches and the popular media.

All this thickens the rich texture of a national culture, providing reference points both inspiring and shameful that orient the members of the nation in their everyday life. In particular, myths of triumph and disaster in war are used metaphorically by political actors to give significance to events (e.g. an economic crisis), to sustain communities in hardship, to call for sacrifice and to justify political innovations. British politics is suffused with memories of the Second World War, in particular its isolated defiance of Nazi Germany in 1940, which gave rise to several myths: the Dunkirk spirit (the popular defiance expressed in the spontaneous rescue of stranded British troops on the coast of Dunkirk by civilian ships); the spirit of the Blitz (the temporary abandonment of class differences and sense of national community under German bombing); the Battle of Britain (the defeat of German invasion plans because of the individual heroism of pilots of the Royal Air Force). The democratic camaraderie of the Blitz was used to justify the introduction of the British welfare state after the war; the Dunkirk spirit was invoked by Harold Wilson to mobilise an economic nationalism to save the British economy in the late 1960s; and the Battle of Britain evoked a spirit of heroism that counteracted a sense of depression following Britain's precipitate decline as a world power after 1945 (M. Smith, 2000: chs 7, 8). These myths are connected to still older myths – of Henry V's triumph at Agincourt against the French in the Hundred Years War, and of the golden age of Elizabeth I confronting the Spanish Armada – to create a national continuity of glory and sacrifice.

Banal Nationalism

Does this not suggest after all the emergence of an enveloping national identity that is able to incorporate all sectors of the population? Is this not the picture of the settled national state so well described by Michael Billig (1995), in which a national identity is so deeply institutionalised in the rhetoric of politicians, the editorials and organisation of newspapers, and the marketing brands that we are scarcely aware of it at all?

Not really. As we have observed, a nationalist mobilisation may have denationalising consequences (in the case of the Germans). It may result in class stigmatism (of disloyal workers or aristocrats). Although in wartime crises nationalists may be able to mobilise the national members into rigidly bounded societies, after the crises fade, the demobilised individuals return to their multiple and competing loyalties of family, class, religion and region. Moreover, the myth of the nation as a unitary and autonomous society remains just that – a myth.

Yet for much of the time, this gap between myth and reality is not a problem. Taking the nation for granted as a category means that there is little questioning of its meaning and coherence. Individuals, when times are stable, are normatively and socially integrated by their membership of the many institutions (familial, economic, religious) of modern societies and, in general, have no need for overarching appeals to the nation (Mann, 1975: 280). There is no incongruity felt by most members of the nation in being national and in pursuing sectional interests. The use by most social groups of national symbols implies that a national identity is the ground on which other loyalties rest. As Barth (1969) argues for ethnic groups, so is the case for nations: they tend to deliberately exaggerate differences with others and minimise differences within. Hence a sense of common identity is compatible with internal differences. To have an national identity is not necessarily to regulate all sectors of life by national norms. Collective national identities are compatible with passing (i.e. in or out) migration, for identities are processual rather than a particular *state of affairs*.

This is not to maintain that nations are fluid categories of self-ascription that are maintained by marking boundaries with 'others'. What holds nations together and drives them to engage in boundary maintenance is a sense of group honour that comes from being the bearer of certain unique values. Banal nationalists will become 'hot' in defending national cultural distinctiveness, homeland integrity, economic power and political autonomy. But in most circumstances all nationalists are selective in interpreting what

147

in practice is crucial to achievement of these goals, and this will vary considerably from case to case. For example, a nation defining itself as a great power is likely to focus on defending its military and political autonomy, and a nation defining itself as a custodian of religious values in the realm of culture. Because we have observed the multiple and sometimes competing heritages of nations, the targets of nationalist mobilisation will vary over time depending on the nature of the perceived threat. With changes in the internal machinery of nations, e.g. the rise of state educational and welfare systems, new battlegrounds of national identity form.

A position stating that there are core features of nations (though they will vary in content from case to case and will change over time) is compatible with one that allows for the co-existence of other loyalties over which nations make no overarching claims. In short, ethnicities and nations vary considerably in the social niches they wish to regulate and their salience fluctuates for individuals. Banton (1994) reasons that a switch, say, from avowedly national to international class loyalties (for example, industrial action against a co-national employer in support of foreign workers) may not indicate changes in the values attributed to national affiliations, but rather a changing conception of what relationships should be governed by national norms. An adherence to the nation may not fluctuate much despite apparent changes in behaviour. Here Banton is speaking at the level of *individuals*. Switches at the level of collectivities (national states, nationalist movements) are generally regarded as less common and more significant, but as we have seen, they do occur. Such a model, deriving from the study of ethnic groups, can more readily combine an understanding of the persistence and powerful national loyalties with their varying penetration of social strata and institutions.

At the collective level national states, although focused on certain goal objectives (defence of national territory, cultural distinctiveness and political autonomy), make strategic choices about how best to achieve this. They have differed throughout the modern period in their willingness to pool sovereignty through military alliances, in their support for liberal internationalist as opposed to avowedly economic nationalist (i.e. protectionist) strategies, and in their support for regionalism. This says nothing about the potency of national identities *per se*. In practice, national states have never been the autonomous actors sometimes portrayed and have always acknowledged the limitations of their sovereignty and pursued different strategies so as to achieve their national objectives. As William Wallace (1997) has noted, national states have differed enormously in how they have articulated state–society, state–economy and state–interstate relations. Successful states, such as nineteenth-century Britain, remained a world power in part because of their skill in mustering coalitions of states against the dominant great power on the European subcontinent. Periods of 'splendid isolation' when Britain would enjoy a relative autonomy as a global power have alternated with a pooling of sovereignty in the two world wars. In the economic sphere states have employed different means to compete in transnational economic markets, depending on their relative strengths and the degree of 'openness' of the world market itself. As the pioneering industrial society Britain saw it was in its national interest to promote free trade, though it had to shift to protectionism after the First World War destroyed the 'golden age' of liberal internationalism. By contrast, 'late comer' Germany rejected liberal markets to pursue more protectionist policies that shifted into a territorial mercantilism by 1900 (Mann, 1993: 298–301).

It is when these pragmatic arrangements to secure the primary goals of the nation fail that we see the resurgence of nationalist movements to develop new strategies, harness new energies and redraw boundaries. Clearly there are two issues that must not be conflated: why national groups make strategic choices over the range of roles they wish to regulate, and why there are fluctuations in the salience of national loyalties. Differentiating between the two may be complex, but such major shifts are usually accompanied by explicit justifications and controversy.

Conclusions

I have argued that we must reject top-down and teleological explanations that perceive nation-formation as a process in which elites steadily incorporate ever-more extensive elements of a population into a mass unitary and sovereign state. There is a general tendency for the state to increasingly regulate the life of its members and to incorporate them by extending citizenship rights (though it is important to point out that in many countries there are reverses, for example after the restoration of the French Bourbon monarchy in 1815). But this is a *statist* rather than a nationalist process, though in practice (where the state is in the hands of its dominant nationality) it might be hard to distinguish between the two. Cultural nationalisms alone could not create the nation, and statist strategies, co-opting the ideals and symbols of cultural nationalists, were important diffusers of national identities through their language policies, educational systems and use of the military. But such co-options, driven by imperial, class and regional interests provoked divisions (and frequently new cultural nationalisms seeking to re-authenticate the nation as community).

As we have seen, populations could use their citizenship rights to organise nationally against the state. Where this was a cultural nationalism of the dominant nationality, it was usually an attempt to 'rebalance' community and state or to implant an alternative vision of the nation in society. Where it was the nationalism of a minority, it could threaten the territorial cohesion of the state. In any case, as the state expanded its regulatory reach – defining the language of the state, establishing an educational system, promoting social welfare, and so forth – so the number of domains in which a national contestation could occur increased.

When times were stable, there could be a blurring of state and national identities, and nationalism would lose salience as a mobilising device. An ideological nationalism was an episodic phenomenon, provoked by the incapacity of states (which were never autonomous) to protect the interests of the nation from unpredictable threat. This nationalism engaged in an intensive and extensive regulation of social boundaries. Of long-term significance was the consumption of national myths, images and symbols by an increasingly educated public, for whom they provided meaning, status and direction in the practice of everyday life. The degree to which these national identities could regulate existing or emerging identities of religion, class and family was affected by the scope of older ethnic identifications on which nationalism built. In stable circumstances, national co-existed with these other identities in an unselfconscious fashion. Rather than this being a product of ideological nationalism, such national consciousness co-existed with it, indeed could even have preceded it, since national symbols and stereotypes are to be found before the period of modern ideological movements.

My analysis suggests that there are at least two types of nationalism at work in national identity formation. One is the 'hot' didactic and transformative nationalism that aims to instil the idea of the nation as a sacred and transcendent object of worship for which people must make sacrifices. This is a recurring phenomenon that is self-conscious, systematic and prescriptive, providing exemplary forms of conduct in order to unify all the components (of class, region, religion and gender) of the purported nation. Revivalists find allies (and rivals) in political ideologues who use cultural nationalism to construct political communities, demarcated from others by multiple boundaries. The other type is the informal or 'banal' nationalism of populations who 'consume' nationalism in a relatively unselfconscious manner in decorating their homes, constructing their gardens and expressing their allegiances in international sporting contests (see Yoshino, 1999).

150

As we saw, institutions such as churches, local governments and businesses also use national styles and symbols to define themselves and to present themselves to their target groups.

Scholars have tended to dichotomise these two modes as elite and mass, creative and passive, and there is a tendency to view them in linear terms: the first belonging to the early and heroic nation-building stage, the second to the everyday existence of settled national states (Billig, 1995). In fact, they operate together in an interactive relationship to form the identities of the mass nation.

As we saw in Chapter 2, revivalists were inspired to 'recreate' the nation as a unique culture, by discovering the distinctive habits and experiences of 'the people'. From this they constructed 'idealised types' by which to regenerate and unify their contemporary societies. Populations drew on these cultural repertoires in an eclectic manner in order to feel distinctive and rooted while coping with a changing world. But this is not to suggest a transmission belt account of identity-formation or, alternatively, the relationship between the two nationalisms as one between production and consumption, in which the sacred objects identified by the elite are trivialised.

It is true that there is a tension between the two, as the heroic archetypes of the revivalists are transformed into stereotypical commodities to feed the tastes of mass consumers. For the latter, having a national identity added meaning to their everyday life, but if they drew on the symbols furnished by revivalists, they normally looked askance at ideologues who demanded sacrifice in the name of the nation. Commodification, however, does not of itself imply a lack of feeling: if popular use of iconic images, artistic styles, legends and heroes was imitative and even comic, this does not necessarily mean that the identifications were not deeply felt. They created a repertoire through which the world was imagined and experienced as national.

The problem, one could argue, lay with the revivalist project itself: the ideal of 'authenticating' all social life was in itself impossible – a golden past by its very nature cannot easily supply models for a radically new secular urbanising nation. Herderian nationalists acknowledged this by arguing that national cultures must be continually renovated by a borrowing from other cultures: a certain eclecticism, even incoherence, is therefore built into nationalism. A culture of everyday life, although informed by revivalist images, had to be constructed on the ground, and Mosse (1990) shows in his study of mass warfare how ordinary individuals themselves engage in myth construction in order to overcome the fear of meaningless and death generated by unendurable experiences. The means of this myth construction – ribald songs, diary entries and letters, and later vehicles such as comic postcards, press cartoons and commercial films – may be banal, but the trivialisation of war experiences, he suggested, was a way of reducing over-whelming suffering. Such popular mythication of moments of heroism and solidarity could also provide the legendary base by which a high national culture can be renewed in, say, the novels of a Tolstoy or the films of a John Ford.

The distinction then is not between high and low, and elite and mass, but rather nation-creating and nation-reinforcing processes. Nation-recreation occurs when the community appears in need of salvation, facing crises such as defeat in war, internal social conflict, falling birth rates and the rise of immigration. This might be called a hot nationalism, and although it is initiated by elites, also may have a mass character. Such movements often invoked the sacred, and inbuilt into the idea of the sacred is the idea of separation from but also the reformation of the profane world. The positive pole of hot nationalism is the idea of regeneration, returning to some authentic touchstone – a golden age of exemplary cultural achievement by which self and society would be transformed. The negative pole is the idea of purification of the present, casting out the corrupting forces, such as Franglais (or equivalents), alien religious ideas and immigrants. Community-formation entails that both positive and negative rites operate to energise and form the boundaries of the group and so prevent its dissolution. Whether the positive or negative will predominate will vary, with the positive being emphasised if the problem is perceived to derive from an internal moral crisis, and the negative if the danger comes from outside.

In contrast, for banal nationalists the nation is a taken-for-granted entity that, when consumed, gives meaning to the practice of everyday experi-ences. This is not just by injecting symbols eclectically into the profane world. It is recreated by the assumptions that underlie the organisation of information and the analysis of social problems. Kosaku Yoshino explores the role of cultural intermediaries such as business people in contemporary Japan who assume the existence of unique national types in training their employees how to negotiate with 'Westerners' (Yoshino, 1999); Michael Billig (1995) the unexamined assumptions of politicians and newspapers when using shared metaphors and idioms with which to persuade their audience. This mention of cultural intermediaries highlights the need to go beyond elite–mass dichotomies.

Hot nationalism seeks to nationally transfigure the entire social world, but a national life cannot be long lived to the exclusion of other loyalties and needs, whether these are familial, class or religious. There must be a return to the everyday plurality of existence in which national identities return to a background role. To sustain themselves from the attrition of the banal, even routinised nations have their scheduled moments of transcendence, commemorative ceremonies such as Remembrance Day to recall past sacrifices and bind the living to the dead. The capacity of such events to move and define collective identity is demonstrated by the struggle of excluded groups to be recognised and included in their ceremonies. When such struggles intensify, they often prefigure a new wave of hot nationalism.

5

Nationalism and the Conflict of Civilisations

Introduction

In this chapter I wish to address the future of nations, applying the *longue durée* perspective developed so far. I have argued that nationalism has become the surrogate religion of modernity that sustains its members against unpredictable change by attaching them to a historically embedded unit, with a special cultural destiny, that is capable of continuous innovation. In the modern period the nation has become the hegemonic cultural and political unit, and the national state remains the major institution (via its membership of international organisations) through which the great planetary problems are addressed. In recent decades, however, the apparent global diffusion of the national model has been accompanied by debates about its future. In particular, many scholars question the survival both of nations and sovereign national states in the face of globalisation, regionalisation (the rise of entities such as the EU), and the current religious resurgence.

This chapter will examine these debates, which are closely related. Three arguments will be considered: first, globalisation is leading to the supersession of nations as relevant political actors; second, nations are being subsumed into larger regional units; and third, rapidly gaining an audience since the recent terrorist attacks on the USA, the major battleground in the world is not between nations and their states but between civilisations, in particular religious civilisations. What I wish to do in this chapter is to expose the lack of a long-range historical perspective displayed by many social scientists (including historians) who assert the declining salience of nations.

Many social scientists suffer from a tendency to (in John Breuilly's words) 'eternalise the present' (Breuilly, 2000). Social scientists cannot pretend to offer authoritative answers to any of these debates. Karl Popper has rightly argued that since the action of human beings is shaped by their knowledge of the world, a successful long-range historical prediction would require us to know now what people will know in the future and the conditions they will encounter (Popper, 1960). Forecasting, then, in any strict sense is impossible. All we can do is examine if there are indications to be drawn from present or past experience that the nation is being superseded by other forms of collective identification. A longer historical perspective indicates a much more dynamic vision of nation-formation than is current, that recognises that ethnies and nations have inaugurated globalisation processes and been formed and reformed in a response to them. It will show that ethnic and national agents (in Europe) have historically defined and been defined by 'Europe', and that judged by past experience the current religious resurgence is as likely to contribute to nation-formation as to undermine it.

In short, it is a mistake to exaggerate the uniqueness of the nation to the modern world and the potency of nations and national states within modernity. Prophecies about the fading of nations are predicated on a mythic contrast: between a past of sovereign and unitary national states and a present of unprecedented global interdependence, since the authority of nations (and national states) has always been qualified domestically and externally. We require a much more calibrated discussion that charts the changing characteristics of ethnic communities and nations over historical periods and their fluctuating strength *vis-à-vis* other collective attachments. At present there is no diminution in the drive of nations to establish sovereignty over those areas conceived to be of vital interest, despite the growth of regional institutions. Although it is likely that nations and national states will change, predictions about their demise are unlikely to be fulfilled.

Nations, as entities based on conceptions of popular sovereignty and commitments to common citizenship rights, the possession of a distinctive high public culture and a consolidated territory, are generally post-eighteenth-century formations. But they are also communities of sentiment that in large part rest on ethnic cultures that predate the modern period. These provide the nation with a collective name, myths of unique origin, a sense of belonging to a homeland, of shared history and culture and common political fate. It is the sense of belonging to an ancient, 'timeless' community that gives the ideology of nationalism such potency in a modern world where science has eroded religious sacralisations. Nationalism is able to bind individuals into a society through which they can overcome contingency and death: they achieve immortality by adding their story to that of an eternal unit (Smith, 1999: 88).

Globalisation and Nationalism

In 1919 John Maynard Keynes recalled the liberal Europe before the First World War:

> What an extraordinary episode in the economic progress of man that age was which came to an end in August 1914! The inhabitant of London could order by telephone, sipping his morning tea in bed, the various products of the whole earth, in such quantity as he might see fit, and reasonably expect their delivery early upon his doorstep; he could at the same moment and by the same means adventure his wealth in the natural resources and new enterprises of any quarter of the world ... he could secure forthwith, if he wished it, cheap and comfortable means of transit to any country or climate without passport or other formality ... But, most important of all, he regarded this state of affairs as normal, certain, and permanent, except in the direction of further improvement. (Keynes, 1920: 9–10)

What is interesting in this passage is Keynes' nostalgic presentation of this cosmopolitan free trading civilisation as a golden *past*, destroyed by war and fanatical ideologies (nationalism and Bolshevism).

This should make us cautious about the claims of scholars (for example, Albrow, 1996; Castells, 1996; Giddens, 1990) who argue that we have recently entered a new period of world history, a shift from modernity to postmodernity, engendered by globalisation. 'Globalisation' is defined here as an intensification of interconnectedness between the populations of the world that might be economic, political, cultural, military or natural (including biological and ecological processes). As Montserrat Guibernau (2001) outlines, theorists of globalisation argue that contemporary advances in technology and communications have intensified the contacts between the world's populations to such an extent that time and space have been compressed to form human populations into one world, transforming our sense of the 'local'. When does globalisation begin? Some prefer 1950, others the early 1970s (Hopkins, 2002: 34), but the list of characteristics of an emerging globalism is much the same:

1. A global liberal economy, regulated by bodies such as WTO, the IMF and the World Bank, marked by the following: free trade; a dominant post-industrial service sector; the power of transnational corporations; a large proportion of world trade devoted to exports; the growth in size and velocity of world capital markets; global cities.
2. World political and legal organisations such as the UN, the International Court at the Hague; and regional associations of states such as the EU and NAFTA.

3. A global civil society of transnational non-governmental agencies, advancing solutions to human rights abuses, civil conflict and poverty.
4. A world language (English) and transnational media organisations promoting a universal popular culture.
5. The growth of diaspora communities and their salience as important economic and ideological actors.
6. A widening range of planetary problems, including nuclear prolife-ration, terrorism, long-distance economic migrations and refugee flows and climate change.

Many argue that the nation and national state, those central institutions of modernity, are ceasing to be our primary political and cultural reference points because of these new horizons, organisations and problems that cut across their territorial boundaries.

There are various versions of this thesis, but they all presume the exis-tence during the nineteenth and early twentieth centuries of a 'classical' nation state, which was politically sovereign, militarily autonomous, territo-rially bounded, culturally homogeneous and economically integrated. A radi-cal version, heavily economic in its assumptions, predicts the erosion of such national states by institutions of global and regional governance as they become increasingly powerless to regulate the new borderless world of economic transactions (Ohmae, 1996; Wriston, 1992). A more qualified version argues for a transformation, not a destruction, of the classical national state (Giddens, 1990; Held et al., 1999). According to this, the autonomy of the national state is qualified by the growth of transnational institutions that has resulted in a pooling or loss of sovereignty. The identity of nations has also been recast. The unlikelihood of large-scale war between great powers leads to 'internal' others such as immigrants and refugees substituting for 'exter-nal' enemies for purposes of collective differentiation; the greater visibility of immigrants and national minorities means that homogeneous national cultures are being pluralised and hybridised; and the rise of English as the world language, carried by transnational media channels, encourages a global consciousness and culture at elite and popular levels. There are countervail-ing tendencies that are strengthening nations and national states, but the overall effect is weakened national states having to come to terms with mul-ticulturalism (on all this, see Guibernau, 2001).

My chief target will be the radical thesis, for transformationalists recog-nise the long duration of globalisation, its different forms and its incoherent character (Held et al., 1999). I argue, however, that the general focus on the prospective crisis of the national state set in train by emerging global forces is misdirected. Globalisation long preceded the era of nation-formation, and nations have always allied or competed with regional or global networks. We should instead be examining the effects of globalisation on the *origins* of nations. Doing so gives us a very different view of the future of nations and national states. Although globalisation historically has blurred or destroyed ethnicities, it has also resulted in the crystallisation of those ethnic solidarities that have been a prerequisite for modern nation-formation. Nationalism is one manifestation of modern globalisation, and having a nationality and, better still, a national state is essential for participating in the contemporary world. We may therefore predict that the intensification of globalisation will not bring the era of nations to an end. It will result in new struggles for nation-formation.

Adopting a *longue durée* framework for examining the relationships between nation and globalisation will revise our understanding of the crisis of the national state. It will highlight the interactive dynamic, in which ethnic groups and nations have been sponsors of global processes, and globalisation has been a catalyst in ethnogenesis. Until recently our understanding of globalisation has been flawed in three respects. Scholars have associated it with Western modernity or postmodernity (post-1945), they have privileged technological and economic processes, and they assume globalisation is unitary and coherent.

World history, national states and the global

In his magisterial study, *The Rise of the West*, W. H. McNeill (1963) argued that a global society formed in the twentieth century out of the world dominance of the West (first in the guise of European national states, then the USA). The origins of globalism lay in fifteenth-century Europe when militaristic national states, forming out of a competitive subcontinental state system, expanded overseas. This was given impetus by revolutions in science and communications until, by the twentieth century, Europe had overthrown all other civilisations. The revolutionary disruptions engendered by the scientific ideas could be seen as either a threat to all older religiously-based civilisations, including the West, or as a continuation of the West's revolutionary potential. What was undeniable was the emergence for the first time of a single cosmopolitan humanity, one that would make politically obsolete the European national states themselves. In McNeill's treatment national states precede and indirectly engender globalisation only to be superseded by it, and globalisation is defined as Western in origin and secular in character (McNeill, 1963: chs 11–13).

McNeill's account is richly illuminating and it contains many of the assumptions of many current globalisation theorists (though they would attribute a later date to the origins): namely that contemporary globalisation is unprecedented; it is defined by science and technology; and it is Western. Each of these assumptions can be criticised. Globalisation should not be seen as a modern revolutionary development but as a recurring and evolutionary process. It is not a unitary and secular process, but takes multiple and contradictory forms. Moreover, it is always transformed in the way it is received, resulting as much in differentiation as homogenisation. By exploring the implications of these criticisms one can hope to throw a different light on the relationship between globalisation and nations.

First, world historians now set back the beginnings of global processes, before the eighteenth-century revolutions, or even the sixteenth century, to very early periods in human history. Janet Abu-Lughod (1989) has criticised not only McNeill but also the world systems interpretation of Immanuel Wallerstein (1974), that argued that modernity began in the sixteenth century with the rise of the Western world economic system. She argues that this system built on earlier world networks, emerging in 1250 and coming to a peak in 1400, that were organised round three to four overlapping core regions and eight overlapping trade circuits, stretching from Western Europe to the Far East and having its centre in China. McNeill, himself, influenced by such criticisms, revised his earlier views to admit precursors of the Western world system on which the latter formed. The first developed in the Middle East from the second millennium BC until its decay by AD 200. A second, again centred on the Middle East, accompanied the rise of Islam from AD 600–1000. Between 1000 and 1500 China, borrowing from the Middle East became the centre of gravity of a third world economic network, stretching through the Middle East to Western Europe (McNeill, 1990). Moving beyond economic definitions of a world system, Richard Eaton (1990: 17) argues that Islam can be regarded as history's first global civilisation (although one omitting the New World): over one thousand years from the seventh to the seventeenth centuries, Islam brought together for the first time all the major civilisations of the Old World – Greco-Roman, Irano-Semitic, Sanskritic, Malay-Javanese and Chinese – within an overarching civilisation.

Secondly, globalisation cannot be defined as a unitary and secular process. C.A.M. Adshead, in dating the origins of world history to the Mongolian 'explosion' of the thirteenth century in Central Asia, argues that the contemporary world system was built on successive layers of interlocking networks: information, microbial and military circuits, religious internationals, the republic of letters, the global armoury, the world commodity market, the world technological bank, and a common consciousness expressed through the use of English (Adshead, 1993: 3–4). Whether or not one can so easily identify a chronological overlaying of different circuits in this way, the relevant point is that globalisation includes, as well as secular sciences, technologies and ideologies, processes such as missionary religious expansion, imperial conquest and colonisation, migrations and long-distance trade that often cut across each other (one of the outstanding students of these phenomena has been McNeill himself!) Michael Mann (1986), we have already noted, has analysed patterns of world history through the interaction of four overlapping and competing networks of power – the economic, the political, the ideological and the military – each of which has its own technologies and boundaries.

Thirdly, Marshall Hodgson (1993) has argued that globalisation cannot be equated with 'Western' characteristics. In Hodgson's interregional model, world history is the story of the interactions of four major culture zones over a period of 2,800 years, each of which emerged for a time as the leading edge before its innovations were (over a period of 500 years) assimilated by the other zones. This interaction was both peaceful (trade and the diffusion of ideas) and violent (warfare and imperial conquest). One of the implications is that the rise of the 'West' (a marginal actor until the sixteenth century) is not unprecedented or final. It is only the latest of a series of recurring 'jumps' in global social power, to use the term of Mann (1986: 31), which is at present being absorbed world wide. A second point is that globalisation is not unitary but differentiated. Even if we view the USA and European states as a single 'Western' civilisation, the hegemony of the West has not obliterated other civilisations, and, indeed, has at times enabled their expansion. Islam spread during the nineteenth century in Africa, often under the protection of Christian Empires. Free trade and imperial security allowed the growth of a Chinese trading diaspora in South East Asia and the expansion of an Indian diaspora into new areas such as East and South Africa (Hopkins, 2002: 32–3). In the 1980s it appeared that Japan as the second biggest industrial economy had developed an alternative mode of development to the (American-dominated) 'West', leading some to speak of its impact on Asian societies as a form of 'Easternisation'.

This should make us reconsider the causal relationship between globalisation, ethnic formations and nations in three ways. If globalisation has been in process for a millennium or more, then claims that it will result in the supersession of nations become problematic. It is possible that ethnic- and nation-formation accompany and, perhaps, are active agents of globalisation.

161

Secondly, although missionary religions, long distance trade and so forth threaten to erode ethnic and national identities, they always come laden with the assumptions of an originating region and are transformed into the specificities of the 'receiving' culture as it seeks to compete with its challengers. In McNeill's 'contact model', world history is marked by a shift from isolated individuals to increasing social interdependence, and through this an enhancement of human power over nature. Such contacts have engendered conflict as well as harmony (Costello, 1993: 197–9), and as we saw in Chapter 1, they have been catalysts of ethnic crystallisations that have often provided the basis of the modern nation. Thirdly, because there are multiple agents and processes of interconnectedness, there is an inherent unevenness and unpredictability in world history. The *intensification* of globalisation in the modern world, together with its multicentred character, is perhaps the key factor in the rise of nationalism, a revolutionary and activist form of ethnicity that promotes an ideology of progress on the basis of a selective appropriation of other cultures to favour the distinctive traditions of the historical community.

This lends to three claims:

1. Ethnic and national societies accompany and, indeed, have been agents of global processes, continually evolving in their forms.
2. Global processes in combination with continental and regional networks are often central for the crystallisation of ethnic communities.
3. The multiple cross-cutting character of global processes (economic, military, religious, political, ecological) although producing unpredictability also permits agency to ethnic and national actors.

Ethnic agents of globalisation

Ethnic groups have been active in the formation of long distance networks from early recorded history, as creators of 'world empires', inventors and diffusers of world religions and enablers of world trade.

As C. A. Bayly (2002) argues, tribal warrior leaders (Alexander the Great, Attila, Genghis Khan, Tamerlane), inspired by ideas of cosmic kingship, have had an enormous political impact, bringing together novel combinations of men and weaponry to overthrow established empires, and creating new or unifying established trade routes. Alexander's wars were underpinned by a Hellenising mission that had the ultimate objective of a transethnic 'world' empire fusing Greek and Persian elites. Although these visions dissolved with his death, he constructed a web of political, military and economic relationships, sustained by his creation of numerous Greek cities, that extended from the central Mediterranean to northern India, from the fourth century BC to 146 BC. A Greek-Oriental syncretism formed, in which the Greek *koine* became the *lingua franca* of the Middle East (McNeill, 1963: 304–15). Among those inspired by Alexander's dream of universal empire was Genghis Khan, the leader of the greatest of many waves of Central Asian steppe invaders of the wealthy agrarian civilisations of Asia and Europe. The Mongol Empire, extending at its height from the Black Sea to China in the mid-thirteenth century, came closest to uniting the Eurasian continent. It unified the crucial land-based routes of inter-regional trade and created an information circuit linking Asia and Europe (Adshead, 1993: ch. 3). Osmanli or Turkish steppe warriors from Anatolia founded the Ottoman Empire, which resulted in the expansion of Islam into South Eastern Europe.

Ethnic peoples were founders and diffusers of world religions. From Greek-speaking Jews sprang Christianity that rapidly advanced within the mercantile cities of the Roman Empire. Islam was spread by an alliance of Bedouin tribesmen and Arab merchants, who defeated Byzantine and Persian armies in a series of conquests that by AD 750 reached into North Africa, Spain and China. With Arabic as its sacred language, Islam united hitherto distinct religious and language communities in a global civilisation of urban networks linking India, China, the Middle East and Mediterranean Europe. As a creative hub, it received, absorbed and transmitted to its counterparts cultures and technology, such as paper making, agricultural products, medicine, astronomy and mathematics (Eaton, 1990). We can note, too, the role of Germanic Catholic military orders in Eastern Europe in the forced evangelism of that region.

These remarks also highlight the ethnic contribution, sometimes indirect, to the development of long distance trade. A central role was played (see Chapter 1) by ethnic minorities and ethnic diaspora: Armenians, Jews, Greeks, Chinese, Muslim Kashmiris and Hindu Khattri acted as bankers, merchants, sea-borne traders and translators before the rise of imperial national states (Bayly, 2002: 60–2).

From the early sixteenth century incipiently national states played an increasingly important part in global processes. The completion of the Spanish reconquest of 1492 and the expulsion of the Muslims and Jews was followed by the remarkable seizure of South America and the Catholic conversion of its peoples. The rivalry of the European national states spurred the quest by the Spanish, Dutch, Portuguese, English and French to explore, trade with and conquer the non-European world. By the nineteenth century Britain was becoming the pre-eminent global economic and political actor.

It was the foremost proponent of a free trading world economy, the centre of the world financial markets, the main carrier through its merchant navy of world trade, and its empire sponsored the Protestant Christian missions to Africa and Asia. The global institutions of capitalism, democracy, liberalism and Christianity were carried in the late nineteenth century from Europe to the rest of the world by imperial states who gave them a national inflection, just as their messianic successor, the USA, does today.

Globalisation and ethnic crystallisation

Ethnic identities, however, might well be eroded or blurred by the very processes they advanced. The transformation of the Mongol tribal confederations into empires led to the assimilation of the warrior elite into the more sophisticated urban civilisations, and to their conversion from shamanism to the religions of their subjects. As non-Arab populations converted and Islam was universalised, so Arabs ceased to be the primary bearers of the religion, to the extent that an Arab nationalism today co-exists in tension with Pan-Islamic sentiments.

Nonetheless, we observed earlier how missionary religions, imperial expansions, long distance trade and migrations have in turn been catalysts of ethnic crystallisations.

Christian evangelism, inspired by the biblical recognition of linguistic diversity, effected the translation of the scriptures into local languages and the proliferation of written vernaculars (Hastings, 1997: ch. 1). In presenting Israel as the exemplary political community of unified kingdom, sacred territory and holy people bound by their distinctive scriptural culture, the Old Testament diffused the model of the nation, first in (Western), Europe then, as Christianity expanded with European imperialism, world wide. All the great religions 'fell' into schism and internal differentiation, which were used to transform ethnic categories into rival ethnic communities. Religions were employed by rulers to construct culturally cohesive populations, differentiated from neighbouring groups, and, above all, they became vehicles of a sacred group identity when populations found themselves on the fault lines between different religious civilisations.

The rooting of Shi'ite Islam in Iran was accompanied by a rejection of Arab dominance and a Persian ethnocultural revival, given intensity by the wars of the Sunni Ottoman Empire against the Safavid Empire of Persia. The conflict between Islam and Christianity over 1,000 years saw several polities claim the status of border guard: on the Christian side, Byzantium, Castilian Spain and Tsarist Russia, and on the Muslim, Mameluke Egypt.

The *antemurale* myth also re-emerged from wars between Catholic and Orthodox and between Catholic and Protestant states. All of these identifications have strongly shaped the trajectories of the modern nations.

Imperial expansions, although normally a threat to ethnic consciousness, could also provoke ethnic revivals. A powerful ethnicity was forged in Armenian and Jewish populations, caught on exposed trade and communication routes between rival Roman and Persian empires, and who suffered collective subjugation and 'exile' (Armstrong, 1981: ch. 7). Empires can consolidate ethnic communities through systems of indirect rule that reinforce indigenous leaderships, as under the Ottoman *millet* system (Hechter, 2000: chs 2, 3). Memories of imperial greatness, in being transferred during democratisation from dynasty to the dominant nationality, contributed to a sense of national honour as a world actor on the part of the French, Spanish, Russian and British.

The development of long distance trade also excited the ambitions of groups to control it and brought far distant cultures into contact and often conflict. We have already noted steppe invasions of the wealthy agrarian civilisations of Asia and Europe that followed the land-based silk and spice routes, and how the Mongol drive for world empire in the thirteenth century has been explained by historians as motivated in part by a desire to seize control of the silk route. The memory of the 'Mongol/Tatar yoke' had a deep impact on Muscovite Russia and Magyar Hungary. The Mongol unification of the silk route created an information circuit linking Asia and Europe and a literature of travellers' accounts that inspired Western states to seek out a seaward route to the riches of the East (Adshead, 1993: ch. 3). Out of this came the European 'discovery' of America, large-scale colonisations that led to new ethnic crystallisations, and wars between the European great powers in their struggle for overseas wealth and empire.

A drive for world empire and for commercial advantages inevitably generated interstate warfare that has intensified ethnic differences. There are distinctions to be made between the effects of limited wars based on mercenaries, small aristocratic strata, professional armies, and large-scale mass warfare. But recurring and protracted interstate wars, even between feudal states such as the Hundred Years War between the French and English kingdoms, has resulted in a social penetration of ethnic sentiments. This was intensified during the modern period. Even when wars result in the overthrow of a state, an ethnic consciousness may persist, especially where groups define themselves in religious terms, interpreting their defeat, like the Serbs at the Battle of Kosovo, as a test of their commitment to the true religion. A religious sense of election thus explains away defeat, and indeed instils a reinforced drive to defend collective traditions as a means of eventually regaining divine favour.

In short, globalisation when conceived in the *longue durée* has gone hand-in-hand with an ethnic differentiation of populations. To adopt such a stance is to accept a *non essentialist* concept of ethnicity: to acknowledge that ethnic formations even when strongly institutionalised are subject to recurring external challenges of different kinds, which may result in internally generated innovation, imposed syncretisation through conquest, or possibly dissolution through voluntary or coerced assimilation and ethnocidal programmes. The multiple and disaggregated nature of these challenges entails that ethnic formations may often contain a repertoire of many different pasts and cultural heritages, and hence models of individual and collective identity to which they can turn in order to negotiate change. Ireland had such heritages as the pagan era of aristocratic warriors, encoded in epic poetry (derived from Celtic settlement); the '*insula sacra*' of St Patrick and Irish saints from the incursion of Christianity; the heritage of parliamentary autonomy resulting from Anglo-Norman settlement; and the legends of the martyred people from the English conquest and later Famine. The Anglo-British nation draws on multiple heritages as the land of Anglo-Saxon liberties; as the elect Protestant people during Elizabethan times; as an Imperial world power; and later as the global exemplar of liberal economic and political freedoms. Russians claim to be the upholders of Orthodoxy against the Latin West; the defenders of Europe against the Asiatic peoples of the steppes; and the creators of an Imperial Eurasian civilisation.

National differentiation and modernisation

It is arguable, however, that the scientific-technological revolutions create novel forms of globalisation (the modern bureaucratic states, the industrial capitalism, military machines and cosmopolitan ideologies) that erode former ethnic identities. In part I agree: I reasoned in Chapter 2 that nationalism was a novel revolutionary form of ethnicity that preaches a continuous innovation through selective borrowing in order to overcome the unprecedented challenges of the modern world. Nationalists' level of success depends on several factors.

Globalisation itself in its modern forms remained multiple and contradictory in its effects. It was not uniform but developed within a multi-actor system of competing European national states (e.g. Britain and France) that suggested the possibility of different paths to development. There was no single acting 'West' but rather rival (imperial and national) centres of power, and European imperialism could not obliterate the non-European cultures and civilisations over which they ruled. Indeed the several forms of interconnectedness (political, economic, cultural) they provided offered opportunities to indigenous actors. We have noted the growth of Islam in Africa and of a Chinese trading diaspora in South East Asia under imperial auspices (Hopkins, 2002: 32–3). Moreover, the effects of Christian missions, protected by European states, were unpredictable. In India they stirred a Hindu revivalism that gave momentum to a secular Indian nationalism, and here, as in much of Africa and Asia, they also inspired an ethnic and national consciousness by constructing written native vernaculars through which the scriptures could be presented. The fruits of one form of globalisation (religious) could be used by nationalists to fend off another (political imperialism).

If globalisation processes offered opportunities as well as dangers for nationalists, their capacity to exploit them was itself affected by their ability to appeal to (or appropriate) 'memories' of high civilisational achievement. By mobilising these, they could reject received practices, justify innovation and be inspired to stick with these innovations in spite of conservative resistance. This was an ideology ideally suited to an increasingly interactive world where unpredictable inventions had impacts that were rapid and disconcerting. Most nationalists came to the conclusion that to secure their goals – the preservation of the identity, territorial integrity and autonomy of the historical community – they required a state. But such states themselves were faced with recurring crises that generated national mobilisations of the population for or against existing regimes. The possession of multiple heritages, we saw in Chapter 3, provided a varied repertoire to which groups might appeal, should the prevailing model fail. At different times, English nationalists (sometimes the same figures) have appealed to a defensive myth of uniqueness (of Anglo-Saxon liberties), an exclusive but more aggressive sense of British world prestige (the Imperial heritage), and a more open liberal ideal as a global economic actor (the Victorian period). Plural heritages limit the threat that the nation will die or be absorbed into a stronger culture, if the prevailing model fails. This also preserves the nation from falling victim to a model's success: the possibility of the English nation being absorbed into an Imperial, even global identity was countered by the persistence of a 'little England' tradition of the Anglo-Saxon liberties. As we saw, several nations (Czechs, Finns, Greeks, Russians) have developed a sense of mission as a mediating nation between culture zones, reflecting a history of periodic subjection to different more powerful neighbours. This reinforces a self-image of the community as a creative synthesiser and participant in world affairs, countering fears that it might face being torn apart by the pressures of rival blocs.

The success of nationalists in engaging with a continuously changing world has ensured the planetary diffusion of the national model. The triumph of this model is itself an example of the globalisation process. The advance of the European national state model has accompanied industrialisation, and the enhanced resources available to states have enabled the development of structures and policies (e.g. the welfare state) that have deepened social identification with the nation. But what of claims we are now moving from a period of *internationalisation,* in which the world was constructed into national states that then formed a world civil order, into one of *globalisation?* In this latter period it is suggested that because of the scale, speed and intensity of interactions, these international institutions are being detached from their national moorings to develop a life and rationale of their own in the resolution of global problems. Have we not reached a new stage in the post-1945 world when the rise of transnational and international alliances indicates that the era of the national state is passing? Do we not see emerging a new planetary consciousness, expressed through the rise of English (or American), the UN and WTO, and global cities such as New York, London, Paris and Geneva that are homes to mobile transnational financial, business, legal and intellectual elites? Does this not demonstrate that existing national states cannot resolve problems such as nuclear proliferation, environmental threats, large-scale international migratory and refugee flows, and terrorism?

Such interpretations tend to rely on the notion of a 'golden age' of largely autonomous national states in control of their economic, political and military destiny, but this conception is a myth. Modern nations and national states, we have seen, from their very beginnings have operated in alliance or contest with the transnational institutions of empires, the great religions, revolutionary internationals and capitalism. Stein Tonnesson (2004) maintains that national states in an open market economy have indeed lost some of their power to tax and regulate business, especially transnational corporations, and that national elites are now more occupied in foreign negotiations with in international institutions. Others (see Weiss, 1998) argue forcefully that the national state remains the pre-eminent actor in the sphere of political economy.

So far there is little evidence of a global consciousness superseding national interests; rather national interests are being negotiated through global agencies. Small- to medium-size powers such as Ireland, Australia and Sweden view participation in organisations such as the United Nations as an effective means of achieving national goals. The larger national states also use their imperial legacy to buttress a global mission, Britain through the Commonwealth, France as leader of Francophone African states, and Spain as mediator between Europe and Latin America. The USA, in particular, shows no signs of being willing to subordinate national interests to 'world opinion'. The negotiating games of national elites are complex. National states in Europe can use the *global* as an instrument in their struggles for autonomy against the *regional* pressures of 'Europe' or against a dominant regional power. Thus the global military reach of the USA, made possible by technology, is welcomed by many states, both in Europe and Asia. International covenants may strengthen the powers of national governments over their peoples. In Australia the Hawke government in 1983 was able to prevent the state of Tasmania from constructing a dam by invoking treaty obligations covering world heritage sites that overrode the constitutional rights of the Australian states. Tonnesson, however, suggests that as state elites become preoccupied with the global stage, they are likely to alienate themselves from their national societies and to face nationalist challengers from below.

The strategies of national elites are evolving with the new more complex transnational environment. But many of the new issues have a familiar face. Was not a romantic nationalism born in the great cosmopolitan cities of Western Europe, and did it not have a global vision? Was there not then a focus on the cultural rights of minorities against the state? Did this not lead then, as it now does, to support for the suppressed or neglected heritages of marginalised peoples? Almost all national states have ethnic minorities, and attempts to protect their rights has led to the intensification and proliferation of nationalist movements, including those of 'indigenous peoples'.

The very growth of transnational institutions has provoked a widespread reaction against the 'Western' values that they seem to embody in Asia, Africa and Latin America. In much of the world globalisation is associated with Americanisation, that is to say, with a covert nationalist agenda. Reacting against this, strands within Chinese elites present a neo-Confucianism, emphasizing harmonious co-operation, as a non-exclusionary principle of world order superior to the competitive messianism of the West (Zheng, 1999: ch. 4). It is not inconceivable that China, now rapidly developing its vast population, could eventually become once again the global centre of gravity. A growing sense of threat from China has evoked at times an ethnocentric response from the supposedly global civilisation of the USA. In short, current global currents come with their own ethnocultural assumptions, and provoke countervailing visions and, in turn, rival nationalisms.

The perception that world political and economic institutions are captured by great power and largely western interests fuels the religious resurgence in the non-European world that is as much nationalist as religious. In the contemporary period religious organisations such as Islam and Evangelical Protestantism, their reach extended by modern communication systems, remain among the most potent globalising agents and offer a rival vision to that of secular modernity. The recent attacks on the USA have shown the unpredictable threats that can arise out of a global interconnectedness. Globalisation has engendered a hostility against the West on the part of large sections of the Muslim world, and whereas the prophets of multiculturalism have viewed the migration of millions of peoples from a historically rival civilisation into the heartlands of the West as encouraging a creative hybridisation of identities, many now fear instead an intensified and perhaps even religio-racial nationalism in the West triggered by conflicts between host communities and 'immigrants'. Already there are calls to 'nationalise' immigrant minorities by teaching them the values of citizenship defined in terms of the dominant culture.

Regionalism

If there is little evidence of a planetary-wide human identity forming as a cultural or political alternative to the national state, can we not see evidence of the advance of globalisation in the increasing tendency of national states to collaborate in regional associations? Might these not be harbingers of a transnational future? In discussing this possibility I will examine the European Union as the most far-reaching of these organisations.

In signing the Treaty of Maastricht (1994) the national states of the European Community bound themselves to a Union that reaches into many of the core functions of the national state – control of borders and territory, the policing of citizens and immigration, currency and taxation, management of the economy and foreign policy and defence (Wallace, 1997: 33). The national state was born in Europe and became through European imperial expansion the global norm. Yet is Europe now pioneering a new political form, embodying the principle of multiple sovereignties, which will supersede the national state and fit humanity for its postmodern future? Does Maastricht represent an 'irreversible move towards real federation' (Anderson, 1997b: 126)? Or is it a doomed experiment, likely to intensify the very thing it is designed to forestall – the resurgence of nationalism at the very heart of the Union?

Taking a sceptical stance, I will argue that most of those championing the European project make the mistake of conflating nation with national state, and equating the potency of the political nation with its modernising rather than with its identity functions. Most analysts also exaggerate the contemporary Europeanisation of nations, failing to note being 'European' has always been enmeshed in national agendas. The concept of 'Europe', I shall suggest, is largely indeterminate, given a common definition only when imposed by the 'great national states', and as such it is unable to provide a directive and solidarist response at time of crises when national interests conflict. What is in doubt is the medium-term viability of the European Union not of its constituent national states, for the historical record reveals federations, like empires, have a poor record in the modern world.

Evolving nations

To many the rise of the European Union since the Second World War is a symptom of the obsolescence of the national state in a global era. National states now have to pool sovereignty to achieve their goals and, at least at the elite level, there is a new sense of a European destiny. The unitary character of national states has given way as minority nationalities and regions have demanded measures of territorial autonomy, and their claims to cultural homogeneity have been undermined by large-scale immigration, fuelling demands for their redefinition as multicultural communities (Guibernau, 2001).

The evidence is indisputable, but in arguing for the decline of national before European loyalties, much of the discussion is predicated on three assumptions. First, nation is conflated with national state, and there is a presumption that collective identification with national states is based on instrumental considerations. Secondly, the claim of a crisis of the national state rests on a contrast with an alleged period in which national states were unitary and bounded societies. Thirdly, the intermeshing of national and European loyalties, evident particularly at the elite level, is assumed to be unprecedented. All three propositions are overstated.

The first argument relates the identification of people with their national state to its capacity to achieve democratic control and economic and social progress. Hence, Alan Milward (1992) argues that membership of the EU rescued European national states that had been all but destroyed by the war by sustaining high levels of economic growth, employment, welfare provision and education. Indeed the national states by these indices enjoyed a mass loyalty unknown in the nineteenth and early twentieth centuries.

William Wallace, although agreeing that the EU reinforced national states up to the 1960s, maintains that since the 1980s recognition of the incapacity of individual national states to deliver such benefits has led to a surrender of core powers and a loosening of their authority (Wallace, 1997). Whatever their differences, each views national identifications as at best the psychological underpinnings of a collective unit (the state) whose justification is the achievement of democratic participation and economic and social progress. This is dubious: as Perry Anderson observes (1997a: 55), the low levels of democracy (and hardships) endured by German (and other) populations did not have discernable effects in their preparedness to die in great numbers for their nation in the Second World War. Nations are, above all, communities of fate, and peoples' attachment to their state rests on its capacity to sustain their deep-seated commitments to the defence of their homeland, unique culture and independence. Even if the EU is associated with economic prosperity this will not in itself undermine the status of national states.

Secondly, pooling of sovereignty is not a revolutionary new development, since nations have continually fluctuated in strength and the degree to which they wish to regulate the various sectors of social life. As we noted in Chapter 4, successful states, such as nineteenth-century Britain, remained a world power in part because of their skill in mustering coalitions of states against the dominant great power on the European subcontinent. Periods of 'splendid isolation', when Britain would enjoy a relative autonomy as a global power, have alternated with a pooling of sovereignty in the two world wars. We also noted that in the economic sphere states have employed different strategies to compete in transnational economic markets. Britain during the nineteenth century saw it in its national interest to promote free trade, whereas 'late comer' Germany pursued more protectionist policies.

Not only strategies have evolved in response to contingent challenges. We have noted oscillations between national and imperial, class, regional and religious identities throughout the modern period (Connor, 1990). Even for Britain and France, the notion of a golden age of sovereign national states is a myth. This is even more the case for small countries. Nations and national states take different decisions over the social niches they wish to regulate by explicit reference to national norms (as in the divergent French and British attitudes to American popular culture), and they vary in their stance over time. Such variations may not indicate changes in the values attributed to national affiliations, but rather a changing conception of what relationships should be governed by national norms. An adherence to the nation may not fluctuate much despite apparent changes in behaviour (Banton, 1994). In Chapter 4 I argued we must distinguish between two issues: why national groups make strategic choices over the range of roles they wish to regulate, and why there are fluctuations in the salience of national loyalties. The former are rational decisions about how to achieve national goals, through, for example, pooling of sovereignty, and such decisions are conditional and, in principle, reversible. The latter represents major shifts of loyalty away from nation to other allegiances, perhaps to a European identity. Differentiating between the two may be complex, but such major shifts are usually accompanied by explicit justifications and controversy. Whether there have been major shifts will be addressed later.

Thirdly, claims that European integration is enmeshing national and European identities so that national identity is now being expressed in terms of European horizons are doubtful. Most commentators admit that such Pan-European consciousness as exists is confined to elite political, business, bureaucratic, trade union and media networks. They have predicted, however, that participation in this project would broaden as European integration deepened. Such perspectives imply a new cultural basis is being created to underpin a European pluricentred system of decision-making. This is doubtful for two reasons. First, there has always been a consciousness at the elite level of belonging to a common European as well as to a local culture. Secondly, from their very beginning nations, aware of their part of a multi-actor civilisation, defined themselves through an involvement in a European mission, and the modern history of Europe is the story of a struggle between the great powers over which nationalist vision of Europe would prevail.

From the early middle ages a Europe existed, at least at the elite level, as a family of cultures, to use the concept of Anthony Smith (1992), knit by Latin Christianity, the heritage of the Roman Empire, dynastic inter-marriage, the rise of a system of diplomacy and, later, international treaties. In the early modern period a royal court culture centred on France defined the codes of the European aristocracy, and later the movements of the Enlightenment and Romanticism provided a common conceptual language of European politics and culture, including for the emerging nationalisms of the subcontinent.

Even before this, when national identities crystallised, they often defined themselves by reference to a European mission, as participants in a European battle of values or in conflict against an extra-European 'other'. We have already noted how several European peoples (the Spanish, Poles, Hungarians, Serbs and Russians) legitimised themselves in centuries of conflict with Muslim powers as *antemurale* defenders of Christian Europe. The wars of the Reformation and Counter-Reformation resulted in English, Dutch, French and Spanish states defining themselves in addition as elect defenders of

Protestantism or Catholicism, but only after civil wars within emerging national states in which proponents of the rival religious causes looked for support in friendly European states. In short the (religious) battles to define the nation and European civilisation were interlinked. Foreign intervention could lead to the triumph of one side: the intervention of William of Orange in England secured the Glorious (Protestant) Revolution in 1688.

Modern national identities crystallised round the French-led Enlightenment assault on the European *ancien régime*, when Republican France perceived itself as the modern bearer of the Roman mission to construct a European civilisational zone of peace and justice. In reaction, an English constitutional-monarchical and German romantic nationalism formed, with the Germans rejecting a rationalist unification of Europe in favour of a Christian confederation of nations on the model of the Holy Roman Empire (Kohn, 1967). As before, these competing ideals of the nation provided a European repertoire for many emerging nationalisms, and the choice of national conceptions was shaped by location within the different politico-cultural zones of Europe. German organic conceptions were influential in many Central and Eastern European nationalities. But there were rival visions within nations which looked for inspiration and sometimes support from 'dominant models'. In Russia, German-inspired Slavophiles admired an English constitutionalism led by a conservative aristocracy, whereas Westerners tended to look to French republicanism.

Indeed, the struggle between models was perceived to be a battle for the identity of Europe. The nationalism of 'great powers' tended to appropriate the traditional ambitions of such states to command the subcontinent. Napoleon sought to unite Europe within a French imperium that in the guise of his 'Continental System' was economic as well as political. After national unification was achieved by the defeat of France, Germany, in the two world wars, made attempts to achieve a European Empire, again using economic as well as military instruments to secure its ends. The nationalism of stateless nations or small national states, by contrast, was often expressed in moral terms, with Poles and the Irish viewing themselves in redemptionist fashion as exemplary Christian nations.

What this suggests is that intrinsic to many national identities is a sense of mission to a wider European civilisation, arising from the sense of belonging to a common heritage, characterised by status competition, mutual borrowing and concepts of the balance of power (see Hall, 1985: ch. 5). This Europe is not unitary but multiple, and is perceived through different national prisms. For great powers 'Europe' implies a leadership role, whereas smaller nations have seen relationships with European neighbours as a means to escape the threat of absorption by adjacent great powers – hence Irish nationalists looked to Republican France and Germany (at different times) as a counter to Britain.

Europe also divides into culture zones, often dominated by competing powers, such as France (and also Britain) in the 'West', Germany in the Centre and Imperial Russia in the East, and these states have provided the models through which other communities defined themselves. Those perceiving themselves to be on the margins, especially those on geo-cultural fault lines, such as Poles, Croatians and Greeks, may compensate by demanding recognition for a historic role as frontier guards of Europe.

Because of the interpenetration of European cultures, this multiplicity has been reflected within nations, and rival projects, in their battle to secure their vision of the nation, have looked to 'Europe' both as a source of support and of threats. 'Europe' can be simultaneously 'other' and the means of returning to one's authentic traditions. Hence in nineteenth- and twentieth-century Spain we find a struggle between a conservative conception, based on the *Reconquista*, of the nation as defender of Catholic Europe, and a modernising ideal originating with the Enlightenment for whom 'a return to Europe' entailed a moral regeneration of the nation (Jauregui, 1999).

A counter-argument: the embeddedness of European identities

An alternative perspective maintains that the formation of the EU is a *revival* of civilisation loyalties embedded in the political, legal, religious and intellectual structures of Europe, which have been mobilised periodically to check destructive internal conflict and protect the subcontinent from external threats (see Pagden, 2002a, 2002b). There are certain persistent European values and ideals based on the Roman, Latin Christian and humanist heritages: the idea of uniting Europe in a single legislative order (inspiring powerful rulers from Emperor Justinian to Napoleon); the concept of Europe as a (Christian) zone of peace; and the sense of belonging to a distinctive cultural realm, the legacy not just of Latin but also common vernacular artistic styles (such as Gothic architecture) across Europe (see also Jordan, 2002). 'Europe' has thereby created mechanisms such as first the Papacy, then international law (e.g., the Treaty of Westphalia and the Congress of Vienna) to moderate conflicts between Christian states and to unite them against Islam during the Crusades and against the Turks when the latter besieged Vienna.

Ariane Chebel d'Appollonia (2002) argues that the EU can be regarded as the most systematic mechanism devised by European elites to overcome the greatest internal and external crises facing the subcontinent. Its messianic dream of constructing an exemplary cosmopolitan, democratic and peaceful federation of peoples is a secular version of Christian exceptionalism. It originated from Enlightenment intellectuals who viewed Europe as a great republic of peoples, superior to other civilisations by virtue of its limited government and commitment to civil society. Indeed, the modern European project emerged among enlightened elites as a reaction against the effects of nationalism apparent in the wars and revolutionary upheavals of the early nineteenth century. What gave these minority projects force were the increasingly destructive twentieth-century wars between the European states and also the growing sense of external threat to European hegemony from rising powers on the periphery, first from the USA and then from Bolshevik Russia. A Pan-European movement formed in the interwar period to promote a United States of Europe that would eliminate the nationalist rivalries responsible for the First World War and regenerate the European subcontinent.

This was the precursor of the present EU, whose origins lie in the overwhelming destruction of European societies between 1939–45, the division of Europe into two blocs and the loss of the European Empires. Although its original forms were economic, the larger objectives were to overcome national rivalries, restore Europe as an autonomous global actor, and regenerate its democratic and economic life. However, in seeking to overcome nationalism the European project took two forms from its nineteenth-century beginnings. One sought to create a united Europe that would limit national state sovereignty, in the form of a federal state based on European values that, to a greater or lesser extent, would be supranational. The other expressed the Mazzinian ideal of a Europe built from below on the basis of nations. Although the two were quite different, they now co-exist in the present EU, and either way they represent a threat to existing national states.

This argument, however, invites the response that in either of its forms the European project is one largely of minorities. We may well ask: what popular resonance can it evoke to overcome ingrained national identities, and how can it avoid being 'captured' by national interests, either those of great powers (see Fontana, 2002) or those of stateless peoples, and thus itself become a zone of conflict?

European Union and the National States

Can we then see the rise of the EU as a fundamental revision of the traditional European national states, impelled by global threats and the escalating destruction of modern warfare? Does the federal vision of its founders represent a fundamental revulsion against the national principle in the name of wider (European) civilisational loyalties? Or is the EU a new *strategy* of national elites to maximise their sovereignty in an increasingly globalised world? Or, again, is it a strange new hybrid of the national and European, which will liberate the stateless nations from their national states?

There is evidence for all of these positions. The European Union can be seen as the latest in a series of attempts to politically unite Europe as an instrument of national ambitions. France (under Napoleon) and Germany (under Wilhelm II and Hitler) have each attempted in time of war to establish a European power bloc as a global actor against imperial competitors. In the postwar period the goal, in alliance with the USA, was to forge a stable political and economic bloc to combat the overwhelming threat from the USSR, and the initial instrument, the European Coal and Steel Community, was influenced by the organisation of the German war economy in occupied Europe (Keegan, 1997). What is distinctive about the current project is the *alliance* of the former enemies, France and Germany, and the *voluntary* agreement of other European national states under their leadership to pool their sovereignty in a supranational institution, inspired by the general revulsion against the national rivalries that had brought Europe to the point of destruction.

The formation and accession of states to the European Union and the politics of the European Union can be explained by national motives. The interests of France (to constrain a temporarily weakened Germany within a French-dominated Europe) and Germany (to relegitimise itself as a national state committed to European democracy) are clear. Joining 'Europe' can also be a strategy of freedom from economic dependence on a powerful neighbour (e.g. Ireland in relation to Britain). In some cases, joining 'Europe' was seen as ensuring the victory of one's conception of the nation against internal rivals. Spanish democrats, like their counterparts in Greece, regarded accession as a validation and protection of the authentic 'enlightened' nation against opponents longing for a return to military authoritarianism and religious reaction, and there is a similar story for Eastern European aspirants. For all member states participation in the European Union gives them the status as joint decision-makers on the world stage, particularly compelling for small national states, to which the EU Presidency rotates periodically, giving them their Warholian 'fifteen minutes of fame'.

European Union politics have been driven by the national interest of the larger states, notably France and Germany. Hence power was centred in the Council of Ministers, the Commission was weakened by having a tiny bureaucratic staff and the parliament was little more than a talking shop.

Even the dramatic 'deepening' represented by Maastricht, it can be argued, is dictated by the interests of the European national states, recognising that the sudden collapse of Communism could result in a return to the politics of the 1930s with a re-unified Germany, an unstable Eastern Europe of economically distressed states trying to establish democratic traditions but with problematic national minorities and, further east, an insecure and bellicose Russia. Strengthening the European Union arose from the French desire to constrain a re-united Germany within a 'European' set of economic institutions and the German willingness to offer up its economic autonomy in return for admission of the former communist states, thereby stabilising its eastern borders and extending its influence (Anderson, 1997a).

Nonetheless, the EU has a supranational as well as an intergovernmental character, and its range of regulatory functions, including, now, monetary policy, is steadily increasing. This suggests a European-wide federation may arise as an *indirect effect* of the competitive goals and fears of the European national states, just as before the nations of Europe arose in part as an unintended consequence of the competition of dynastic states. The question is then, can the European dimension co-exist with the national dimension, and on what basis?

Can a European identity be found that will eventually transcend national loyalties and underpin a European state? Or is the emerging EU *sui generis*, a novel entity recognising the multiple sovereignties of postmodernity? Or again, is the future likely to be based on a European order acknowledging the primacy of national states in a constitution that regulates the respective powers of supranational and national institutions?

The introduction of symbols such as a EU flag and anthem and the preoccupation with a European demos suggests the desire to create a European *national* community. But symbols in themselves have no efficacy unless they evoke a sense of a concrete collectivity, and even the outstanding civic nation, France, I have argued, is founded on an ethnic substratum – a historic political capital – Paris, the prestige of French language and culture, a history of *gloire*, and clear boundaries 'naturalised' by war and physical barriers. Whereas nations evoke heroic images of collective will, a concrete cultural community and a sacred homeland, the 'European' identity the EU wishes to create is vague and contested. As political centres, Brussels and Strasbourg evoke no sacral aura, and the EU lacks cultural sites and clear geographic boundaries. It offers no equivalence to national commemorations of 'fallen soldiers' that have such a powerful popular resonance. The European project is articulated by reference to an indefinite future-oriented telos (the image of a train moving towards ever-closer union that one must get on) that represents a rejection of the past of national rivalries.

Can a European constitutional patriotism guaranteeing civil rights and progress be realised subjectively as an act of faith in the future? The model of the USA is often invoked as a successful ideological project that founded a new society based on universal enlightenment principles and a deliberate rejection of the (European) past (d'Appollonia, 2002: 176–70). Like the architects of the USA, European federalists veer between conceiving of the project as a heroic act of will and as following a telos. The USA, however, could plausibly differentiate itself from the past because it was a 'New World' nation of emigrants who consciously left their places of origin, possessed a myth of auto-emancipation by virtue of its war of independence against Britain, and generated a canon of revolutionary heroes and sacred texts (the Declaration of Independence and its Constitution) that inspired allegiance. The only pre-existing ethno-territorial opposition it faced (from the indigenous inhabitants) was pulverised by war and expropriation. In contrast, the EU was founded by the elites of *defeated* national states, and has at best a pragmatic rationale, administered by bureaucrats.

For John Pocock (1997), it is this trauma of defeat that has justified the European Union and has also crippled it. The ideology of Europeanism on which it rests is postmodernist, directed against moral absolutisms and the grand narratives of European national states. It is largely deconstructionist in character, retaining for itself an essential lack of identity. It offers no synthetic or universal history to replace those of the national states. The very indeterminacy of 'Europe' presents tactical advantages, since, like a text, it can be 'read' in very different ways by the different constituent nationalities, and its borders can be extended elastically to fit the needs of a developing project (Pocock, 2002: 67–70). But this lack of clear criteria of membership enhances the manipulative capacity of powerful states in what is essentially a pragmatic imperial project, seeking to override the resistance of routinised national identities.

Postmodernists might reply that the European Union neither can nor should attempt to be a supernation, because in a global age the idea of a territorially bounded sovereign actor is obsolete and dangerous (see Passerini, 2002: 200–8). The EU is based on a recognition of the catastrophic consequences of the national rivalries of Europe and of the vital need to discipline them in a political framework that would also recognise transnational (or subcontinental) and (intrastate) regional identities and interests (Pagden, 2002a: 27–32). What hold it together are not just the *rational* advantages perceived by *elites* in pooling sovereignty, but a deeper *moral* revulsion of *peoples* against nationalism, combined with a sense that national identities are more securely preserved by detaching them from national states whose wars nearly destroyed their peoples. The European Union thus does not need to be conceived as a surrogate national state with all the absolutisms that implies, including a moral messianism (*pace* the USA). Its justification is as a pioneer of a new form of democratic political community, acknowledging the reality that the contemporary world is characterised by multiple and overlapping centres of power. It is governed according to the principle of subsidiarity – that authority is located appropriately to the problem at hand. The European Union liberates both dominant and minority nations from their fetish of the national state, and this is reflected in the trend to regional devolution. Moreover, a citizenship conceived in European terms, because of its thinness, would be less exclusive of immigrant minorities and compatible with the multicultural realities of contemporary industrial societies.

There is something in these arguments. A loyalty to the 'European' ideal is visible particularly in the case of discredited aggressor states (Germany, Italy) and the smaller (Benelux) states directly threatened by the quarrels of the great powers. But the postmodernists are open to three objections. First, a Union of peoples cannot be based only on fear (of war, should the Union dissolve): it requires positive founding myths (a point to which I will return). Second, postmodernists underestimate the degree to which national identities remain embedded, and are capable of being re-ignited. The commitment of postwar Germans to a European democratic idealism to overcome the otherwise 'unmasterable past' did not interfere with the impetus to national re-unification in 1990, in spite of opposition from other European leaders. Third, they do not explain how an indefinite ideology can mobilise European populations to collective action in a crisis. A postmodernist celebration of the multiplicity of identities is possible in a stable and prosperous world without obvious external or internal threats. But only a potent and definite identity is capable of orienting and mobilising collective action in order to respond to the eruption of wars (e.g. in the Balkans), Islamist terrorist threats, economic recessions, large-scale immigration and, more recently, the crisis in Iraq and the Middle East. To unite disparate polities by constructing a threatening 'other' in the form of the USA could be dangerously destabilising in the current world crisis and in any case will not work, as the split between 'Old' and 'New' Europe has revealed.

The very expansion of powers by the European Union intensifies a need to find some form of legitimation for their exercise. For monetary union to be successful the EU requires enhanced powers of fiscal co-ordination and also of taxation to distribute resources from richer to poorer regions of Europe to compensate for the loss of exchange rate adjustments. The stronger the EU centre grows, the more it requires such cultural power to mobilise consent. But it does not possess even a common language, let alone a bank of myths, memories and symbols to convey a sense of belonging to a community of sentiment. At the moment, the EU judged by a range of measures, including electoral turnouts, lacks popular legitimacy compared with the national states. The question remains then: how is the European dimension as exemplified by the EU to co-exist with this national dimension?

If it is implausible to construct a strong sense of Europeanness in its own terms, can one conceive of a Europe as a family of nations, gradually developing common values on a continental scale through a sense of quasi-kinship? The analogy is with conglomerate states such as Britain, which may be conceived as a supernation built upon a family network of English, Welsh and Scottish ethnonational ties. There does seem to be a tendency for conglomerate states to use a language of kinship. Even the USSR, organised on avowedly supranational principles, depicted the Russians as the elder brother of the Soviet nationalities.

The very notion of an 'elder brother' acknowledges that such states were built upon a dominant national community which supplied the linguistic and cultural cement of the state, though the conflation of Britishness with Englishness and Soviet identities with Russian values was hidden (see Hutchinson, 1994: 130–3). It is inconceivable for the EU to be based on a single hegemon, given the memories that this would evoke, though France continues to claim leadership by virtue of its historical pre-eminence in Europe. Is there a core quasi-ethnic grouping available to the EU? Possibly, in the loose sense of the original member states who share a founding myth and the sense of status that this implies. Within this group there is the coupling of the two national states that fought for European hegemony during the nineteenth and twentieth centuries, France and Germany, who have dominated EU decision-making since its origin. At points of crisis, German and French opinion-makers and politicians have called for a renewal of this alliance and the formation, with the Benelux countries, of an inner core to further advance integration (see Lamers, 1997).

The problem is that a kinship system implies hierarchy rather than equality and can build up centrifugal resentments, as the case of the USSR and, lately, the UK demonstrates. Although this is reduced by the dual axis of power, the questions remain: who is to be the elder brother, and who is perceived as belonging to the inner core of the family, as opposed to being a distant cousin, or even an adopted orphan (e.g. Turkey)? The EU's project of 'widening' and 'deepening' as it expands to take in Eastern European countries revives these questions as the existing status order is shaken both by territorial expansion and by the struggle for dominance over the strengthened institutions. The Franco-German accommodation (like the former Austrio-Hungarian Habsburg alliance) has always been pragmatic rather than fraternal: there are tensions at the elite level between the French centralist and the German federalist visions of the EU and popular suspicions below the surface. These fears have been exacerbated by the combination of German re-unification with EU expansion to the East that has awakened French fears of a revived German hegemony shifting the centre of gravity of the Union from the West. The very multiplication of actors within the EU following the entry of smaller and poorer eastern states would seem to presage not only the loss of national vetoes through proposed majority voting but also threats to the power of the richer and larger states.

Increasing centralisation raises the stakes in the battle of whose national conception of Europe is to prevail, which, when combined with the increase of members, intensifies the need to find a cement for this arrangement. Will the countries from what has been regarded as the periphery (or even the outside) of Europe perceive the 'integration process' as a form of imperialism, in which they have to submit to an onerous framework designed for advanced industrial states? Can Europe rely on institutional brokering and a conjured rhetoric of common interest, or will the very expansion of the EU increasingly expose its empty heart?

The danger that the EU, as presently constituted, may collapse from its own contradictions is all the more likely as an unaccountable, elite-driven integration process gathers momentum in spite of the absence of a substantiated European democracy (with a demos) that might legitimise the surrender of national state powers. Widening gaps with popular opinion have been exposed already by referendums in France, Ireland, Denmark and Sweden. The incapacity of national representative institutions to regulate such central areas as monetary policy and frontier controls makes it all too probable that grievances over unemployment, immigration and race and ethnicity will generate populist direct action.

One answer to this widening gap between the peoples of Europe and the expanding EU political sphere is a written constitution that would authoritatively define the respective national and Union jurisdictions, and return substantial authority to the only credible repositories of democratic practice, the national states (Weiler, 1997). Different versions of such an arrangement enshrining the ideal of 'ever closer union of peoples' are presently being debated. But constitutions have to have within them the potential for adaptation so that they can address circumstances unimaginable to their formulators. The experience of the USA, Canada and Australia suggests a written constitution becomes a battleground between ideological groups seeking to expand or limit the central state and alter its rulings on fundamental rights, and that the supposedly neutral Constitutional Courts become politicised in the process. In the USA such conflicts over states' rights tied to the issue of slavery led to civil war. More recently, rulings by the Australian High Court in the 1990s on the status of Aboriginal land claims have fuelled the rise of xenophobic populist political movements.

A major difficulty of codifying in a decisive way the respective spheres of the EU and national states is that, as we have seen, nations change in what they perceive to be their core regulatory concerns as they encounter the challenges of an ever-changing world. If that is so even within a single state, a constitution formulated for a union of many national states will almost certainly be the site of perpetual political conflict.

The future of the EU

The movement for European integration over much of the subcontinent is justified by several rhetorics – the extension of democracy and human rights, enhancing economic progress, becoming a world actor, and taking responsibility for European security. But this is an elite-driven and now tottering Imperial (Franco-German) project, infused with a strong subterranean desire to contain the resurgence of 'unmasterable' national differences at the very centre of Europe, as well as on its eastern fringes. The drive to integrate, however, exacerbates the problem. Centralising powers in European institutions raises expectations of what the EU can deliver while multiplying the problems they must resolve, and it widens the gap between elites and peoples by transferring powers from national parliaments to arcane and all but unaccountable institutions. A resentment of an invasive Imperial centre is the classic breeding ground of nationalisms, especially when the Imperial elites have divergent visions of Europe based on national interest.

Myths and symbols provide key components of understanding and negotiating change. Even in normal times, as Michael Billig (1995) has demonstrated, the discourse of politicians is laden with national myths, images and a national rhetoric, often derived from warfare, which insiders take for granted. The legend of the nation is of a community knit by love and common sacrifice. Its myths and symbols orient its members to fundamental values – to homeland, the defence of 'irreplaceable values', and to the freedom of its people. Images establish a common bond between leaders and led and legitimise even in 'normal times' difficult decisions – the imposition of heavier taxes in economic difficulties, the redistribution of resources between richer and poorer regions or classes. At times of extraordinary crisis – the outbreak of war or economic collapse – mythic images of kinship can inspire great sacrifice on behalf of the national state. One of the characteristics of such myth-symbol complexes is that they remain empty or alien to the outsider.

What images will the politicians of an increasingly differentiated European Union invoke to secure collective sacrifice for the European good? And how will they deal with extraordinary crises? Large-scale surveys indicate there is indeed a consciousness of being European, but an identity is more than a sense: it supplies fundamental prescriptions about conduct and a sense of direction for the future. A sense of common fate as *Europeans* is built largely on images of traumatic 'civil war', hardly the basis of a confident collective identity. A European consciousness, too, is largely mediated through the different and often competing national identities of Europeans. We know that nations and national states have a good track record for surviving great adversities. Has the EU similar moral and political stamina? If it fails, nations remain available as potent bases of political action.

The Clash of Civilisations

If a single world united by cosmopolitan values seems some way off, is nationalism not threatened by a globalisation in religious form: namely, a resurgence of religious movements in much of the Middle East, Asia and Latin America? Mark Juergensmeyer (1993) has asked if this religious revival represents a new Cold War against the West. The current Islamist revival against Western secularism, highlighted in the Iranian Revolution, has not only reshaped the politics of states with a Muslim majority, but also fanned a widely based ethnocentric reaction in European national states against Muslim immigrants, including in France where politicians of the left and right have expressed fears about the erosion of secular republican traditions by militant Islam. Samuel Huntington (1997: chs 1, 6), while rejecting the notion of a binary conflict between a secular West and a religious non-West, warns, should the West act with insensitivity, of the danger of a battle of civilisations, underpinned for the most part (though not exclusively) by antagonistic religious heritages. In such a vision, states (and national states) play a secondary role as leading political actors within their civilisation.

Civilisations without leading states will be politically flaccid, but equally, states that seek to escape their historic civilisation such as Greece (which should be in the Orthodox camp but seeks to be Western) or Turkey (which also seeks to be European but is within Islam) will be perpetually torn. Those interstate or intrastate conflicts that coincide with religio-civilisational fault-lines are likely to be the most intense.

There are obvious criticisms one can make of Huntington's associations of conflict with civilisational difference. He defines the European world of Latin Christianity as a single civilisation, but, from the sixteenth century, the most ferocious conflicts conducted by Latin Europeans were not with Muslim, Confucian or Orthodox Christian civilisations but rather against themselves, first in the wars of Reformation and Counter-reformation in the sixteenth and seventeenth centuries, and then in the world wars of the twentieth century.

However, the current phase of Islamist militancy seems partially to confirm Huntington's thesis of civilisation conflict. Islam was the most global civilisation from the seventh century to the seventeenth century, extending from North Africa through the Middle East into sub-Saharan Africa, the Balkans, Central Asia, the Indian subcontinent and Indonesia. It was decentralised, oriented to the *umma* rather than an ethnic or territorial community, and knit by trans-state travelling religious scholars, brotherhoods, schools of law, merchant networks and pilgrimages to the sacred sites of Mecca and Jerusalem. A triumphant military religion, it gave rise to Muslim states such as the Ottoman Empire that were formidable threats to European hegemony up to 1685 when its armies besieged Vienna. European imperial expansion into sacred Muslim lands at the end of the eighteenth century, beginning with Napoleon's incursion into Egypt, was a shock to Muslims. Faced with the threat of colonisation, rulers tried to adopt European models of the territorial state, a rational bureaucracy and, within limits, nationalism as a means to rebuff European infidels. A minority of intellectuals, exposed to Western science and learning, turned first to various forms of Islamic reformism and Pan-Islamic movements. Then, as the British and French absorbed Muslim lands in the Middle East into their empires, they looked to nationalism, rejecting Islam in favour of first liberal, then socialist ideologies that would politically liberate their peoples and rescue them from economic neo-colonialism (Bennison, 2002).

This, however, was an elite reaction: the largely uneducated Muslim masses remained opposed, and by the 1930s militant organisations such as the Muslim Brotherhood formed, which repudiated national models as infidel European concepts that would divide the *umma* and perpetuate

European dominance. The Islamic revolution in Iran has contributed to a resurgence of radical Pan-Islamic movements. Using modern technologies such as transport, mass literacy, radio cassettes and videos, these reach across states into Muslim communities worldwide, aspiring to overthrow the current world order in the name of a universal Islam (Haddad, 1991: 9). The catalyst was the humiliating defeat of the Arab armies in the Six Day War against Israel and the loss of the holy places in Jerusalem. This for many Muslims was a sign of God's judgement against impious elites who had forsaken Islam in favour of secular ideologies such as nationalism and socialism.

Does this not support a Huntington analysis of civilisational allegiances that override national loyalties? This is doubtful. Although modern religious movements can be directed against the West, even where they critique external 'others' the 'real' enemy is generally not global but particular. Their main target is *within*, since they wish to morally regenerate a traditional culture being eroded by secular forces allied to alien cosmopolitan principles. The Islamist movements of the Middle East, Africa and Pakistan and Hindu revivalism in India were born out of the failure of secular (socialist) nationalism to deliver the promises of social and economic emancipation of the masses, to free them from Western 'neo-colonialist' capitalism and to provide law and order (see Hutchinson, 1994, ch. 3). In each case there has been a 'return' to older religious traditions and institutions long predating the Western colonial impact in order to provide more 'authentic' models of development and delivery of basic social services, including justice (hence the appeal for Muslims of shariah law), education and the relief of poverty. The objective of these movements has been focused on a transformation of an existing political community rather than a worldwide crusade. Even 'universal' Islam, we saw in Chapter 1, differentiated into Sunni and Shi'a that gave form to opposing Persian and Arab ethnicities, and has married with indigenous animist traditions in South East Asia. Such rivalries resulted in the failure of Pan-Islamic movements in the nineteenth century. Where the target is also external this is as often a neighbouring country (Israel for Middle Eastern Muslims, India for Pakistanis), and, just as in the case of medieval *antemurale* kingdoms, this has reinforced a sense of nationality by defining the community as a unique custodian of spiritual values now under threat.

It is also a mistake to view such religious revivals as the domain of 'backward' non-Western countries. Religion has been one of the sources of national identity for many avowedly secular states such as Holland and France, and it remains a powerful force in many contemporary Western societies, including Germany, Italy, Ireland and Greece. The American drive for democracy worldwide is couched in the Puritan language of 'crusade' and manifest destiny. The current religious revival can be viewed as the most recent manifestation of a long-recurring conflict between secular and religious concepts *within* nations. Internal conflicts erupted in Europe at the very beginning of modern nationalism as part of a general reaction against the secularism of the French Revolution, and they continued through the nineteenth century, including within France itself. Today the struggle continues in France, most visibly in the campaigns of Le Pen's Front National against the Fifth Republic. Such contestations, we observed, were often an integral part of the nation-building process in Russia, France and Greece. These divisions reflected radically different views of the structure of politics, the status of social groups, relations between regions, the countryside and the city, economic and social policies and foreign policy. They also reflect the diverse heritages of populations whose geopolitical setting continues to expose them to unpredictable changes from several directions. These visions have alternated in power with groups at times switching positions. But it might fairly be asked what prevents such internal conflicts, *especially when religiously based*, leading to social breakdown and civil wars?

This is a pressing question today in many parts of the world. The short answer might be that there must be a common ethnic heritage to which both secular and religious movements can appeal. In the Middle East and Asia the secular national state is threatened because it is seen to be a derivative of Western colonial rule, compared to 'rooted' religious traditions that can claim to be more 'authentic' at times of crises. Often, as we saw, the nationalist initiative was taken by religious minorities – the Copts in Egypt and Maronite Christians and Druze in Lebanon – who find in a secular nationalism, based on a historic period before that of the dominant religion, an instrument that allows them participation as (at least) equals in the political community. The danger is that this ethnic vision has little resonance with the majority. In those national states or state-nations with multiple ethnoreligious or religious communities, an ethnoreligious rejection on the part of the dominant group of secular nationalism threatens to dissolve the state.

Even in contemporary Israel, a national state that claims legitimation by reference to an ancient kingdom and a myth of chosenness, the conflict with Palestinian and Arab nationalism only barely keeps the lid on an internal battle between secular Zionists and Orthodox Jews and religious nationalists about the character of the state. Zionism, of course, was secular in having as its objective the establishment of state and the transformation of Jews from a vulnerable diaspora into Israeli citizens, but their vision of an ingathering in the promised land was religious. Initially, the founding of Israel in war and the victory of 1967 generated a pantheon of heroes and legends of sacrifice that legitimised the Labour Zionist regime. But as with the Arabs in 1967, near defeat in 1973 eroded the secular vision, propelling to power Likud governments allied to religious nationalist movements, for whom it was an imperative to settle the holy land. The Israeli example illustrates two important points: first it reveals the inability of secular nationalism to override an old and institutionalised ethnoreligious heritage. Secondly, accommodation, although at times precarious, has been possible between bitter secular and religious rivals because of a common ethnoreligious heritage to which they refer (as well as a common external threat), but there has been an increasing shift in the identity of the state from its original more secular and socialist orientation.

One may wonder whether the qualified 'success' of the Israeli case is something of an exception in those non-European countries where secular nationalism aggressively confronts a traditional religious heritage with weak or non-existent ethnic moorings. States, however, remain the potent instruments of politics, with the result that religious movements tend to become particularised, and the world religions lack transnational institutions and foci capable of mobilising the faithful in alternative political formations. That said, the emergence of a world of 'real' national states, if it ever comes, is likely to be a protracted, uncertain and potentially reversible process.

Conclusions

We can agree with some points of the three positions we have examined. Undoubtedly, the strategies and perhaps the forms of the national state are changing to face the new international environment. States in many contexts pool sovereignty; international institutions and doctrines have emerged restricting sovereignty, though uncertainly; and trends in democracy and human rights have enabled ethnoregional movements to become more visible and salient. But much discussion of the post-national state remains West Eurocentric, and the conditions which allow such national 'weakening' may remain temporary, even in Europe. I have expressed scepticism about the erosion of the national principle in the face of globalisation.

Globalisation is a much longer phenomenon than most theorists of the subject are willing to acknowledge, and the agents and processes are not simply secular but include religion and warfare, both of which encourage differentiation. Before the modern world such factors resulted in large-scale ethnic phenomena, much of which has shaped the way that modern societies have evolved. The rise of nationalism was in turn produced by more intense forms of interaction, engendered by scientific and technological revolutions, but the empowerment of states came through not an eradication but a transformation of older ethnic heritages. Although the state principle is widely regarded as obsolete in the face of transnational entities, the major world actors remain national states or would-be national states. Nations may have to realise their goals by going beyond the national state, but it remains true that without the possession of a state, the capacities of national populations to negotiate on a larger stage are limited. In the developed world there is little evidence of a fundamental revision of the national state; in the developing world one of the main goals of populations will be to achieve an effective national state. New threats will intensify nationalism in many parts of the world, such as the effects of global climatic changes on states already locked in conflict over such natural resources as water, a major issue between Israel and Jordan and between India and Bangladesh.

Regional groupings of states have emerged as one strategy employed by national elites to manage the instabilities of an increasingly interdependent world. The European Union is the latest form of long-established mechanisms developed by European elites to ensure co-operation and regulate conflict on the subcontinent, but the idea of Europe has long been captured by national interests. A European ideal built on collective trauma does not have the 'sacred' authority that can subordinate the conflicting national interests of its constituent members in developing an autonomous set of collective projects. The 'widening' and 'deepening' will merely multiply and intensify the competing national agenda, while provoking a populist backlash at the loss of democratic accountability. The paralysis of the European Union in recent crises is more representative of a decaying premodern Empire than a pioneering postmodern institution. Whether it can be transformed into a looser arrangement, returning autonomy to national states, remains to be seen.

Religions remain potent global agents in the contemporary world, including the West. The recent religious resurgence has revealed that in much of the world nationalism is thinly based, statist and bears little relation to ethnic and other traditional realities. Nonetheless, the current religious revival does not offer a significant threat to the system of national states. In many cases religious movements have become ethnicised and another variety of nationalism. Religious conflict has as often as not intensified ethnic or national identity between neighbouring states (India and Pakistan). Much of the current religious revival is directed internally at the supposed inauthenticity of secular nationalism in relation to native heritages. Its effects vary according to context. In some cases it is a reflection of the multiple heritage of communities and can provide an alternative option to populations at times of crisis when established ideas and institutions have failed. In other cases, where there are no common ethnic memories to which the rival projects can appeal, internal conflict becomes problematic. The result is likely to be long-term instability and state paralysis.

Conclusion

The central problem addressed by this book is to explain how nations can appear to their members as enduring groups when the identities they maintain are continuously evolving and are subject to regular contestation, and to expansion and contraction. In my account nations are much more potent and also more limited than modernists would like to believe. They are potent because they are able to mobilise powerful sentiments and formulate a variety of routes by which to navigate through the perilous seas of the modern world. They are not mere outgrowths of deeper forces. But, at the same time, even in their guise as national states they never have been autonomous or unitary, but have always been subject to challenges and have always had to pool sovereignty with other actors. Their resilience in the past suggests that much of the discussion about the crisis of the contemporary national state is hyperbole.

I have suggested that what gives nations their enduring character in the modern world is a sense of historical mission, exemplified over centuries, that enables nationalists to plan and act over a long period even when faced with great difficulties over the short- to medium-term. This long time sense is not simply an artefact of romantic historiography, that somehow or other has become lodged in our consciousness, in spite of the best efforts of scientific historians to deconstruct it. Romanticism builds on memories that are carried into the modern period by religious organisations, legal systems, vernacular literatures, constitutions and states, urban architecture and monuments. These institutions have purposes and identities that were not necessarily ethnic, at least in their origins, but, as such memories have become part of the living culture of communities, they have come to assume an ethnic character. Because populations have been subject to multiple shocks, those ethnic communities that do survive have layered pasts that offer several foci of identification and resistance against adversity.

The sense of being part of a community that has survived and that has achieved moments of greatness as well as of decline explains much of the capacity of helpless peoples in the premodern and modern period to survive conquest and absorption into imperial systems. What sustains them is a knowledge that power passes, and this enables elites to work for the day, perhaps not in their lifetimes, that their great oppressor will fall and the ethnic group or nation will be redeemed. Where an ethnicity is infused with a sense of religious election, such visions may last virtually indefinitely (short of mass conversion). Such visions have extra force in the modern world because the uneven impact, intensity and rapidity of technological change of all kinds destabilises established states, as the collapse of the great empires in the twentieth century demonstrates. I therefore depart from Roger Brubaker's concept of nations as contingent and fluctuating events (Brubaker, 1996: 19). His 'new institutionalism' is overly focused on the state, neglecting the many other and often more powerful institutions through which identities become socially embedded.

If nationalists are able to build on such memories, they are often confronted by the 'guardians' of tradition. The conflicts within nations between the dynamic and modernising projects of nationalism and the peculiar stickiness of ethnic traditionalism have been underplayed, certainly by those who are committed to the idea of the nation as an invention. I argued that the rise of national revivalism or cultural nationalism produced an intellectual revolution, repudiating the hegemonic claims of European Christendom as the primary world civilisation in favour of a multicentred world civilisation whose creative origins were non-Western. This, in part, explains the attraction of nationalism to intellectuals outside Europe who felt their cultures and their own status to be increasingly marginalised by European imperialism. But these intellectuals, like their counterparts in Europe, were a small minority, often of a different religion from the majority. This meant that the struggle to culturally transform their societies was a difficult and protracted process, only made possible because many conservatives came to realise that they faced a choice between saving either their peoples or their traditions in the new science-based world.

Even so, one of the essential tools of the revivalists was having a layered ethnic past with alternative traditions that could be used to legitimise as 'authentic' an ideology of innovation through selective borrowing from more advanced cultures. Rather than inventors, I have called such cultural nationalists 'moral innovators' engaged in an internal transformation of tradition, a process I showed was unpredictable and operated in part through trial and error, because the search for the nation revealed unsuspected pasts, cultural practices, 'hidden' sacred sites and communities that then became reference points round which nationalists mobilised. I suggested that a second means by which revivalists established the nation over the older ethnies was through a process of mythic overlaying, inspired by a new cult of sacrifice devoted to the emerging 'god' of the people. In many contexts, this has only had a partial success and we see deep tensions between secular nationalism and ethnoreligious and religious cultures in countries such as Ireland, Israel and the Arab Middle East.

Such divisions, we observed in the chapter on cultural wars, render nation-formation an unfinished and evolving process. All nations, to a lesser or greater extent, contain plural ethnic repertoires that in the modern period become systemised into competing cultural and political projects. These are not reducible to religious–secular differences. They reflect the different heritages possessed by populations, created by formative experiences of triumph or disaster. The activation of such heritages as rival (and sometimes alternating) options demonstrates the intimate involvement of nationalists in the construction of modernity. This undermines the modernist overemphasis on the homogeneity of nations in favour of a picture that shows nationalisms acting on modernisation to produce a differentiation of the human world. Does this not support the claims of postmodernists who view national formation as a construct, though one of many possible 'plays of difference', with the implication that it can be deconstructed? I suggest that this is not the case, for these alternatives have not been plucked from the air of history but have been institutionalised as a result of powerful experiences and they remain live because they address continuing problems. It is the sense of historical constraint that makes these contestations so intense, as the protagonists on each side seek to throw off a particular incubus that lies so heavily upon the present.

Much of the historical discussion of nation-formation is predicated on a heroic myth of how political elites, marching in step with the extension in scale of political and economic communications, absorb ever-broader groups into a unitary and sovereign national society, by programmes of conscription, universal education and the extension of democratic citizenship. I have suggested that this movement can be dubbed 'statism' rather than nationalism, and that national formation is a much more complex and episodic process. The evidence indicates that national identities often emerged before the modern state, and that states have never been bounded power containers capable of inventing nations. Nationalists have used new political rights to mobilise against the state in the name of the national community, especially at times when states have lacked the capacity or willingness to defend the nation against external forces.

In short, I identify two forms of nationalism, a 'hot' or 'sacred' nationalism that is society-forming in mobilising boundaries, and a 'banal', or 'profane' nationalism (or national identity) that is used eclectically and unselfconsciously

193

by individuals and institutions to give meaning and a sense of distinctiveness to their diurnal existence. The latter is not a product of the former; the two exist in tension and interaction with each other. The sense of gap is not so much between a creative high culture versus a commodified popular culture (though this gap can be a stimulus of cultural innovation). Rather the contrast is between those who believe the nation must be recreated so that it regulates in an explicit manner other loyalties and those who take a national identity for granted in their social existence. Because we cannot identify the existence of a nation then with mass mobilisation, since a sense of national identity may exist among large sections of a given population in a more piecemeal fashion (identifying with national stereotypes, singing patriotic songs, rioting against foreign workers, holidaying in national sites), it raises the possibility that in certain cases a mass nation comes into being well before the late nineteenth century.

If historically there is considerable fluctuation in the range of spheres regulated explicitly by national norms, this renders problematic many of the indicators of national incapacities employed by scholars to demonstrate the march of globalisation. I argued that ethnic formation and globalisation have operated together for millennia, and that the triumph of nationalism (as an ideology that legitimises progress through cultural exchange) is intrinsically linked to the rise of an increasingly interactive world. Indeed, we can see something of a cycle operating whereby global processes lead to ethnic crystallisations and ethnic agents sponsor long range interactions that result in new ethnic and national formations. The implications are that though nations may adopt new regulatory strategies in the contemporary world, more intensive forms of global interchange will lead to an intensification and proliferation of nationalisms and nations in the future.

A still more important conclusion is that the concern with globalisation as an emerging threat to the future of the national state is misplaced. *The focus should be on the global past.* The viability of national projects in the contemporary world depends on whether they can draw on the ethnic crystallisations of earlier globalisations. Without such heritages, establishing a cohesive community that can act as the base of modernisation will be difficult and long drawn out.

Yet there is one caveat, and it is a big one. What about the examples of *soi-disant* multicultural nations such as the USA, Australia and Canada? Are they not successful modern societies? I have argued elsewhere (Hutchinson, 1994: ch. 6), that these are special cases that have developed a future-oriented national myth, as 'young' countries destined to exemplify how a diverse humanity can live together. But this is a national myth, based on originating ethnic cores (Anglo-Celtic and, in Canada's case, French), and employed to justify their novelty in a world of nations where status is governed by an ancestral antiquity. In the USA a sense of religious destiny derived from the Puritan heritage has helped underpin this 'New World' identity. Moreover, in recent decades they have been torn by status and political competition between the originating settler ethnies, the waves of newer immigrants who seek to de-anglicise the dominant national culture, and the indigenous peoples.

But what of those cases where, as in the Middle East, older ethnic identities were largely effaced at the popular level by transethnic religious loyalties, which remain strong competitors to nations? Or, alternatively, what of ethnic formations in parts of Africa that threaten to fragment existing states and that are too small to form the basis of an effective alternative polity? Does this not suggest that in many parts of the non-European world nations will be thinly-based elite formations, or will be unviable? To a degree. The problem is to find an alternative to the ethnically-based nation: there appears to be no other plausible model. The imperial principle no longer works, and the federal idea is stable only within states possessing a demographically dominant ethnic core.

This is not to say that populations without premodern ethnic traditions cannot become nations. Ethnogenesis continues in the contemporary period. It is also true that many states or populations claiming to be nations do not fit the above definition, but I suggest that part of the disruption in world politics is an attempt to create such nations. Rather than, as some commentators suggest, reaching the end of the era of nations, I would argue that many areas of Eurasia, Africa and Latin America are still in the early period of nation-formation, and that this will be accompanied by social and political upheavals. But this is a topic for another book.

Bibliography

Abu-Lughod, J. 1989 *Before European Hegemony*, Oxford: Oxford University Press

Abu-Lughod, J. 1993 'The World System in the Thirteenth Century: Dead-End or Precursor', in M. Adas (ed.) *Islamic and European Expansion*, Philadelphia: Temple University Press

Adshead, C. M. 1993 *Central Asia in World History*, London: Macmillan

Agulhon, M. 1998 'Paris: A Traversal from East to West', in P. Nora (ed.) *Realms of Memory: Vol. 3 Symbols*, New York: Columbia University Press

Akenson, D. H. 1992 *God's Peoples: Covenant and Land in South Africa, Israel, and Ulster*, Ithaca, NY: Cornell University Press

Albrow, M. 1996 *The Global Age*, Cambridge: Cambridge University Press

Alter, P. 1985 *Nationalism*, London: Edward Arnold

Anderson, B. 1991 *Imagined Communities*, London: Verso

Anderson, P. 1997a 'Under the Sign of the Interim', in P. Gowers and P. Anderson (eds) *The Question of Europe*, London: Verso

Anderson, P. 1997b 'The Europe to Come', in P. Gowers and P. Anderson (eds) *The Question of Europe*, London: Verso

Argyle, W. J. 1976 'Size and Scale as Factors in the Development of Nationalist Movements', in A. D. Smith (ed.) *Nationalist Movements*, London: Macmillan

Armstrong, J. 1982 *Nations Before Nationalism*, Chapel Hill, NC: University of North Carolina Press

Auerbach, J. A. 1999 *The Great Exhibition of 1851*, New Haven, CT: Yale University Press

Augustinos, G. 1977 *Consciousness and History: Nationalist Critics of Greek Society 1897–1914*, New York: East European Quarterly

Banton, M. 1994 'Modelling Ethnic and National Relations', *Ethnic and Racial Studies*, 17 (1), pp. 1–29

Barth, F. 1969 (ed.) *Ethnic Groups and Boundaries*, Boston, MA: Little Brown and Co.

Bartlett, R. 1993 *The Making of Europe: Conquest, Colonisation and Cultural Change 950–1350*, Harmondsworth: Penguin

Bate, J. 1997 *The Genius of Shakespeare*, London: Picador

Bayly, C. A. 2002 '"Archaic" and "Modern" Globalization in the Eurasian and African Arena, c. 1750–1850', in A. G. Hopkins (ed.) *Globalization in World History*, London: Pimlico

Beckett, J. C. 1966 *The Making of Modern Ireland, 1603–1923*, London: Faber & Faber

Beckett, J. C. 1976 *The Anglo-Irish Tradition*, London: Faber and Faber

Bell, D. 2001 *The Cult of the Nation in France*, Cambridge, MA: Harvard University Press

Bennison, A. K. 2002 'Muslim Universalism and Western Globalization', in A. G. Hopkins (ed.) *Globalization in World History*, London: Pimlico

Billig, M. 1995 *Banal Nationalism*, London: Sage

Bond, B. 1984 *War and Society in Europe (1810–1970)*, London: Fortune

Boyce, D. G. 1982 *Nationalism in Ireland*, London: Croom Helm

Breuilly, J. 1982 *Nationalism and the State*, Manchester: Manchester University Press

Breuilly, J. 1996 'Approaches to Nationalism', in Balakrishnan, G. (ed.) *Mapping the Nation*, London: Verso

Breuilly, J. 2000 Panel discussion ASEN Conference: 'Nationalism and the State', 24 March, London School of Economics

Briggs, A. 1968 *Victorian Cities*, Harmondsworth: Penguin

Brock, P. 1976 *The Slovak National Revival*, Toronto: East European Monographs

Brubaker, R. 1996 *Nationalism Reframed*, Cambridge: Cambridge University Press

Burke, P. 1994 *The Fabrication of Louis XIV*, New Haven, CT: Yale University Press

Burrin, P. 1996 'Vichy', in P. Nora (ed.) *Realms of Memory: Vol. 1 Conflicts and Divisions*, Ithaca, NY: Columbia University Press

Calhoun, C. 1994 'National Traditions: Created or Primordial?' in Ø. Sørensen (ed.) *Nasjonal Identitet – Kunstproduct?*, Oslo: Norges Forskningsrad

Campbell, J. and Sherrard, P. 1968 *Modern Greece*, New York: Praeger

Carr, E. H. 1964 *What is History?*, Harmondsworth: Penguin

Carrithers, M. B. 1984 '"They will be Lords upon the Island": Buddhism in Sri Lanka', in H. Bechert and R. Gombrich (eds) *The World of Buddhism*, London: Thames and Hudson

Castells, M. 1996 *The Rise of the Network Society*, Oxford: Blackwell

Cauthen, B. 2004 'Covenant and Continuity: Ethnosymbolism and the Myth of Divine Election', *Nations and Nationalism*, 10 (1–2), pp. 19–34

Colley, L. 1992 *Britons: Forging the Nation*, New Haven, CT: Yale University Press

Collins, R. 2000 *Macrohistory*, Palo Alto, CA: Stanford University Press

Connor, W. 1990 'When is a Nation?', *Ethnic and Racial Studies*, 13 (1), pp. 92–103

Corbin, A. 1996 'Divisions of time and space', in P. Nora (ed.) *Realms of Memory: Vol. 1 Conflicts and Divisions*, New York: Columbia University Press

Costello, P. 1993 *World Historians and Their Goals*, DeKalb, IL: Northern Illinois University Press

Curtis, P. 1984 *Cross-Cultural Trade in World History*, Cambridge: Cambridge University Press

Curtis, L. P. 1968 *Anglo-Saxons and Celts: A Study of Anti-Irish Prejudice in Victorian England*, Bridgeport, CT: University of Bridgeport

d'Appollonia, A. C. 2002 'European Nationalism and the European Union', in A. Pagden (ed.) *The Idea of Europe: From Antiquity to the European Union*, Cambridge: Cambridge University Press

Darby, W. 2000 *Landscape and Identity: Geographics of Nation and Class in England*, Oxford: Berg

Davies, N. 1997 'Polish National Mythologies', in G. Hosking and G. Schopflin (eds) *Myths and Nationhood*, London: Hurst and Co

Eaton, R. M. 1990 *Islam in World History*, Washington, DC: American Historical Association

Eley, G. 1986 *From Unification to Nazism*, London: Allen & Unwin

Enloe, C. 1980 *Ethnic Soldiers: State Security in Divided Societies*, Harmondsworth: Penguin

Farmer, E. L., Hambly, G.R., Kopf, D., Marshall, B.K. and Taylor R. (eds) 1986 *Comparative History of Civilizations in Asia*, Boulder, CU: Westview Press

Fontana, B. 2002 'The Napoleonic Empire and the Europe of Nations', in A. Pagden (ed.) *The Idea of Europe: From Antiquity to the European Union*, Cambridge: Cambridge University Press

Foster, R. F. 1988 *Modern Ireland 1600–1972*, Harmondsworth: Penguin

Frazee, C. A. 1969 *The Orthodox Church and Independent Greece*, Cambridge: Cambridge University Press

Friedman, E. 1995 *National Identity and Democratic Prospects in Socialist China*, New York: M. E. Sharpe

Fulbrook, M. 1999 *German National Identity After the Holocaust*, Oxford: Polity

Garvin, T. 1981 *The Evolution of Irish Nationalist Politics*, Dublin: Gill and Macmillan

Garvin, T. 1987 *Nationalist Revolutionaries in Ireland 1858–1928*, Oxford: Clarendon Press

Geary, P. J. 2002 *The Myth of Nations: The Medieval Origins of Europe*, Princeton, N.J.: Princeton University Press

Gellner, E. 1964 *Thought and Change*, London: Weidenfeld and Nicolson

Gellner, E. 1983 *Nations and Nationalism*, Oxford: Blackwell

Gellner, E. 1996 'Do Nations have Navels?', *Nations and Nationalism*, 2 (3), pp. 366–70

Geertz, C. 1963 'The Integrative Revolution: Primordial Sentiment and Civil Politics in the New States', in C. Geertz (ed.) *Old Societies and New States: The Quest for Modernity in Asia and Africa*, New York: Free Press

Gershoni, I. 1997 'Rethinking the Formation of Arab Nationalism in the Middle East, 1920–45', in J. Jankowkski and I. Gershoni (eds) *Rethinking Nationalism in the Arab Middle East*, New York: Columbia Unversity Press

Giddens, A. 1985 *The Nation-State and Violence*, Cambridge: Polity Press

Giddens, A. 1990 *The Consequences of Modernity*, Cambridge: Polity Press

Gildea, R. 1994 *The Past in French History*, New Haven, CT: Yale University Press

Gorski, P. S. 2000 'The Mosaic Moment: An Early Modernist Critique of Modernist Theories of Nationalism', *American Journal of Sociology*, CV (5), pp. 1428–68

Grant, S.-M. 1997 'Making History: Myth and the Construction of American Nationhood', in G. Hosking and G. Schopflin (eds) *Myths and Nationhood*, London: Hurst and Co

Grillo, R. D. 1989 *Dominant Languages: Language and Hierarchy in Britain and France*, Cambridge: Cambridge University Press

Grosby, S. 1995 'Territoriality: The Transcendental, Primordial Feature of Modern Societies', *Nations and Nationalism*, 1 (2), pp. 143–62

Grosby, S. 2002 *Biblical Ideas of the Nation: Ancient and Modern*, Winona Lake, IN: Eisenbrauns

Guibernau, M. 2001 'Globalisation and the Nation-state', in M. Guibernau and J. Hutchinson (eds) *Understanding Nationalism*, Cambridge: Polity Press

Haddad, Y. Y. 1991 'The Revivalist Literature and the Literature on Revival', in Y. Y. Haddad, J. O. Voll and J. L. Esposito (eds) *The Contemporary Islamic Revival*, New York: Greenwood

Hall, J. 1985 *Powers and Liberties: The Causes and Consequences of the Rise of the West*, Harmondsworth: Penguin

Hastings, A. 1997 *The Construction of Nationhood: Ethnicity, Religion and Nationalism*, Cambridge: Cambridge University Press

Haugen, E. 1966 *Language Conflict and Language Planning: The Case of Modern Norwegian*, Cambridge, MA: Harvard University Press

Haugland, K. 1980 'An Outline of Norwegian Cultural Nationalism', in R. Mitchison (ed.) *The Roots of Nationalism: Studies in Northern Europe*, Edinburgh: John Donald

Hechter, M. 1975 *Internal Colonialism: The Celtic Fringe in British National Development, 1536–1966*, London: Routledge

Hechter, M. 2000 *Containing Nationalism*, Oxford: Oxford University Press

Heimsath, C. 1964 *Indian Nationalism and Hindu Social Reform*, Princeton, NJ: Princeton University Press

Held, D., McGrew, A., Goldblatt, D. and Perraton, J. 1999 *Global Transformations*, Cambridge: Polity Press

Helleiner, E. 2003 *The Making of National Money: Territorial Currencies in Historical Perspective*, Ithaca, NY: Cornell University Press

Herder, J. G. 1968 *Reflections on the Philosophy of History*, ed. F. Manuel, Chicago: Chicago University Press

Herzfeld, M. 1982 *Ours Once More: Folklore, Ideology and the Making of Modern Greece*, Austin, TX: Texas University Press

Hill, C. 1968 *Puritanism and Liberty*, London: Panther

Hobsbawm, E. J. 1962 *The Age of Revolution*, London: Weidenfeld and Nicolson

Hobsbawm, E. J. 1983 'Mass-Producing Traditions, Europe 1870–1914', in E. J. Hobsbawm and T. Ranger (eds) *The Invention of Tradition*, Cambridge: Cambridge University Press

Hobsbawm, E. J. 1990 *Nations and Nationalism Since 1780*, Cambridge: Cambridge University Press

Hodgson, M. 1993 *Rethinking World History*, Cambridge: Cambridge University Press

Holy, L. 1996 *The Little Czech and the Great Czech Nation*, Cambridge: Cambridge University Press

Hopkins, A. G. 2002 'The History of Globalization and the Globalization of History', in A. G. Hopkins (ed.) *Globalization in World History*, London: Pimlico

Hosking, G. 1997 'The Russian National Myth Repudiated', in G. Hosking and G. Schopflin (eds) *Myths and Nationhood*, London: Hurst and Co

Hosking, G. and Schopflin, G. 1997 *Myths and Nationhood*, London: Hurst and Co

Howard, M. 1976 *War in European History*, London: Oxford University Press

Hroch, M. 1985 *The Social Preconditions of National Revivals in Europe*, Cambridge: Cambridge University Press

Hunt, L. 1992 *The Family Romance of the French Revolution*, Berkeley, CA: University of California Press

Huntington, S. 1997 *The Clash of Civilisations and the Remaking of World Order*, London: Touchstone Books

Hutchinson, J. 1987 *The Dynamics of Cultural Nationalism: The Gaelic Revival and the Creation of the Irish Nation State*, London: Allen & Unwin

Hutchinson, J. 1994 *Modern Nationalism*, London: Fontana

Hutchinson, J. 1999 'Re-interpreting Cultural Nationalism', *Australian Journal of Politics and History*, 45 (3), pp. 392–407

Ichijo, A. 2002 'The Scope of Theories of Nationalism: Comments on the Scottish and Japanese Experiences', *Geopolitics*, 7 (2), pp. 53–75

Jarausch, K. H. and Geyer, M. 2003 *Shattered Past: Reconstructing German Histories*, Princeton, NJ: Princeton University Press

Jarausch, K. H., Seeba, H. C. and Conradt, D. P. 1997 'The Presence of the Past: Culture, Opinion and Identity in Germany', in K. H. Jarausch (ed.) *After Unity: Reconfiguring German Identities*, Providence, R. I.: Bergahn Books

Jauregui, P. 1999 'National Pride and the Meaning of "Europe": A Comparative Study of Britain and Spain', in D. Smith and S. Wright (eds) *Whose Europe? The Turn Towards Democracy*, Oxford: Blackwell/The Sociological Review

Johnson, D. 1993 'The Making of the French Nation', in M. Teich and R. Porter (eds) *The National Question in Europe in Historical Context*, Cambridge: Cambridge University Press

Jordan, W. C. 2002 '"Europe" in the Middle Ages', in A. Pagden (ed.) *The Idea of Europe: From Antiquity to the European Union*, Cambridge: Cambridge University Press

Jusdanis, G. 2001 *The Necessary Nation*, Princeton, NJ: Princeton University Press

Juergensmeyer, M. 1993 *The New Cold War?* Berkeley, CA: University of California Press

Karl, R. E. 2002 *Staging the World: Chinese Nationalism at the Turn of the Twentieth Century*, Durham, NC: Duke University Press

Kaufmann, E. and Zimmer, O. 1998 'In Search of the Authentic Nation: Landscape and National Identity in Canada and Switzerland', *Nations and Nationalism*, (4), pp. 483–510

Kedourie, E. 1960 *Nationalism*, London: Hutchinson

Keegan, J. 1997 'From Albert Speer to Jacques Delors', in P. Gowers and P. Anderson (eds) *The Question of Europe*, London: Verso

Keynes, J. M. 1920 *The Economic Consequences of the Peace*, London: Macmillan and Co.

Kiberd, D. 1996 *Inventing Ireland: The Literature of the Modern Nation*, London: Vintage

Kidd, C. 1999 *British Identities Before Nationalism: Ethnicity and Nationhood in the Atlantic World, 1600–1800*, Cambridge: Cambridge University Press

Kohn, H. 1967 *Prelude to Nation-states: The French and German Experience 1789–1815*, New York: Van Nostrand

Koksalakis, N. and Psimmenos, I. 2003 'Modern Greece: A Profile of Identity and Nationalism', in B. Strath and A. Triandafyllidou (eds) *Representations of Europe and the Nation in Current and Prospective Members*, Brussels: European Commission

Kopf, D. 1969 *British Orientalism and the Bengali Cultural Renaissance*, Berkeley, CA: University of California Press

Koshar, R. 1998 *Germany's Transient Pasts: Preservation and National Memory in the Twentieth Century*, Chapel Hill, NC: University of North Carolina

Krejci, J. and Velimsky, V. 1981 *Ethnic and Political Nations in Europe*, London: Croom Helm

Kristof, L. D. 1994 'Poland: The Image and the Vision of the Fatherland', in D. Hooson (ed.) *Geography and National Identity*, Oxford: Blackwell

Lamers, K. 1997 'Strengthening the Hard Core', in P. Gowers and P. Anderson (eds) *The Question of Europe*, London:Verso

Landes, J. 1988 *Women in the Public Sphere in the Age of the French Revolution*, Ithaca, NY: Cornell University Press

Langlands, R. 1999 'Britishness or Englishness? The Historical Problem of National Identity in Britain', *Nations and Nationalism*, 5 (1), pp. 53–69

Langlois, C. 1996 'Catholics and Seculars', in P. Nora (ed.) *Realms of Memory: Vol. 1 Conflicts and Divisions*, New York: Columbia University Press

Levenson, J. 1959 *Liang Ch'i -ch'ao and the Mind of Modern China*, Berkeley, CA: University of California Press

Lewis, B. 1998 *Multiple Identities of the Middle East*, New York: Schocken Books

Lieven, D. 2000 *Empire: The Russian Empire and its Rivals*, London: John Murray

Llobera, J. 1994 *The God of Modernity*, Oxford: Berg

Lowenthal, D. 1985 *The Past is a Foreign Country*, Cambridge: Cambridge University Press

Lowenthal, D. 1994 'European and English Landscapes', in D. Hooson (ed.) *Geography and National Identity*, Oxford: Blackwell

Lyons, F. S. L. 1979 *Culture and Anarchy in Ireland 1890–1939*, Oxford: Clarendon Press

McCrone, D. 1998 *The Sociology of Nationalism*, London: Routledge

McDaniel, T. 1996 *The Agony of the Russian Idea*, Princeton, NJ: Princeton University Press

MacDougall, H. A. 1982 *Racial Myth in English History*, Hanover, NE: University Press of New England

McNeill, W. H. 1963 *The Rise of the West*, Chicago: University of Chicago Press

McNeill, W. H. 1984 *The Pursuit of Power: Technology, Armed Forces and Society Since AD 1000*, Chicago, Chicago University Press

McNeill, W. H. 1986 *Polyethnicity and National Unity in World History*, Toronto: Toronto University Press

McNeill, W. H. 1990 'The Rise of the West after Twenty-Five Years', *Journal of World History*, 1 (1), pp. 1–21

Mann, M. 1975 'The Ideology of Intellectuals and Other People in the Development of Capitalism', in Lindberg, L. R. Alford, C. Crouch and C. Offe (eds) *Stress and Contradiction in Modern Capitalism*, London: Heath

Mann, M. 1986 *The Sources of Social Power* Vol. 1, Cambridge: Cambridge University Press

Mann, M. 1993 *The Sources of Social Power* Vol. 2, Cambridge: Cambridge University Press

Mansergh, N. 1968 *The Irish Question*, London: Unwin University Books

Marvin, C. and Ingle, D. 1999 *Blood Sacrifice and the Flag*, Cambridge: Cambridge University Press

Meinander, H. 2002 'On the Brink or In-between? The Concept of Europe in Finnish Identity', in M. af Malmborg and B. Strath (eds) *The Meaning of Europe*, Oxford: Berg

Mercer, C. 1992 'Regular Imaginings: The Newspaper and the Nation', in T. Bennett, P. Buckridge, D. Carter and C. Mercer (eds) *Celebrating the Nation: A Critical Study of Australia's Bicentenary*, Sydney: Allen & Unwin

Milward, A. 1992 *The European Rescue of the Nation State*, London: Routledge

Milward, A. 1997 'The Springs of Integration', in P. Gowan and P. Anderson (eds) *The Question of Europe*, London: Verso

Mosse, G. 1975 *The Nationalization of the Masses*, New York: New American Library

Mosse, G. 1976 'Mass Politics and the Political Liturgy of Nationalism', in E. Kamenka (ed.) *Nationalism: The Nature and Evolution of an Idea*, London: Edward Arnold

Mosse, G. 1990 *Fallen Soldiers: Reshaping the Memory of the World Wars*, London: Oxford University Press

Mukherjee, S. N. 1968 *Sir William Jones*, Cambridge: Cambridge University Press

Nairn, T. 1975 *The Break-up of Britain*, London: New Left Books

Neumann, I. B. 1996 *Russia and the Idea of Europe*, London: Routledge

Neumann, I. B. 2002 'From the USSR to Gorbachev to Putin: "Perestroika" as a Failed Excursion from "the West" to "Europe" in Russian Discourse', in M. af Malmborg and B. Strath (eds) *The Meaning of Europe*, Oxford: Berg

Newman, G. 1987 *The Rise of English Nationalism: A Cultural History*, London: Weidenfeld and Nicolson

O'Farrell, P. 1976 'Millenialism, Messianism and Utopianism in Irish History', *Anglo-Irish Studies*, 2, pp. 45–68

Ohmae, K. 1996 *The End of the Nation State*, New York: Free Press

Ostergard, U. 1994 'Nation-Building Danish Style', in Ø. Sørensen (ed.) *Nordic Paths to National Identity in the Nineteenth Century*, Oslo: The Research Council of Norway

Özkirimli, U. 2000 *Theories of Nationalism*, London: Macmillan

Ozouf, J. and Ozouf, M. 1997 'Le Tour de la France par deux enfants': The Little Red Book of the Republic', in P. Nora (ed.) *Realms of Memory, Vol. 2, Traditions*, New York: Columbia University Press

Pagden, A. 2002a 'Introduction', in A. Pagden (ed.) *The Idea of Europe: From Antiquity to the European Union*, Cambridge: Cambridge University Press

Pagden, A. 2002b 'Europe: Conceptualising a Continent', in A. Pagden (ed.) *The Idea of Europe: From Antiquity to the European Union*, Cambridge: Cambridge University Press

Paris, M. 2000 *Warrior Nation: Images of War in British Popular Culture 1850–2000*, London: Reaktion Books

Passerini, L. 2002 'From the Ironies of Identity to the Identities of Irony', in A. Pagden (ed.) *The Idea of Europe: From Antiquity to the European Union*, Cambridge: Cambridge University Press

Pastoureau, M. 1998 'The Gallic Cock', in P. Nora (ed.) *Realms of Memory: Vol. 3 Symbols*, New York: Columbia University Press

Pearson, R. 1983 *National Minorities in Eastern Europe 1848–1945*, London: Macmillan

Pearson, R. 1996 'Hungary: A State Truncated, A Nation Dismembered', in S. Deane and T. G. Fraser (eds) *Europe and Ethnicity*, London: Routledge

Pepelassis, A. 1958 'The Image of the Past and Economic Backwardness', *Human Organisation*, 17 (9), pp. 19–27

Petrovich, M. B. 2000 'Religion and Ethnicity in Eastern Europe', in J. Hutchinson and A. D. Smith (eds) *Nationalism* Vol. IV, London: Routledge

Pfaff, W. 1993 *The Wrath of Nations*, New York: Simon and Schuster

Pipes, R. 1977 *Russia under the Old Regime*, Harmondsworth: Penguin

Plakans, A. 1974 'Peasants, Intellectuals, and Nationalism in the Russian Baltic Provinces 1820–90', *Journal of Modern History*, 46, pp. 464–9

Pocock, J. G. A. 1997 'Deconstructing Europe', in P. Gowers and P. Anderson (eds) *The Question of Europe*, London: Verso

Pocock, J. G. A. 2002 'Some Europes in Their History', in A. Pagden (ed.) *The Idea of Europe: From Antiquity to the European Union*, Cambridge: Cambridge University Press

Poliakov, L. 1974 *The Aryan Myth*, New York: Basic Books

Pomian, K. 1996 'Franks and Gauls', in P. Nora (ed.) *Realms of Memory: Vol.1 Conflicts and Divisions*, New York: Columbia University Press

Popielovsky, D. 1989 'The "Russian Orientation" and the Orthodox Church', in P. Ramet (ed.) *Religion and Nationalism in the Soviet Union and Eastern Europe*, Durham, NC: Duke University Press

Popper, K. R. 1960 *The Poverty of Historism*, London: Routlage, Kegan Paul

Posen, B. 1995 'Nationalism, the Mass Army and Military Power', in J. L. Comaroff and P. C. Stern (eds) *Perspectives on Nationalism*, Amsterdam: Gordon and Breach Science Publishers

Prizel, I. 1998 *National Identity and Foreign Policy*, Cambridge: Cambridge University Press

Puymège, G. de 1997 'The Good Soldier Chauvin', in P. Nora (ed.) *Realms of Memory, Vol. 2, Traditions*, New York: Columbia University Press

Ramet (ed.) *Religion and Nationalism in the Soviet Union and Eastern Europe*, Durham, NC: Duke University Press

Rabow-Edling, S. 2001 *The Intellectuals and the Idea of the Nation in Slavophile Thought*, Stockholm: Stockholm University Press

Reid, D. 1997 'Nationalizing the Pharaonic Past: Egyptology, Imperialism, and Egyptian Nationalism 1922–52', in J. Jankowkski and I. Gershoni (eds) *Rethinking Nationalism in the Arab Middle East*, New York: Columbia University Press

Reynolds, S. 1997 *Kingdoms and Communities in Western Europe 900–1300*, London: Oxford University Press

Riasonovsky, N. V. 1952 *Russia and the West in the Teaching of the Slavophiles*, Cambridge, MA: Harvard University Press

Riasonovsky, N. V. 1985 *The Image of Peter the Great in Russian History and Thought*, London: Oxford University Press

Richter, M. 1998 *Medieval Ireland: The Enduring Tradition*, Dublin: Gill and Macmillan

Roberts, M. 1967 *Europe 1880–1945*, London: Longmans

Rudnytski, I. L. 1977 'The Ukrainian National Movement on the Eve of the First World War', *East European Quarterly*, 11 (2), pp. 141–54

Savory, R.M. 1992 'Land of the Lion and the Sun', in B. Lewis (ed.) *The World of Islam*, London: Thames and Hudson

Schama, S. 1995 *Landscape and Memory*, London: Fontana

Schenk, H. G. 1966 *The Mind of the European Romantics*, London: Oxford University Press

Schwab, R. 1984 *The Oriental Renaissance: Europe's Rediscovery of India and the East 1680–1880*, New York: Columbia University Press

Seton-Watson, H. 1977 *Nations and States*, London: Methuen

Sharp, A. 1996 'The Genie that Would Not Go Back into the Bottle', in S. Dunn and T. G. Fraser (eds) *Europe and Ethnicity*, London: Routledge

Sheehy, J. 1980 *The Rediscovery of Ireland's Past: The Celtic Revival (1830–1930)*, London: Thames and Hudson

Skinner, Q. 1974 'Some Problems in the Analysis of Political Thought and Action', *Political Theory*, 2 (3), pp. 277–303

Sluga, G. 1998 'Identity, Gender, and the History of European Nations and Nationalism', *Nations and Nationalism*, 4 (1), pp. 87–111

Smith, A. D. 1971 *Theories of Nationalism*, London: Duckworth

Smith, A. D. 1981 'War and Ethnicity: The Role of Warfare in the Formation, Self-images and Cohesion of Ethnic Communities', *Ethnic and Racial Studies*, 4 (4), pp. 375–97

Smith, A. D. 1984 'National Identity and Myths of Ethnic Descent', *Research in Social Movements, Conflict, Change*, 7, pp. 95–130

Smith, A. D. 1986 *The Ethnic Origins of Nations*, Oxford: Blackwell

Smith, A. D. 1992 'National Identity and the Idea of European Unity', *International Affairs*, 68 (1), pp. 55–76

Smith, A. D. 1999 *Myths and Memories of the Nation*, London: Oxford University Press

Smith, A. D. 2001 'Nations in History', in M. Guibernau and J. Hutchinson (eds) *Understanding Nationalism*, Cambridge: Polity

Smith, A. D. 2002 'When is a Nation?, *Geopolitics*, 7 (2), pp. 5–32

Smith, G., Law, V., Wilson, A., Bohr, A., and Allworth, E. 1998 *Nation-building in the Post-Soviet Borderlands*, Cambridge: Cambridge University Press

Smith, M. 2000 *Britain and 1940: History, Myth and Popular Memory*, London: Routledge

Sørensen, Ø. 1994 'The Development of a Norwegian National Identity During the Nineteeenth Century', in Ø. Sørensen (ed.) *Nordic Paths to National Identity in the Nineteenth Century*, Oslo: The Research Council of Norway

Sorenson, M. L. 1996 'The Fall of a Nation, the Birth of a Subject: The National Use of Archaeology in Nineteenth Century Denmark', in M. Diaz-Andreu and T. Champion (eds) *Nationalism and Archaeology in Europe*. London: UCL Press.

Sternhell, Z. 1999 *The Founding Myths of Israel*, Princeton, NJ: Princeton University Press

Stokes, W. 1868 *The Life and Labours in Art and Archaeology of George Petrie*, Dublin

Thaden, E. 1964 *Conservative Nationalism in Nineteenth Century Russia*, Seattle: University of Washington Press

Thompson, E. P. 1968 *The Making of the English Working Class*, Harmondsworth: Penguin

Tilly, C. (ed.) 1975 *The Formation of National States in Western Europe*, Princeton, NJ: Princeton University Press

Tilly, C. 1995 'States and Nationalism in Europe, 1492–1992', in J. L. Comaroff and P. C. Stern (eds) *Perspectives on Nationalism*, Amsterdam: Gordon and Breach Science Publishers

Tonnesson, S. 2004 'Globalising National States', *Nations and Nationalism*, 10 (1–2), pp. 179–94

Tsoukalas, C. 2002 'The Irony of Symbolic Reciprocities – the Greek Meaning of "Europe" as a Historical Inversion of the European Meaning of "Greece"', in M. af Malmborg and B. Strath (eds) *The Meaning of Europe*, Oxford: Berg

van der Veer, P. 1994 *Religious Nationalism: Hindus and Muslims in India*, Berkely: University of California Press

van der Veer, P. 1999 'The Moral State: Religion, Nation and Empire in Victorian Britain and British India', in P. van der Veer and H. Lehmann (eds) *Nation and Religion*, Princeton, NJ: Princeton University Press

Vauchez, A. 1992 'The Cathedral', in P. Nora (ed.) *Realms of Memory, Vol. 2 Traditions*, New York: Columbia University Press

Wallace, W. 1997 'The Nation-state – Rescue or Retreat?', in P. Gowers and P. Anderson (eds) *The Question of Europe*, London: Verso

Wallerstein, I. 1974 *The Modern World System: Volume 1*, New York: Academic Press

Weber, E. 1976 *Peasants into Frenchmen: The Modernization of Rural France (1870–1914)*, Palo Alto, CA: Stanford University Press

Weiler, J. H. H. 1997 'Demos, Telos, Ethos and the Maastricht Decision', in P. Gowers and P. Anderson (eds) *The Question of Europe*, London: Verso

Weiss, L. 1998 *The Myth of the Powerless State*, Cambridge: Polity Press

Wiener, M. J. 1981 *English Culture and the Decline of the Industrial Spirit 1850–1980*, Cambridge: Cambridge University Press

Wilson, W. A. 1976 *Folklore and Nationalism in Modern Finland*, Bloomington, IN: Indiana University Press

Wimmer, A. 2002 *Nationalism and its Exclusions*, Cambridge: Cambridge University Press

Winock, M. 1998 'Joan of Arc', in P. Nora (ed.) *Realms of Memory: Vol. 3 Symbols*, New York: Columbia University Press

Winter, J. 1995 *Sites of Memory, Sites of Mourning: The Great War in European History*, Cambridge: Cambridge University Press

Woodruff, W. 1973 'The Emergence of an International Economy 1700–1914', in C. Cipolla (ed.) *The Fontana Economic History of Europe: The Emergence of Industrial Societies Part 2*, London: Collins

Wriston, W. 1992 *The Twilight of Sovereignty*, New York: Charles Scribner's Sons

Yahil, L. 1992 'National Pride and Defeat: A Comparison of Danish and German Nationalism', in J. Reinharz and G. Mosse (eds) *The Impact of Western Nationalisms*, London: Sage

Yoshino, K. 1999 'Rethinking Theories of Nationalism: Japanese Nationalism in a Market-place Perspective', in K. Yoshino (ed.) *Consuming Ethnicity and Nationalism: Asian Experiences*, Richmond: Curzon Press

Young, C. (ed.) 1993 *The Rising Tide of Cultural Pluralism: The Nation-State at Bay?*, Madison, WI: University of Wisconsin

Yuval-Davis, N. 1997 *Gender and Nation*, London: Sage

Zerubavel, Y. 1995 *Recovered Roots: Collective Memory and the Making of the Israeli Nation*, Chicago: University of Chicago Press

Zheng, Y. 1999 *Discovering Nationalism in China: Modernisation, Identity and International Relations*, Cambridge: Cambridge University Press

Index